ENVIRONMENTAL INFORMATION REGULATIONS

A Practical Guide

Susan Wolf

The Law Society

© The Law Society 2011

Crown copyright material is reproduced with the permission of the Controller of Her Majesty's Stationery Office

ISBN-13: 978-1-85328-639-1

Published in 2011 by the Law Society
113 Chancery Lane, London WC2A 1PL

Typeset by Columns Design XML Ltd, Reading
Printed by Hobbs the Printer, Ltd, Totton, Hants

The paper used for the text pages of this book is FSC certified. FSC (the Forest Stewardship Council) is an international network to promote responsible management of the world's forests.

For Betty and Alex

Environmental Information Regulations

Other titles available from Law Society Publishing:

Commercial Law Handbook
Edited by David Berry

Data Protection Handbook, 2nd edn
General Editor: Peter Carey

Environmental Law Handbook, 7th edn
Valerie Fogleman, Trevor Hellawell and Andrew Wiseman

Freedom of Information Handbook, 2nd edn
General Editors: Peter Carey and Marcus Turle

Information Sharing Handbook
Edited by Claire Bessant; Consultant Editor: Phil Tompkins

Privacy Law Handbook
Edited by Keith Mathieson

Titles from Law Society Publishing can be ordered from all good bookshops or direct (telephone 0870 850 1422, email **lawsociety@prolog.uk.com** or visit our online shop at **www.lawsociety.org.uk/bookshop**).

Contents

Foreword

If freedom of information has changed the fabric of public life since 2005, the Environmental Information Regulations 2004 (EIR 2004) are having a parallel effect on the fabric of our environment. The Regulations have been less familiar, sometimes to public authorities as well as to politicians, the media and the general public. But – where they apply – they generally go further down the road of disclosure and need to be taken with ever-greater seriousness.

Susan Wolf's book is a masterpiece and it is a privilege to be asked to provide a foreword. It is written as a practical guide, but is much more than that. It is comprehensive, clearly-written and accessible both for beginners and experienced information practitioners. It is also very timely. Some six years after their introduction, sufficient cases have now come forward to public authorities, to the Commissioner, to the Tribunal and to the higher courts to make coherent sense of EIR 2004. It has not been easy to appreciate their full impact. The Regulations have suffered 'Cinderella' status in the shadow of the Freedom of Information Act which came into effect on the same day. The inter-relationship between the two regimes (and with data protection law) is complex and subtle. The similarities, and the important differences, between the detailed wording of the two laws calls for a nuanced approach. And the purposive influence of the parent EU Directive can never be neglected.

Recital 16 of the Directive is fundamental and forthright:

> The right to information means that the disclosure of information should be the general rule and that public authorities, should be permitted to refuse a request for environmental information in specific and clearly defined cases. Grounds for refusal should be interpreted in a restrictive way...

It is welcome that so much emphasis of this book is placed on practical guidance. The user will find clear expositions of the challenging definition of environmental information, the bodies to which EIR 2004 apply, the various exceptions and the crucial impact of the Public Interest Test. There is also very helpful material on the practicalities of handling requests, the procedures for complaints and appeals and the enforcement arrangements. The growing body of both binding and influential jurisprudence is skilfully inter-woven, alongside numerous practical examples and references to official guidance.

Transparency is now a permanent feature of public life and the law. The rationales in terms of access, accountability, public participation and exposing or deterring impropriety are well-established. The Regulations seek to apply these principles and bring transparency to information about air, water, land, biological diversity and all the other elements of the environment and about releases, discharges, emissions and so on. As the boundaries continue to develop, everyone working across this vast and crucial field needs to understand EIR 2004.

I can only regret that Susan Wolf's book could obviously not have been available to steer all of us through the first six years of the life of these far-reaching Regulations.

Richard Thomas CBE
Information Commissioner, 2002–2009
September 2011

Acknowledgements

Particular thanks are due to my colleague Andrew Watson for kindly agreeing to write the chapter on personal data. I also wish to thank my colleagues Helen Morris and Jennifer Stephens for their valuable comments and support.

Thanks also to my son, Alex, for preparing one of the tables and my husband, Alastair, for giving me the time, space and support to write this book.

Table of cases

Table of statutes

Table of statutory instruments

Table of European and international legislation

Abbreviations

AAC	Administrative Appeals Chamber
BERR	Department for Business, Enterprise and Regulatory Reform
CBI	Confederation for British Industry
CDPA 1998	Copyright, Designs and Patents Act 1998
COPA 1974	Control of Pollution Act 1974
CPSR 2008	Local Authorities (England) (Charges for Property Searches) Regulations 2008, SI 2008/3248
DEFRA	Department for Environment, Food and Rural Affairs
DMPO 2010	Town and Country Planning (Development Management Procedure) (England) Order 2010, SI 2010/2184
DPA 1998	Data Protection Act 1998
ECHR	European Convention on Human Rights
ECJ	European Court of Justice
ECtHR	European Court of Human Rights
EIR 2004	Environmental Information Regulations 2004, SI 2004/3391
EPA 1990	Environmental Protection Act 1990
EPR 2010	Environmental Permitting (England and Wales) Regulations 2010, SI 2010/675
FCO	Foreign and Commonwealth Office
FOIA 2000	Freedom of Information Act 2000
GRC	General Regulatory Chamber
HSE	Health and Safety Executive
IAR	Information Asset Register
IPPC	Integrated Pollution Prevention Control Directive
LGA 1972	Local Government Act 1972
LLCA 1975	Local Land Charges Act 1975
LLCR	Local Land Charges Register
LPP	Legal professional privilege
MNOs	Mobile network operators
MTUA	Mersey Tunnels Users Association
NAEI	National Atmospheric Emissions Inventory
NGOs	Non-governmental organisations

NoA	Notice of Appeal
Ofcom	Office of Communications
OFWAT	Office of Water Services
OPSI	Office of Public Sector Information
PSIR 2005	Re-use of Public Sector Information Regulations 2005, SI 2005/1515
PIT	Public interest test
RANE	Regional Assembly for the North East of England
RCEP	Royal Commission on Environmental Pollution
SSSI	Sites of Special Scientific Interest
UNECE	United Nations Economic Commission for Europe
WEEE	Waste Electrical and Electronic Equipment Regulations 2006, SI 2006/3289
WIA 1991	Water Industry Act 1991
WIPO	World Intellectual Property Convention

CHAPTER 1

Introduction and background to EIR 2004

1.1 INTRODUCTION

This book is about access to environmental information and very specifically about the Environmental Information Regulations 2004, SI 2004/3391 (EIR 2004).

There is little doubt that when most people think about access to information their attention will focus on the much heralded Freedom of Information Act 2000 (FOIA 2000). It is almost unimaginable that anyone could have escaped the exposés and media stories that have resulted from information released under FOIA 2000. In contrast, EIR 2004 are relatively inconspicuous. Some practitioners have likened EIR 2004 to a Cinderella regime and that analogy is apt; after all, EIR 2004 are not primary legislation and in comparison to FOIA 2000 they have attracted virtually no media attention. However, these factors should not mask the significant importance of EIR 2004 on the information rights landscape. In fact, EIR 2004 are being used by members of the public and non-governmental organisations (NGOs) to access a wide array of environmental information which traditionally would have been classed as secret or confidential. The reasons for accessing the information are myriad, but it certainly appears that EIR 2004 are being used to provide the public with the information they need to challenge public authorities and the environmental decisions that they take. Moreover, EIR 2004 provide a more generous access-to-information regime than FOIA 2000 and they impact on a larger number of bodies than the Act. It is estimated that over 100,000 bodies are subject to the obligations of EIR 2004, including private sector organisations that fall within the regulations' expansive definition of 'a public authority'.

Unfortunately, one only has to look at some of the Decision Notices issued by the Information Commissioner and decisions of the First-tier Tribunal (Information Rights) to know that many public authorities do not always recognise requests for environmental information and consequently fail to deal with them under the 'correct' information rights regime. In some cases, it appears that public authorities seem to automatically default to FOIA 2000 with little or no regard for EIR 2004. It has been said that this is not a problem where the public authority intends to disclose all of the information requested. Pragmatically that may be correct, but as a matter of law it cannot be right since environmental information is excluded from the ambit of FOIA 2000. Problems arise when public authorities misapply FOIA exemptions to requests for environmental information, not least because more exemptions are available under the Act than under EIR 2004, and this could result in information being withheld under the Act which should have been disclosed under the regulations.

The aim of this handbook is relatively simple: to provide a user-friendly and practical guide to EIR 2004. The book is aimed at information rights practitioners and anyone else in a public authority (including lawyers) who is charged with making decisions about the disclosure of environmental information. The book also aims to provide a useful guide to applicants or prospective applicants. Where applicable, tips and suggestions are included. Applicants are not expected to be well versed in the law even to the extent that an applicant is not required to say that he or she is making a request for environmental information. The task of working out how to deal with a request for information, and the applicable legislative regime, falls to the public authority receiving the request. However, it is hoped that this handbook will provide some guidance to anyone who wishes to utilise EIR 2004 to access environmental information.

This book is not about FOIA 2000, which has been considered at length elsewhere (for example, the Law Society's companion *Freedom of Information Handbook* (2008) and *Information Sharing Handbook* (2009). However, on occasion it has been necessary or useful to draw comparisons with corresponding provisions of FOIA 2000, although such references have been kept to a minimum. The book also includes an examination of other statutory provisions which can be used by the public to access environmental information held by public authorities.

1.2 BACKGROUND TO EIR 2004

Environmental regulation was traditionally shrouded in secrecy, with some legislative provisions expressly making it an offence for officials to disclose information about the exercise of their statutory duties and others only allowing disclosure about emissions if expressly permitted by the 'polluter'. The view of industry (as reflected, for example, by the Confederation for British Industry) was that the greater release of information would increase the prospects of misinterpretation and the threat of ill-judged legal proceedings against polluters. Industrialists were also concerned that the release of more information about their activities would enable competitors to unearth trade secrets; this was soundly rejected by the Royal Commission on Environmental Pollution (RCEP), which took the view that that 'legislation which protects secrecy over industrial effluents and wastes no longer safeguards genuine trade secrets'. More particularly, in 1984 the RCEP recommended that:

> a guiding principle behind all legislative and administrative controls relating to environmental pollution should be a presumption in favour of unrestricted access for the public to information which the pollution control authorities obtain or receive by virtue of their

statutory powers, with protection for secrecy only in those circumstances where a genuine case can be substantiated.

The calls for greater openness in environmental regulation were part of the more general move towards freedom of information, notably with the Franks Committee Report and the Younger Committee Report, both in 1972.

1.2.1 The public registers

The first 'inroads' into this culture of secrecy came with the advent of modern day statutes which required the pollution control regulatory bodies to maintain public registers of information about the various regulated activities. The Control of Pollution Act 1974 introduced public registers in relation to consented water pollution. The scope of the public registers was extended further with the enactment of a raft of environmental legislation in the 1990s. For example, the Environmental Protection Act (EPA) 1990, the Water Resources Act (WRA) 1991 and the Water Industry Act (WIA) 1991 made provision for the regulators to maintain public registers of, *inter alia*, pollution control authorisations, water discharge consents, water abstraction licenses and sewage effluent consents. Although much of this legislation has now been repealed and replaced with a more streamlined Environmental Permitting regime, the public registers remain an important source of information about polluting activities in England and Wales. The public registers will be examined in **Chapter 11**.

Although the public registers provided a start in the right direction, they did not confer a general right of access to information other than that prescribed in the legislation, and this was almost exclusively about the polluting activities authorised or consented by the regulatory bodies. The registers did not, and do not, provide a right to information about wider environmental issues, such as the state of the environment or policy. In the 1980s, the government's Pollution Paper 23 tacitly recognised the 'guiding principle' referred to in the RCEP's 1984 Report, but rejected the need for a general right of access to environmental information.

1.3 DIRECTIVE 90/313/EEC AND THE ENVIRONMENTAL INFORMATION REGULATIONS 1992

At the European level there was also an increasing recognition that the public should have access to environmental information. The Third Environmental Action Programme for 1982–1986 mandated that '[t]he requisite knowledge and information must be improved and made readily available to decision makers and all interested parties, including the public'. By the time the Fourth Environmental Action Programme (1987–1992) was published, the European Commission announced that it should be possible to improve public access to information held by environmental authorities whilst at the same time protecting confidential information.

The result of the call for greater access to environmental information was the enactment of Council Directive 90/313/EEC on the freedom of access to information on the Environment (1990 Directive). Member States were required to transpose the Directive into national law by 31 December 1992. The 1990 Directive intended to facilitate a right of access to information about the environment but left the Member States to define their own procedural rules.

The European Court of Justice (ECJ) was called upon to give a number of interpretive rulings (preliminary rulings) of the 1990 Directive and it soon became clear that the Court was willing to give a broad purposive interpretation of the rights granted by the Directive (see, for example, *Wilhelm Mecklenburg* v. *Kreis Pinneberg-Der Landrat* (Case C-321/96) [1998] ECR I-3809). In contrast, the ECJ took a restrictive approach to the interpretation of the exceptions, so as to ensure the widest possible access to information about the environment. Some of these earlier preliminary rulings will be examined, where appropriate, throughout this book.

In 2000 the European Commission completed a review of the 1990 Directive, based on the shared experiences of the Member States. The review identified the principle 'weaknesses' of the 1990 Directive, identifying, *inter alia*, the need to provide clearer definitions of 'environmental information' and 'public authority', and to make the exceptions to disclosure more restrictive. The findings of the 2000 review informed the European Union's position during the negotiations leading to the adoption of the Aarhus Convention (see **1.4**), which would further pave the way for greater transparency and democracy in relation to environmental matters.

1.3.1 The Environmental Information Regulations 1992

The 1990 Directive was implemented into domestic law by the Environmental Information Regulations 1992, SI 1992/3240 (EIR 1992), which came into force on 31 December 1992. Although broadly similar to EIR 2004, the 1992 regulations included a narrower definition of 'environmental information' and 'public authority'. In contrast, the exceptions to disclosure were quite broadly cast and, in particular, were not subject to a public interest test. There is very little substantive evidence about the use of EIR 1992 other than some apocryphal stories which suggest that many public authorities were either unaware of their obligations or that they simply ignored or refused requests. The principal problem with this earlier regime was that it lacked teeth. The only way in which an applicant could challenge a decision refusing a request for information was by way of judicial review; an extremely risky and costly exercise to try and secure information. This explains why there is so little case law concerning EIR 1992. (See *R* v. *British Coal Corporation*, ex parte *Ibstock Building Products Ltd* [1995] Env LR 277; *R* v. *Secretary of State for the Environment, Transport and the Regions & Midland Expressway Ltd* (No.1) [1999] Env LR 447; *Maile* v. *Wigan MBC* [2001] Env LR 11.)

1.4   THE INTERNATIONAL DIMENSION AND THE AARHUS CONVENTION

In 1998 the UK and the EU signed the UNECE Convention on Access to Information, Public Participation in Decision Making and Access to Justice in Environmental Matters, or, as it is more commonly known, the Aarhus Convention.

The Convention was described by the then UN Secretary-General Kofi Anan as the 'most impressive elaboration of Principle 10 of the Rio Declaration' because it fleshes out the rights identified in Principle 10 and gives them a legal substance.

Principal 10 of the Rio Declaration 1992

Environmental issues are best handled with the participation of all concerned citizens, at the relevant level. At the national level, each individual shall have appropriate access to information concerning the environment that is held by public authorities, including information on hazardous materials and activities in their communities, and the opportunity to participate in decision-making processes. States shall facilitate and encourage public awareness and participation by making information widely available. Effective access to judicial and administrative proceedings, including redress and remedy, shall be provided.

The Aarhus Convention is broken down into three distinct pillars, of which environmental information is the first. The pillars can be briefly summarised as follows.

1.4.1   Access to environmental information

The Aarhus Convention recognises that public authorities hold a great deal of environmental information in the public interest. It provides that the public have the right, subject to limited exceptions, to access this information. The Convention defines both 'environmental information' and 'public authority', and lists the limited exceptions to disclosure. Article 4 provides that public authorities that hold environmental information make it available to the public on request, subject to the limited exceptions within art.4. A requestor is not required to state their interest. The public authority may make a reasonable charge for supplying the information. The information must be supplied as soon as possible and in any event within one month of the request unless the volume and complexity of the request requires an extension of up to two months. Article 5 deals with the collection and progressive dissemination of environmental information. The EU, which played a key role in shaping and drafting the Convention, sought to ensure that the access to information limb of the Convention did not repeat the defects and weaknesses of the 1990 Directive.

1.4.2   Public participation in environmental decision making

Recalling Principle 10 of the Rio Declaration, the Aarhus Convention asserts that the public have a right to participate in certain types of environmental decisions. This requires, *inter alia*, that the public are notified when decisions are going to be taken, and are given reasonable time frames to make their representations known.

Public participation should be at an early stage when all options are open. Article 6 deals with certain projects which are likely to have significant effects on the environment, art.7 deals with programmes, policies and plans and art.8 deals with legislation. The rights that are articulated in these three articles have been implemented into EU law by a number of Directives (Council Directive 2001/35/EC which amends Council Directive 85/337/EEC of 27 June 1985 on the assessment of the effects of certain public and private projects on the environment and also Council Directive 2001/42/EC on the assessment of the effects of certain plans and programmes on the environment). These Directives have been transposed into domestic law via a range of statutory instruments, each of which sets out the procedural mechanisms for securing public participation in the specific decision making. It is not difficult to see the link between this limb and the access to information limb; for the public to participate in a meaningful way in environmental decision making they need access to the environmental information held by public authorities.

1.4.3 Access to justice in environmental matters

Article 9 of the Convention is misleadingly brief given its substantive content. It has also generated a considerable body of academic and practitioner discussion about the extent to which the UK complies with all aspects of art.9. (For example, see The Sullivan Report, *Ensuring Access to Environmental Justice in England and Wales* (2008) and Update 2010. In late 2010, the Aarhus Compliance Committee found that the UK was in breach of various aspects of art.9, specifically in relation to the costs of judicial review, and the European Commission has issued a Reasoned Opinion alleging similar breaches.

Article 9(1) provides that each signatory party must, within the framework of its own national legislation, ensure that any person who considers that his or her request for information under art.4 has:

> been ignored, wrongfully refused, whether in part or in full, inadequately answered, or otherwise not dealt with in accordance with the provisions of that article, has access to a review procedure before a court of law or another independent and impartial body established by law.

Articles 9(4) and (5) attach conditions to these procedures and remedies, notably that the procedures must be fair, timely and not prohibitively expensive.

The review and appeal procedures under EIR 2004 are considered in **Chapter 10**.

1.4.4 Relevance of the Convention to information rights practitioners

Although the Aarhus Convention, as an international treaty, has no direct effect within the domestic legal system, it should not be disregarded as irrelevant by information rights practitioners. It is important to see EIR 2004 in their broader context and, as will be seen below, it is necessary to interpret their provisions purposively. *The Aarhus Convention: An Implementation Guide* (the Aarhus Implementation Guide), which is available via the United Nations Economic Commission for Europe (UNECE) website (**www.unece.org**), provides a useful aide to practitioners, particularly as it goes through each article of the Convention and emphasises throughout the overall objectives of the Convention. That said, the Information Commissioner or Information Rights Tribunal rarely make reference to it. On the other hand, they both frequently refer to Directive 2003/4/EC, which implements the first limb of the Convention.

1.5 DIRECTIVE 2003/4/EC: THE ENVIRONMENTAL INFORMATION DIRECTIVE

Both the EU and the UK were signatories to the Convention. This meant both were required, by art.3, to take the necessary legislative, regulatory and other measures to ensure compliance with the obligations and also to ensure proper enforcement of those measures. In order to fulfil its obligations under the Convention it was necessary for the EU to adopt new Convention-compliant legislation.

Directive 90/313/EEC was repealed and replaced with Directive 2003/4/EC on public access to environmental information, the wording of which is almost entirely identical to the relevant provisions of the Convention. Member States of the EU were required to transpose the provisions of Directive 2003/4/EC into the domestic law by 14 February 2005. The UK found itself doubly bound to implement EIR 2004 by virtue of its own obligations under the Convention and the EU Directive. EIR 1992 were repealed and replaced with EIR 2004. EIR 2004 came into force on 1 January 2005 (the same day as the whole of FOIA 2000).

1.5.1 Relevance of the Directive in the interpretation of EIR 2004; the duty of sympathetic interpretation

EIR 2004 practically mirror the provisions of the Directive. However, EIR 2004 do not include the recitals to the Directive, which are sometimes useful to legal practitioners because they provide evidence about the purpose of the Directive. The recitals can act as an aid to interpretation, for example Recital 16, which given its importance is cited below:

> The right to information means that the disclosure of information should be the general rule and that public authorities should be permitted to refuse a request for environmental information in specific and clearly defined cases. Grounds for refusal should be interpreted in a restrictive way, whereby the public interest served by disclosure should be weighed against the interest served by the refusal. The reasons for a refusal should be provided to the applicant within the time limit laid down in this Directive.

When a national court or tribunal is tasked with applying national law which implements the requirements of a Directive the court or tribunal must interpret the national law, as far as possible, in the light of the wording and the purpose of the

Directive (*Marleasing SA* v. *La Comercial Internacional de Alimentacion SA* (Case C-106/89) [1990] ECR I-4135). This duty of sympathetic interpretation (generally referred to as indirect effect) was recognised by Laws LJ when he stated that if the interpretation of EIR 2004 'is to be coloured by anything it must be by the Directive' (*R (on the application of Office of Communications)* v. *Information Commissioner* [2008] EWHC 1445 (Admin); [2009] Env LR 1). When the same case was on appeal from the Court of Appeal, the Supreme Court (*Office of Communications* v. *Information Commissioner* [2010] UKSC 3; [2010] Env LR 20) concluded that the requirements of the Directive (in relation to the public interest test) were not clear. The Supreme Court sought a preliminary ruling which was delivered by the European Court of Justice on 28 July 2011 (Case C-71/10 – at the time of writing the decision is only available via the Court's website at **http://curia.europa.eu** (See **Chapters 7** and **8** for further discussion of this case).

1.6 FOIA 2000 AND ENVIRONMENTAL INFORMATION

Both FOIA 2000 and EIR 2004 came into force on 1 January 2005. Given the higher profile that FOIA 2000 enjoys, it is much more likely that if a person is going to cite any legislation as the basis for his request, he will refer to the Act rather than EIR 2004. A glance at many of the Information Commissioner's decision notices suggests that very few applicants ever refer to EIR 2004 when making their requests. This should not be a problem for the applicant; the public is not actually required or expected to know about either FOIA 2000 or EIR 2004 or indeed the differences between the two. Applicants do not even have to cite any legislation when they make a request for information, let alone the correct one. However, public authorities are expected to know the difference. When a public authority receives a request for information (other than a request for personal data by the data subject) it should, irrespective of whether the applicant has cited FOIA 2000, consider whether the request is for environmental information. If the request is for environmental information then the public authority handling the request should proceed in accordance with the rules laid down in EIR 2004 and not FOIA 2000. If it is not a request for environmental information then it should be handled in accordance with FOIA 2000.

This begs the question: Why do we have two information rights regimes, one of which is perfectly capable of embracing the other?

1.6.1 Why can't requests for environmental information be dealt with under FOIA 2000?

There is no doubt that it would have been a great deal simpler for public authorities had the two regimes been enacted as a single piece of legislation, conferring a general right to all information, including environmental information. It would have been open to the government to enact a Freedom of Information Act that included environmental information within its scope. Certainly other Western European countries, such as Sweden, Finland and the Netherlands, have not differentiated between environmental information and other kinds of information held by public authorities, making the question of which regime to apply wholly unnecessary. However, the Labour government of the day chose to enact two separate pieces of legislation, both coming into force on the same day. A full account of the reasons why we have two separate regimes falls outside the scope of this book, but is largely to do with the fact that, as far as environmental information is concerned, the legislation had to comply with the limited exceptions laid down in Directive 2003/4/EC. To incorporate environmental information into FOIA 2000 would have meant either applying the limited exceptions in the Directive to all information or having a separate set of exceptions for environmental information. Presumably the first was unpalatable to the government and the second would have resulted in a particularly unwieldy FOIA 2000.

The decision to have two separate pieces of legislation meant that a mechanism had to be found to ensure that requests for environmental information were covered by EIR 2004 rather than FOIA 2000. The answer to this was to make environmental information 'exempt' from the wide-ranging scope of the Act.

1.6.2 FOIA 2000, s.39: Environmental information exemption

FOIA 2000, s.39 provides that information is exempt from the Act (there is no duty to disclose it) if the public authority holding it:

- is obliged to make the information available under EIR 2004; or
- would be obliged to disclose it under EIR 2004 but for the operation of any exception contained in the Regulations.

The effect of this is that 'where a request for information is made under FOIA there is an exemption under s.39 where EIR 2004 apply, and the public authority is obliged to deal with the request under EIR' (*Kirkaldie* v. *Information Commissioner & Thanet District Council* (EA 2006/01)).

In short, a public authority should consider, on receipt of a request for information, whether the request is for environmental information. If the request is for environmental information then the public authority must deal with under EIR 2004.

However, and somewhat curiously, the FOIA 2000, s.39 exemption is not an absolute exemption. FOIA 2000 has two different types of exemption; absolute and qualified. Where information falls within an 'absolute exemption', then the public authority is not obliged to disclose the information. For example, information contained in a court record is an absolute exemption (FOIA 2000, s.23) as is information provided in confidence (FOIA 2000, s.41). The absolute exemptions apply to all information which falls within the categories listed in the exemption. Another absolute exemption is information that is reasonably accessible by other means (FOIA 2000, s.21). This means that if information is reasonably accessible to the applicant by other means then the public authority does not have to disclose it.

Exemptions that are not absolute are referred to as 'qualified' (although that term never actually appears in FOIA 2000 itself). To apply a qualified exemption the public authority must first consider whether the information requested falls into the type covered by the exemption. For example, national security (FOIA 2000, s.24) health and safety (FOIA 2000, s.38), or environmental information (FOIA 2000, s.39). If the information falls within one of the qualified exemptions then the public authority must go on to consider the public interest test; it must consider whether the public interest in withholding the information outweighs the public interest in disclosing it. If the public interest in disclosure outweighs the public interest in maintaining the exemption then the information must be disclosed.

It should also be noted that FOIA 2000 includes a further categorisation of exemptions; those that are class based and those that are prejudice based. As far as prejudice-based exemptions are concerned, the public authority can only engage the exemption if disclosure would, or would be likely to, prejudice the interest protected by the exemption. An example of a prejudice-based exemption is FOIA 2000, s.27 where information is exempt if its disclosure would, or would be likely to, prejudice relations between the United Kingdom and any other state.

Section 39 is a qualified exemption

As stated earlier, FOIA 2000, s.39 is a qualified exemption, although it really is not clear why this is the case, nor is it entirely clear what the impact of the qualification is. The effect of FOIA 2000, s.39 was considered by the Information Tribunal in the *Rhondda* case :

Rhondda Cynon Taff County Borough Council v. Information Commissioner (EA/2007/0065)

A requestor asked the council for a 'copy of your current working under the Land Drainage Act'. The council understood this to be a request for a copy of the Act itself and so referred the applicant to the OPSI website and invited him to access this via facilities in the public library. The council relied on FOIA 2000, s.21 which exempts information where the information is reasonably accessible to the applicant. It is not clear whether the council ever considered the possibility that the request should fall under the EIR.

Following investigation the Commissioner decided that the requested information was 'environmental' and therefore exempt from FOIA by virtue of s.39 and that the council could not therefore rely on the s.21 exemption. Accordingly the Commissioner instructed the council to disclose information to the applicant. In his Decision Notice the Commissioner takes the view that the two regimes were exclusive of one another (FS50117954).

On appeal the Tribunal did not dispute that the information was 'environmental' but they did not concur with the Commissioner's submissions about the exclusivity of the regimes, preferring to view the regimes as running 'in parallel'. The Tribunal concluded that the effect of s.39 is that if a request for environmental information is refused under the EIR then it should go on to be considered under FOIA 2000. The Tribunal reminded itself that s.39 was subject to the public interest test but never went any further in discussing what this means in practical terms.

If the Tribunal is right, then FOIA 2000, s.39 appears to operate like a gateway taking a request from FOIA 2000 into EIR 2004 and then back into the Act if the information is not released under EIR 2004. However, it is extremely difficult to imagine how, in practice, a request for information that has been denied under EIR 2004 could result in disclosure under FOIA 2000 when the exemptions under FOIA 2000 are more widely cast and it is generally acknowledged that it is harder to withhold information under EIR 2004 than it is under the Act.

Notwithstanding the semantic arguments rehearsed by the Tribunal in the *Rhondda* case, the fact remains that requests for environmental information should not be dealt with under FOIA 2000. Therefore, when a public authority receives a request for information the first thing it should do is ask whether the information requested is 'environmental'. This absolutely demands an understanding of the definition of 'environmental information' on the part of all public authorities. The definition is considered in depth in **Chapter 3**.

1.7   EIR 2004 AND OTHER STATUTORY BARS

Readers should also note a further significant difference between FOIA 2000 and EIR 2004. Under FOIA 2000 a public authority is prohibited from disclosing any information which is subject to a statutory bar. A statutory bar is a restriction or prohibition on the disclosure of information. Examples include CPA 1974, s.94 and WIA 1991, s.206. In contrast, EIR 2004, reg.5(6) states that any enactment or rule of law that would prevent the disclosure of information (i.e. a statutory bar) in accordance with EIR 2004 shall not apply. This means that a statutory bar in other legislation cannot be automatically used to refuse a request for environmental information under EIR 2004. However, the information may be refused under one of the EIR exceptions. The statutory bar may be considered relevant in assessing the public interest and whether an exception is engaged (see **Chapters 7** and **8**).

1.8   OTHER SOURCES OF ENVIRONMENTAL INFORMATION

It would be misleading to imagine that the only way in which the public can access environmental information is via EIR 2004. As noted above, the public registers created under various pieces of environmental legislation remain and provide a further source of information, particularly about emissions into the environment. In addition there are various other legislative provisions which may be utilised to obtain information. These are considered in **Chapter 11**.

CHAPTER 2

Overview of EIR 2004

2.1 INTRODUCTION

This chapter aims to provide an overview of the provisions of EIR 2004. The chapter will introduce some key terms, consider the structure and content of the regulations and briefly examine the range of sources that are available to assist both applicants and public authorities in understanding the respective rights conferred and obligations imposed by EIR 2004.

2.2 KEY TERMS AND DEFINITIONS

The following table lists some (but not all) of the terms that are discussed throughout this handbook.

Term	Comments
The Act FOIA 2000	The Freedom of Information Act 2000. FOIA 2000 came fully into force on 1 January 2005, the same day as EIR 2004. FOIA 2000, s.39 exempts environmental information from the provisions of the Act. However, the enforcement and appeals provisions in FOIA 2000 are 'imported' into EIR (with some modification) by EIR 2004, regs.11 and 18.
Advice and assistance	A public authority is required to provide advice and assistance to applicants and prospective applicants. The duty only extends to the level of advice and assistance that it would be reasonable to expect an authority to provide (EIR 2004, reg.9).
Applicant	The person who makes the request for information.

Term	Comments
Charging	A public authority may charge for the environmental information it provides but any charge must not exceed a reasonable amount. The public authority cannot make any charge for allowing an applicant to access any public register or lists of environmental information or for allowing the applicant to examine the information where it is held by the public authority (EIR 2004, reg.8). See **Chapter 6**.
Code of Practice	The Secretary of State has issued a Code of Practice (under EIR 2004, reg.16). The Code provides guidance as to the practice which it would, in the Secretary of State's opinion, be desirable for public authorities to follow when discharging their obligations under EIR 2004.
Commissioner	The Information Commissioner; his role in relation to EIR 2004 is considered at 10.2.
Convention The Aarhus Convention	The UNECE Convention on Access to Information, Public Participation in Decision Making and Access to Justice in Environmental Matters – known as the Aarhus Convention after the Danish city in which the Convention was signed.
Data, data protection principles, data subject and personal data	These terms have the same meaning as in the Data Protection Act 1998 (DPA 1998). See **9.2**.
Decision notice	Notice issued by the Information Commissioner to a public authority/complainant following a complaint to the Information Commissioner's Office (ICO) about a breach of EIR 2004. The notice is binding on the recipient public authority. See **Chapter 10**.
Defra	The Department for Environment, Food and Rural Affairs.
The Directive	Directive 2003/4/EC on public access to environmental information. EIR 2004 transposes the provisions of this Directive into domestic law. It repealed and replaced the provisions of Directive 90/313/EEC on the freedom of access to information on the environment.
Emissions	Emissions are included within the definition of 'environmental information' in EIR 2004, reg.2 (factors such as substances, energy, noise, radiation or waste, including radioactive waste, emissions). By reg.12(9), if the environmental information relates to emissions, a public authority is not entitled to refuse to disclose that information under the exceptions referred to in EIR 2004, reg. 12(5)(d)–(g).

Term	Comments
Enforcement notice	If the Commissioner is satisfied that a public authority has failed to comply with its obligations under EIR 2004, the Commissioner may serve an enforcement notice requiring the public authority to take particular steps by a particular time to comply with its obligations (FOIA 2000, s.52). See **10.3**.
Environmental information	The definition of 'environmental information' is clearly central to the operation of EIR 2004. The definition is given the same meaning as in art.2(1) of the Directive. See **Chapter 3**.
Exceptions	EIR 2004 provides that certain information may be withheld from disclosure providing an exception to disclosure applies and, in all the circumstances of the case, the public interest in maintaining the exception outweighs the public interest in disclosing the information. The exceptions to disclosure are provided in EIR 2004, reg.12 and are considered in **Chapters 7, 8 and 9**.
Exemption	FOIA 2000 uses the word exemption instead of exception. (See above.)
Form and format of information	An applicant may request that environmental information be provided in a particular form or format (e.g. a hard copy or a specific electronic format such as PDF). EIR 2004, reg.6 requires the public authority to comply with such a request subject to two exceptions. See **Chapter 6**.
Government department	Each government department is to be treated as a person separate from any other government department for the purposes of EIR 2004, Parts 2, 4 and 5. (Part 3 which is omitted from this relates to the exceptions.)
Historical record	Is given the same meaning as in FOIA 2000, s.62(1) and is considered at **6.8**.
Holding information	The duty to disclose environmental information (subject to the application of the exceptions) only applies to environmental information held by a public authority. The definition of 'held' is provided in EIR 2004, reg.3(2) and is considered at **6.2.4**.
ICO	Information Commissioner's Office.
Information notice	The Information Commissioner may serve an information notice under FOIA 2000, s.51 requiring a public authority to provide the information he requires, in the form he requires and within the time specified in the notice. See **10.3**.

Term	Comments
Information Rights Tribunal, First-tier Tribunal (Information Rights)	Properly called the First-tier Tribunal (Information Rights), formerly the Information Tribunal. The Tribunal hears appeals from notices issued by the Information Commissioner. See **10.11** in relation to the role of the Tribunal in the enforcement and appeals procedures.
Internal review	If an applicant is dissatisfied with the way in which a public authority has handled his request for environmental information or considers that the request has been wrongly refused, the applicant may ask the public authority to review its decision. The complainant must make the request in writing and the public authority must complete the internal review and notify the complainant of its decision as soon as possible and within 40 days after the date of the written request. The process is free of charge (EIR 2004, reg.11). See **10.8**.
Ministerial certificate	A certificate issued by a Minister of the Crown which provides conclusive proof that the disclosure of information would adversely affect national security and it would not be in the public interest to disclose the information (EIR reg.15). See **8.3.4**.
Personal data	Has the same meaning as in the Data Protection Act 1998. If the information requested includes personal data and the applicant is not the data subject (the person whom the information is about) then the public authority must not disclose the information if disclosure would breach the DPA 1998 (EIR 2004, reg.13). See **Chapter 9**.
Presumption in favour of disclosure	EIR 2004, reg.12(2) expressly states that public authorities shall apply a presumption in favour of disclosure. See **7.3**.
Publication schemes	Not specifically a requirement under EIR 2004. Public authorities subject to FOIA 2000 are required to publish information proactively via their publication schemes (FOIA 2000, s.19). Public authorities subject to both FOIA 2000 and EIR 2004 may use their publication schemes to actively disseminate environmental information and comply with their obligations under EIR 2004, reg.4. See **Chapter 5**.
Public authority	'Public authority' is defined in EIR 2004, reg.2(2). Only public authorities that fall within this definition are subject to EIR 2004. The definition is wide enough to catch a number of private sector bodies. See **Chapter 4**.

Term	Comments
Public interest test	A public authority may only withhold information under the exceptions listed in EIR 2004, reg.12 if, in all the circumstances of the case, the public interest in maintaining the exception outweighs the public interest in disclosing the information (EIR 2004, reg.12(1)(b)). This is referred to as the public interest test. For further discussion see **7.4**.
Public record	Has the same meaning as FOIA 2000, s.84 which defines it as a public record within the meaning of the Public Records Act 1958 or a public record to which the Public Records Act (Northern Ireland) 1923 applies. See **6.8**.
Public registers	Several pieces of legislation provide for certain prescribed information to be made available on a public register. The key public registers of environmental information are considered in **Chapter 11**.
Scottish public authority	A body referred to in FOIA 2000, s.80(2) and (in so far as the body is not covered by s.80(2)) a Scottish public authority as defined by the Freedom of Information (Scotland) Act 2005.
Transferred public record	Has the same meaning as defined in FOIA 2000, s.15. See **6.8**.
Upper Tribunal (Administrative Appeals Chamber)	The Upper Tribunal (Administrative Appeals Chamber) for the United Kingdom is a Superior Court of Record with UK-wide jurisdiction. Has jurisdiction to decide applications for permission to appeal and appeals on points of law from decisions of the First-tier Tribunal (Information Rights). See **10.13**.
Working day	Has the same meaning as defined in FOIA 2000, s.10(6). It means any day other than a Saturday, Sunday, Christmas day, Good Friday or a day which is a bank holiday under the Banking and Financial Dealings Act 1971 in any part of the UK.

2.3 OVERVIEW OF THE RIGHTS AND DUTIES PRESCRIBED IN EIR 2004

EIR 2004 are broken down into four parts.

1. Part 1 includes the interpretation section and defines the application of the regulations.
2. Part 2 (EIR 2004, regs.4–11) defines the obligations on public authorities in respect of access to environmental information held by public authorities.
3. Part 3 (EIR 2004, regs.12–15) deals with the exceptions to the duty to disclose environmental information.

4.   Part 4 makes provision for the issue of a Code of Practice and historical records.
5.   Part 5 (EIR 2004, regs.18–21) imports the enforcement and appeals provisions of FOIA 2000 into EIR 2004 and also establishes a number of criminal offences in respect of breaches of EIR 2004.

2.3.1   Overview

- Underpinning EIR 2004 is the belief that public authorities hold environmental information in the public interest and that the public has a right to access this information, subject to a limited number of exceptions.
- EIR 2004 impose obligations on public authorities (except any public authority to the extent it is acting in a judicial or legislative capacity) (EIR 2004, reg.3).
- Public authorities are under a duty to actively and systematically make the environmental information that they hold available to the public by electronic means (EIR 2004, reg.4).
- EIR 2004 confer a right on any member of the public to request environmental information held by public authorities. The regulations prescribe how such requests should be handled, including how the information may be supplied, charges and time limits (EIR 2004, regs.5–11).
- Public authorities are under a duty to provide environmental information on request. Any enactment or rule of law that would prevent the disclosure of information in accordance with EIR 2004 is disapplied by EIR 2004, reg.5(6).
- Public authorities are under a duty to provide advice and assistance to applicants and prospective applicants (EIR 2004, reg.9).
- Public authorities must apply a presumption in favour of disclosing environmental information (EIR 2004, reg.12(2)).
- Public authorities may withhold environmental information in certain circumstances. An exception to disclosure must apply and, in all the circumstances of the case, the public interest in maintaining the exception must outweigh the public interest in disclosing the information (EIR 2004, reg. 12(1)).
- If the request for environmental information includes personal data of which the applicant is the data subject then the request must be processed under DPA 1998. If the request includes personal data of which the applicant is not the data subject, then the information must not be disclosed to the applicant unless it conforms with the provisions of DPA 1998 (EIR 2004, regs.12(3) and 13).
- A public authority is not entitled to refuse to disclose information on emissions under some of the exceptions to disclosure (EIR 2004, reg.12(9)).
- A Minister of the Crown may certify that certain information should not be disclosed on the grounds that disclosure would adversely affect national security and it would not be in the public interest to disclose the information (EIR 2004, reg.15).

- Where a public authority refuses to disclose any environmental information requested, then the public authority must notify the applicant, within the specified time period, and state its reasons for refusal (EIR 2004, reg.14).
- If a member of the public considers that a public authority has not complied with the requirements of the regulations when handling his request for environmental information then he has the right to request the public authority concerned to reconsider its decision. This is referred to as an internal review (EIR 2004, reg.11).
- If an applicant is not satisfied with the response by the public authority after the public authority has reconsidered its decision, then the applicant can complain to the Information Commissioner. The enforcement and appeals provisions of FOIA 2000 are imported into EIR 2004 by reg.18.
- The Information Commissioner can investigate complaints and may issue a decision notice either vindicating the public authority's decision or actions or requiring it to take certain steps, including requiring it to disclose information (EIR 2004, reg.18).
- The Information Commissioner may serve an enforcement notice on a public authority if the Commissioner is satisfied that a public authority has failed to comply with Parts 2 and 3 of EIR 2004.
- Both the complainant and the public authority concerned may appeal a decision notice issued by the Information Commissioner. The appeal is heard by the First-tier Tribunal (Information Rights) (hereafter 'the Information Rights Tribunal'). Onward appeals to the Upper Tribunal can be made, with permission, on any point of law arising from the decision of the Information Rights Tribunal. Appeals beyond the Upper Tribunal are to the Court of Appeal on a point of law.

All of the points raised above will be examined throughout the following chapters.

2.3.2 Jurisdictional scope

EIR 2004 apply to public authorities in England and Wales. The regulations do not apply to Scottish public authorities which are subject to the Environmental Information (Scotland) Regulations 2004, SSI 2004/520. This means that EIR 2004 do not apply to the:

- Scottish Parliament;
- any part of the Scottish administration;
- the Scottish Parliamentary Corporate Body;
- any Scottish public authority with mixed functions or no reserved functions within the meaning of the Scotland Act 1998;
- any body defined as a public authority by the Freedom of Information (Scotland) Act 2002.

However, it should be noted that an English or Welsh public authority that is located in Scotland and which does not fall within the definition of 'a Scottish public authority' (above) is subject to EIR 2004.

2.4 SOURCES OF ADVICE AND GUIDANCE

There is no shortage of advice and guidance available for organisations and applicants. In some respects there is arguably too much, with no one source being definitive. With the exception of the Code of Practice (see **2.4.1**), which sets out the standards which the Information Commissioner considers that public authorities should adhere to, the guidance on the interpretation of EIR 2004 is not legally binding.

There are two main sources of guidance. The first is issued by Defra, which is the lead government department for EIR 2004. In addition, the ICO also offers its own advice and EIR 2004 guidance along with guidance on FOIA 2000, DPA 1998 and the Privacy and Electronic Communications (EC Directive) Regulations 2003, SI 2003/2426, as amended. Users should bear in mind that neither source of guidance is *definitive* and there may be subtle differences between the advice offered. The Defra guidance represents the government's view on what it considers is the correct interpretation of the regulations. The Information Commissioner, on the other hand, is independent of government and does not necessarily have to concur with the government's viewpoint.

In addition to the guidance offered by Defra and the ICO we can add into the mix a further source of guidance. It was noted in **Chapter 1** that EIR 2004 give effect to Directive 2003/4/EC on public access to environmental information. The Directive in turn fulfils the requirements of the UNECE Aarhus Convention. Apart from one or two slight differences, EIR 2004 closely correspond to various articles of the Convention. Tthe Aarhus Implementation Guide (available via the UNECE website at **www.unece.org**) provides an overview and detailed analysis of each article of the Convention. For example, it considers the definitions of 'public authority', 'environmental information' and the operation of the exceptions. Although much of the material in the Aarhus Implementation Guide is echoed in either the Defra or ICO guidance, it does constitute a separate source of information which practitioners may find valuable.

2.4.1 Defra guidance

Defra is the lead government department for EIR 2004. The Secretary of State for the Environment was responsible for issuing the EIR Code of Practice and the Defra is responsible for reporting to the European Commission on the operation of EIR 2004. The 2009 report in available on the Defra website.

The Defra website offers the user a relatively easily navigable access point to a considerable body of information about EIR 2004. The material ranges from a list of frequently asked questions, largely directed at applicants, to the detailed technical guidance largely directed at organisations. In addition, Defra has produced various other guidance notes dealing with specific issues. One particularly useful source of information is on the boundaries between environmental information and other information (see **2.8** for useful websites). Another is guidance for public authorities on using the model ICO publication scheme for disseminating environmental information. Throughout this book the reader will be referred to Defra guidance as and when necessary; however, care should be taken since the guidance is subject to revision and may alter after publication of this book. The material on the Defra website can be broadly grouped into three categories:

- Code of Practice on the discharge of the obligations of public authorities under EIR 2004;
- detailed guidance; and
- guidance for applicants.

Detailed guidance

Defra has issued detailed guidance on all aspects of EIR 2004. This is largely directed at organisations but provides very useful information to applicants and any person wishing to 'challenge' the decision of a public authority. The detailed guidance is broken down into the following chapters:

1. Introduction
2. Who is covered by the regulations?
3. What is covered by the regulations?
4. What do the regulations require public and other authorities to do?
5. Proactive dissemination
6. Handling requests for environmental information
7. Exceptions
8. Complaints, reconsideration and appeals
9. Records management and offences
10. Monitoring and reporting

The detailed guidance was originally produced in 2005 following public consultation, but the chapters are revised from time to time to take account of recent decisions of the Information Commissioner, Information Rights Tribunal and the courts. Public authorities using the detailed guidance should check the date of the guidance and do any necessary updating by referring to relevant ICO decision notices or Tribunal decisions.

Guidance for applicants

The Defra web pages list a whole series of frequently asked questions (FAQs) aimed at prospective applicants, with questions ranging from 'What information is covered by the Regulations?' to 'What grounds are there for refusing a request?' By clicking on any of these questions the public are given a brief answer, but there is also a link to the detailed guidance discussed above.

2.4.2 Code of Practice on the discharge of the obligations of public authorities under EIR 2004

Under EIR 2004, reg.16 the Secretary of State may issue a Code of Practice, providing guidance to public authorities as to the practice which would, in the Secretary of State's opinion, be desirable for public authorities to follow. Similar provisions exist under FOIA 2000, s.46 which allow the Secretary of State to issue a Code of Practice relating to FOIA 2000. Any references in this book to the Code of Practice are references to the EIR 2004 Code, unless otherwise stated. The Secretary of State is required to consult the Information Commissioner before issuing or revising the Code. The Code was laid before Parliament on 16 February 2005.

Although the Code of Practice does not form part of EIR 2004 and it purports to offer guidance on how public authorities should discharge their duties, it is a very important yardstick in assessing whether public authorities have fulfilled their statutory obligations under EIR 2004. As the foreword to the Code notes:

> if public authorities do not follow the Code's recommendations it will be difficult for them to meet their obligations under the Regulations.

Similarly, the foreword further states that although the Code is not legislation, authorities are *expected to abide* (author's emphasis) by the Code unless there are good reasons why it would be inappropriate to do so. Moreover, a public authority will be expected to justify to the Information Commissioner any departure from the Code. Anybody considering challenging a public authority's handling of a request for environmental information would therefore be well advised to start with the Code and consider whether the authority has complied with its recommendations.

The Code has several aims, all largely to do with setting out good practice and protecting the rights of the public. It aims to:

- facilitate the disclosure of information by setting out good administrative practice that it is desirable for public authorities to follow when handling requests for information;
- set out good practice in relation to the proactive dissemination of environmental information;
- protect the interests of applicants by setting out standards of advice and assistance that should be offered as a matter of good practice;
- ensure that any third party rights are considered and that authorities consider the implications for access to environmental information before agreeing to

21

confidentiality provisions in contracts and accepting information in confidence from a third party; and
- encourage, as a matter of good practice, the development of effective review and appeal procedures of decisions taken under EIR 2004.

The foreword to the Code (which does not actually form a part of the Code) states that public authorities should refer to the government (Defra) guidance and also the guidance issued by the ICO (these are discussed below).

The Code of Practice on Records Management issued under FOIA 2000, s.46 also applies to environmental information in the same way as other types of information.

2.4.3 ICO guidance

In addition to the government guidance offered by Defra, organisations and applicants should also refer to the guidance issued by the ICO. The Information Commissioner's duty to promote good practice by public authorities under FOIA 2000 also extends to EIR 2004 and EIR public authorities. To this end, the ICO website provides various sources of advice and guidance to applicants and organisations. These are briefly described below.

Advice for applicants

The ICO website offers general advice to applicants and prospective applicants about their rights under FOIA 2000, EIR 2004, DPA 1998 and the Privacy and Electronic Communications (EC Directive) Regulations 2003. This includes general advice on the range of information the public can access and suggestions about how to formulate questions. In addition, the website also provides brief answers to a range of FAQs about EIR 2004.

Advice for organisations

The ICO website offers some advice regarding EIR 2004, in particular on the definition of 'environmental information'; whether a body is subject to EIR 2004; how to answer an information request; what to do if an individual complains about a request; and whether the information should be made available via a publication scheme. The more detailed information about EIR 2004 is available in the document library which includes online documentation on the following:

- What is environmental information?
- Charging for environmental information
- A verbal request log sheet which public authorities can use to log and track verbal requests for environmental information
- Time for compliance (FAQs)
- Advice and assistance (FAQs)

- A brief introduction to the exceptions
- Routinely publishing environmental information
- Guidance on EIR 2004, reg.6 (form and format) is offered via FOIA awareness guidance 29

In addition, the ICO now offers some specific guidance on the use of EIR 2004 in property searches. This is an issue that has generated a considerable amount of controversy and is therefore examined at **11.7**.

2.5 DECISION NOTICES

All of the decision notices issued by the Information Commissioner are accessible online via the ICO website. A decision notice is issued following the investigation of a complaint; a complainant may apply to the Commissioner for a decision about whether a request for information to a public authority has been dealt with in accordance with the requirements of Parts 2 and 3 of EIR 2004. The decision notice, which must be served on both the complainant and the public authority, will set out what steps the public authority has to take, if any, to comply with EIR 2004. A decision notice is legally binding on the public authority but it does not constitute a precedent which must be followed in all cases. Nevertheless, the notices provide a useful source of information about the Commissioner's approach to the various aspects of EIR 2004 and in this respect may be used as a further source of 'guidance' to organisations.

Decision notices may be searched either by reference to the specific provision of EIR 2004 or by the name of the public authority concerned. A public authority seeking to rely on a particular exception would be well advised to refer to relevant decision notices in order to ascertain the approach taken by the Commissioner to that particular exception.

Practical example

In FER0230659 *Environment Agency* the Commissioner sets out his approach to the 'manifestly unreasonable' exception in EIR 2004, reg.12(4)(b). The decision notice confirms that the Commissioner considers a request may be refused under regulation 12(4)(b) if it would be otherwise characterised as vexatious if dealt with under FOIA 2000, s.14.

2.6 TRIBUNAL DECISIONS

Following a decision notice both the complainant and the relevant public authority may appeal to the Information Rights Tribunal. Once again, the decisions of the Tribunal are not precedent setting, although they are, of course, binding on the parties (subject to further appeal). The Tribunal's decisions are published on the

Tribunal's website and are searchable by reference to subject (i.e. definition of 'public authority') or by appeal number or the name of the parties. Onward appeals from the Information Rights Tribunal may be made, with permission, on any point of law arising from the Tribunal's decision. Appeals are to the Upper Tribunal (Administrative Appeals Chamber). These are also available on the Tribunal's website.

The Tribunal decisions provide a very important source of information for practitioners and, in the absence of any decided case law, remain the most authoritative source of information about the interpretation of EIR 2004.

2.7 CASE LAW

Where the Upper Tribunal or a court has considered and interpreted a provision of EIR 2004 then this constitutes a binding precedent on lower courts (and the Information Rights Tribunal). However, it is still relatively early days and a body of case law has yet to emerge. Prior to the establishment of the Upper Tribunal in 2010, which can hear appeals against decisions of the Information Rights Tribunal (on points of law) only two cases had proceeded before the courts. The first case, before the Administrative Court, concerned the Export Credits Guarantee Department and its interpretation of the internal communications exception to disclosure in EIR 2004, reg.12(4)(e) (see *Export Credits Guarantee Department* v. *Friends of the Earth* [2008] EWHC 638 (Admin); [2008] Env LR 40; [2008] JPL 1813). The second case concerned a request to the Office of Communications (Ofcom) for information about the location, ownership and technical attributes of mobile phone base stations. The case is of particular importance since it resulted in an appeal to the Supreme Court (*Office of Communications* v. *Information Commissioner* [2010] UKSC 3; [2010] Env LR 20) and a preliminary ruling from the European Court of Justice (see *Office of Communications* v. *Information Commissioner* (Case C-71/ 10) [OJC 113 of 01.05.2010, p.20]). The ECJ delivered its preliminary ruling on 28 July 201. The importance of this case cannot be understated because it concerns the application of the public interest test in relation to the exceptions to disclosure. The *Ofcom* case is considered in detail at **7.4.2** and **Chapter 8**.

In addition to the Ofcom case noted above the ECJ has given rulings in a number of other cases in relation to the implementation and interpretation of Directive 2003/4/EC. A number of these cases are considered throughout the handbook as and when relevant.

No doubt over time a body of case law on the interpretation of EIR 2004 and FOIA 2000 will develop and should give practitioners greater confidence in how they approach the application of EIR 2004. Until such time as this happens, practitioners would be well advised to consult the relevant decisions of the Information Rights Tribunal (and Upper Tribunal) and the Information Commissioner.

2.8 USEFUL WEBSITES

Please see the list below for useful websites in relation to this chapter.

- Defra: **www.defra.gov.uk**
- The Information Commissioner's Office: **www.ico.gov.uk**
- The First-tier Tribunal (Information Rights) and the Administrative Appeals Chamber of the Upper Tribunal: **www.justice.gov.uk/guidance/courts-and-tribunals/tribunals/information-rights/index.htm**
- The Aarhus Convention: **www.unece.org/env/pp/**
- EU web pages on access to environmental information: **http://ec.europa.eu/environment/aarhus/index.htm#information**

CHAPTER 3

Definition of environmental information

3.1 INTRODUCTION

> What is important is that if information comes within the scope of the EIR, then, as the Tribunal pointed out in *Kirkaldie* v. *Information Commissioner*, it is exempt information under FOIA 2000 (pursuant to section 39) and the public authority is obliged to deal with the request under the EIR. (*Archer* v. *Information Commissioner and Salisbury District Council* (EA/2006/0037))

The definition of 'environmental information', which is to be found in EIR 2004, reg.2(1) is critical because it defines the boundaries of EIR 2004. If the requested information does not fall within the very broad scope of 'environmental information' then the regulations do not apply and the request should be dealt with under FOIA 2000. In order to ensure that a public authority deals with a request for information under the appropriate legislative regime it is essential that it determines whether the request is for environmental information. This would appear to be self-evident. However, a quick glance at the decision notices published on the ICO website reveals many instances where public authorities have failed to consider whether the request is for environmental information, even in cases which are relatively clear cut. It is not entirely clear whether some public authorities find the definition of 'environmental information' confusing or whether the relative lack of publicity and training around EIR 2004 (compared to FOIA 2000) means that some public authorities 'default' to FOIA 2000 without considering the nature of the request. The fact remains though that a public authority should consider, on receipt of a request, whether the information requested is 'environmental'.

3.2 APPROACHING THE DEFINITION OF 'ENVIRONMENTAL INFORMATION': GENERAL OBSERVATIONS

It may be immediately obvious that the requested information is 'environmental'. However, in cases of uncertainty, practitioners can turn to the Defra and ICO guidance and, of course, previous decision notices and cases which have considered similar requests. In most instances the issue can be resolved with little or no difficulty or with a little research.

3.2.1 Duty of sympathetic interpretation

Where there are genuine questions about the extent and scope of the definition then regard should be had to the purpose of the Directive, to enable the purposive approach to interpretation demanded by the ECJ. It has already been noted in **Chapter 1** that courts and tribunals must, as far as is possible, interpret national law in the light of the wording and the purpose of the Directive (*Marleasing SA* v. *La Commercial Internacional de Alimentacion SA* (Case C-106/89) [1990] ECR I-4135). The Information Commissioner's guidance ('What is environmental information?') also advocates such an approach, cautioning that it is more important to take into account the purpose of the regulations than the rules of interpretation built into English law. Of course, such an approach requires some understanding of the purpose of EIR 2004. A useful starting point is Recital 1 of the Directive which states that the Directive aims to facilitate increased public access to environmental information:

> … so as to contribute to a greater awareness of environmental matters, a free exchange of views and more effective participation by the public in environmental decision making and eventually a better environment.

Further, Recital 8 extols the dissemination of environmental information to the general public to 'the widest possible extent'. There is nothing within the recitals to suggest that the definition of 'environmental information' should be given a restrictive interpretation, unlike the exceptions which must be interpreted in a restrictive way (Recital 16). In short, the definition of 'environmental information' should be interpreted broadly, having regard to the aims of the Directive.

A purposive approach requires public authorities to understand how access to environmental information supports the broader environmental protection aims of the Aarhus Convention. It does not, however, require public authorities to have an expert knowledge about environmental issues; a view endorsed by the Tribunal:

> The definition is not intended to set out a scientific test and its words should be given their plain and natural meaning. (*The Office of Communications* v. *Information Commissioner* (EA/2006/0078))

Practical example

An excellent example of the purposive approach to interpretation can be seen in *Halton Borough Council* FER0138940. In deciding whether information about proposals to introduce road tolling constituted environmental information, the Commissioner recalls that one of the purposes of Directive 2003/4/EC is to allow the participation of the public in environmental decision making at the earliest stages. Consequently, the Information Commissioner concluded that:

> information which would help the public contribute to the preparation of a plan which is likely to have an effect on the environment should be dealt with as a environmental information under EIR 2004.

The fact that the plan may not come to fruition does not prevent the information from being environmental. See also *Department for Business, Enterprise and Regulatory Reform* FER0085500.

3.2.2 Earlier case law

To date there have been very few judicial decisions concerning Directive 2003/4/EC or EIR 2004 and these are discussed, where appropriate, elsewhere in this book. However, it is possible to gain some insight into the general approach of the judiciary by reference to some of the earlier case law relating to the 1990 Directive and EIR 1992. Whilst this case law is not binding, the cases demonstrate that both the ECJ and the national courts in England are willing to adopt a robust and purposive approach to the definition of 'environmental information'. In *R* v. *British Coal Corporation* ex parte *Ibstock Building Products Ltd* [1995] Env LR 277, the High Court held:

> It would be strange if the legislature had intended that only the bare information itself should be disclosed without it being possible to ascertain whether it was right, wrong or indifferent.

The applicant in this case wanted to know the name of the person who had supplied British Coal with information concerning the deposit of naval munitions in the land. Similarly, the High Court took a broad view of the definition of 'environmental information' in *R* v. *Secretary of State for the Environment, Transport and the Regions* ex parte *Alliance Against the Birmingham Northern Relief Road (No.1)* [1999] Env LR 447; [1999] JPL 231. The court found little difficulty in concluding that the content of a concession agreement relating to the construction of a motorway was environmental information and, subject to any applicable exceptions, had to be disclosed.

The ECJ adopted a similar approach in a number of cases relating to the 1990 Directive. For example, *Commission* v. *France* (Case C-233/00) [2003] ECR I-6625 and *Mecklenburg* v. *Kreis Pinneberg - Der Landrat* (Case C-321/96) [1998] ECR I-3809. In the latter case, the ECJ held that a statement of 'views' advanced by a public authority made in connection with planning approval for the construction of a proposed ring road constituted environmental information, since the views informed the decision-making process.

However, even a broadly purposive approach will have its limits and in *Glawischnig* v. *Bundesminister für soziale Sicherheit und Generationen* (Case C-316/01) [2003] ECR I- 5995 the ECJ considered that the definition did not 'give a general and unlimited right of access to all information held by public authorities which has a connection, however minimal, with one of the environmental factors mentioned in art.2(a)'. The case is important because it recognises that some information may be too 'remote' from the definition. The request related to information about the enforcement of an EU Directive concerned with the labelling of products containing genetically modified organisms. Since the purpose of the Directive in question was to facilitate free trade and to protect consumers (as opposed to environmental protection) then the connection with the environment was too remote.

3.2.3 Guidance and decisions

There is no shortage of guidance for public authorities on the question 'what is environmental information?'. Both the ICO and Defra produce their own guidance on what is covered by the regulations (Defra's 'What is covered by the Regulations?' and the ICO's 'What is environmental information?'). Defra has also issued a publication on 'The boundaries between EIR 2004 and FOIA', which usefully provides a number of worked examples for public authorities to consider. In addition, the Aarhus Implementation Guide provides yet further guidance on each limb of the definition.

3.2.4 Previous decisions

There is also an increasing number of ICO and Tribunal decisions which can be used to assist public authorities, some of which are examined below. Before considering the definition in detail, the following examples reveal the breadth of the definition and the very wide range of information caught by it:

- Information about payments received by individual Verderers under the Countryside Stewardship Scheme and legal advice obtained by the Verderers of the New Forest on the Countryside Stewardship Scheme, *Rudd* v. *Information Commissioner and The Verderers of the New Forest* (EA/2008/0020).
- Information (minutes and correspondence) relating to plans to build affordable housing: *Denmead Parish Council* FER0285249.
- Information about a local authority's potential financial liability towards the cost of the construction of sea wall defences: *McGlade* v. *ICO and Redcar and Cleveland Borough Council* (EA/2009/0019).
- A copy of a report prepared by the Health and Safety Executive about a possible escape of gas from a fire-fighting appliance in a house: *Health and Safety Executive* FER0293708.
- Information about a tender exercise (including details of the successful tender submission and the tender evaluation report) in respect of wildlife and habitat management at an airport; the applicant was one of the unsuccessful tenders. The tender exercise constituted a measure likely to affect one of the elements of the environment: *Cornwall Airport Ltd* FER0235155.
- A copy of a draft purchase order relating to the compulsory purchase of land: *Department for Business, Enterprise and Regulatory Reform* FS50159087.
- The names, job titles and departments of council officials within Omagh District Council who had drafted and equality impact assessment (EQIA) on the council's policy on 'the disposal of land for the purpose of erecting or retaining a memorial monument'. The monument concerned, commemorated

the deaths of IRA hunger strikers: *Omagh District Council* v. *The Information Commissioner*, EA/2010/0163.

3.3   EIR 2004, REG.2(1): ENVIRONMENTAL INFORMATION

The definition categorises what environmental information can be about, in a non-exhaustive way. The definition, in full, is as follows:

> 'Environmental information' has the same meaning as in Article 2(1) of the Directive, namely any information in written, visual, aural, electronic or any other material form on:
>
> (a)   the state of the elements of the environment, such as air and atmosphere, water, soil, land, landscape and natural sites including wetlands, coastal and marine areas, biological diversity and its components, including genetically modified organisms, and the interaction among these elements;
>
> (b)   factors, such as substances, energy, noise, radiation or waste, including radioactive waste, emissions, discharges and other releases into the environment, affecting or likely to affect the elements of the environment referred to in (a);
>
> (c)   measures (including administrative measures), such as policies, legislation, plans, programmes, environmental agreements, and activities affecting or likely to affect the elements and factors referred to in (a) and (b) as well as measures or activities designed to protect those elements;
>
> (d)   reports on the implementation of environmental legislation;
>
> (e)   cost-benefit and other economic analyses and assumptions used within the framework of the measures and activities referred to in (c); and
>
> (f)   the state of human health and safety, including the contamination of the food chain, where relevant, conditions of human life, cultural sites and built structures inasmuch as they are or may be affected by the state of the elements of the environment referred to in (a) or, through those elements, by any of the matters referred to in (b) and (c).

The various limbs of the definition do not simply list different categories of matter which must be included in the information if it is to fall within the definition. There is a degree of cross-reference between them. This means that information on the factors covered by subparagraph (b) will only bring that information within the definition if the factors affect or are likely to affect the elements of the environment listed in subparagraph (a). Likewise the measures/activities listed in subparagraph (c) will only fall within the definition if they are affecting or likely to affect the elements or factors listed in subparagraphs (a) or (b) (see **Figure 3.1**).

3.3.1   Any information on?

Environmental information is any information in written, visual, aural, electronic or any other material form. The majority of requests will be for written information, either in the form of reports or minutes. However, given the nature of environmental issues, it is entirely probable that an applicant may want to see:

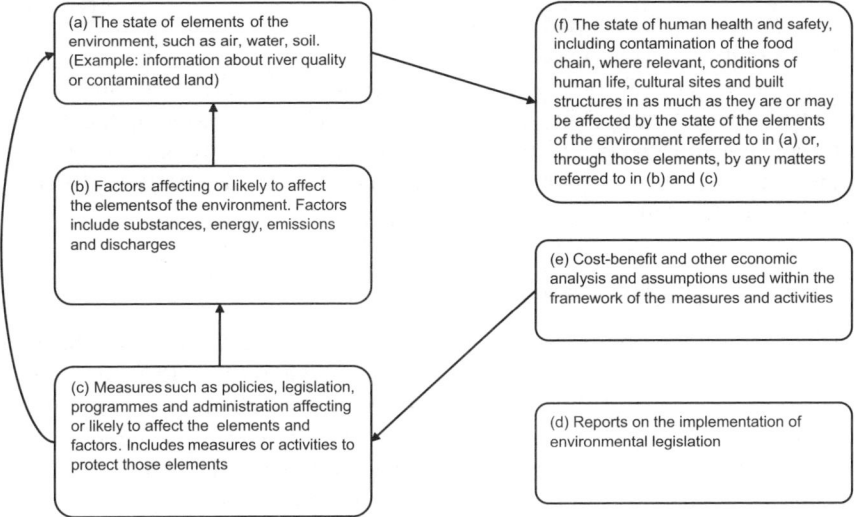

(a) The state of elements of the environment, such as air, water, soil. (Example: information about river quality or contaminated land)

(b) Factors affecting or likely to affect the elements of the environment. Factors include substances, energy, emissions and discharges

(c) Measures such as policies, legislation, programmes and administration affecting or likely to affect the elements and factors. Includes measures or activities to protect those elements

(d) Reports on the implementation of environmental legislation

(e) Cost-benefit and other economic analysis and assumptions used within the framework of the measures and activities

(f) The state of human health and safety, including contamination of the food chain, where relevant, conditions of human life, cultural sites and built structures in as much as they are or may be affected by the state of the elements of the environment referred to in (a) or, through those elements, by any matters referred to in (b) and (c)

Figure 3.1 Definition of 'Environmental Information': EIR 2004, reg.2(1)

- plans (for example, *Chesterfield Borough Council* FS50260693 – photostat copy of plan of allotments);
- maps, drawings, photographs, graphs, monitoring data, satellite images.

The Defra guidance goes as far as saying that no types of information are excluded from the general ambit of environmental information.

The use of the word 'any' informs the way in which the ICO/Tribunal will approach the definition. For example, in *The Office of Communications* v. *Information Commissioner* (EA/2006/0078) ('the *Ofcom* case') the applicant requested the names of the mobile network operators who had supplied raw data held by Ofcom. The Tribunal disagreed with Ofcom's arguments that the names did not constitute environmental information:

> The name of a person or organisation responsible for an installation that emits electromagnetic waves falls comfortably within the meaning of the words 'any information ... on ... radiation'.

Echoing the High Court's reasoning in the *Ibstock* case (see **3.2.2**) the Tribunal held that to accept otherwise would be to create an unacceptable artificiality and that such an narrow interpretation would also be inconsistent with the purpose of the Directive to achieve a greater awareness of environmental matters, a free exchange of views and more effective participation by the public in environmental decision making.

The use of the word 'on' is also significant since it indicates a wide application and will extend to any information about, concerning, or relating to the various parts of the definition. For example, see *Department for Business, Enterprise and Regulatory Reform* FER0085500 where the Commissioner stated that 'information that would inform the public about the matter under consideration and would therefore facilitate effective participation by the public in environmental decision making is likely to be environmental information' (see also *Denmead Parish Council* FER0285249).

No duty to create information

A public authority is obliged to provide any such information that it holds but it is not under an obligation to create information in order to respond to a request. For example, a public authority could be obliged to release raw data, held on a computer in the form of an Excel spreadsheet, without having to prepare any explanatory report or summary. A public authority should not refuse to supply raw data simply because it considers the applicant would not understand it. (See, for example, *Doncaster Metropolitan Borough Council* FS50102786.)

3.3.2 EIR 2004, reg.2(1)(a): Elements of the environment

EIR 2004, reg.2(1)(a), which covers the state of the elements of the environment, may be regarded as the most important part of the definition since paragraphs (b), (c), (e) and (f) all refer back expressly or impliedly to it. The list of elements of the environment is widely stated as including:

- air and atmosphere, this includes air within buildings and other natural and manmade structures above or below ground;
- water, both underground and surface waters, natural or manmade;
- soil, land, and landscape;
- natural sites including wetlands, coastal and marine areas;
- biological diversity and its components, including genetically modified organisms; and
- the interaction among these elements.

The use of the word 'includes' means that the list of elements of the environment is not exhaustive and there may be other elements which are not expressly listed.

It is not necessary to engage in any technical discussion about the precise definitions of the elements listed (e.g. a definitive definition of 'coastal waters') since the definition needs to be approached broadly and from a purposive perspective. For example, the ICO guidance notes:

> there is little to be gained from considering the subtle differences between 'air and atmosphere' or 'discharges and releases'. The examples are there to help identify what is environmental information, not to confuse.

The state of the elements of the environment is not limited to the current state but also includes the past, predicted and future conditions.

Examples of requests falling under this limb include requests for information about river water quality, the state of the pavements and highway, air quality within buildings (and arguably within aircraft (see *Hoyte* v. *Information Commissioner and the Civil Aviation Authority* (EA/2007/0101)). Land includes all land surfaces, buildings, land covered by water and underground strata. In relation to the latter this includes land with natural minerals and deposits, such as salt, coal, limestone, slate and iron.

3.3.3 EIR 2004, reg.2(1)(b): Factors affecting the environment or likely to affect elements of the environment

Information is environmental information under this second limb if it is about 'factors' which affect or are likely to affect the elements of the environment in EIR 2004, reg.2(1)(a). If there is no effect or no likelihood of effect then information about the factors does not fall within the definition. Factors include:

- substances;
- energy;
- noise;
- radiation;
- waste, including radioactive waste;
- emissions;
- discharges and other releases into the environment.

Once again the use of the words 'such as' in the above list makes it clear that the list is non-exhaustive and other things may be considered to be factors. The ICO guidance recognises that elements of the environment can also be factors; for example, water can be a factor which affects land via flooding.

Some of the listed factors have been given a statutory definition in other pieces of legislation but they are not defined within EIR 2004. For example, the definition of 'waste', provided for by the Waste Framework Directive 2006/12/EC (as amended), is very complex and has generated a significant amount of case law from the national courts and the ECJ. This begs the question whether the factors should be defined by reference to other pieces of environmental legislation. We are of the opinion that the answer must be no. First, there is nothing within EIR 2004 to suggest the need for any cross referencing to other statutory provisions and, second, the definitions should be interpreted broadly having regard to the aims of the Directive. In a case concerning information about waste the Commissioner did not engage in any discussion about the legal definition of waste; he simply stated that the term should be broadly interpreted to include a number of different types of waste including sewage sludge (*Bridgnorth District Council* FS50154310). This view appears to be shared by the Tribunal. When faced with arguments about the definition of the term 'emissions', the Tribunal sensibly took the view that it should be given its plain and natural meaning and not be limited by any other statutory definitions (see *The Office of Communications* v. *Information Commissioner* (EA/2006/0078)). In light of this it was accepted that radio frequency waves can be categorised as energy, radiation and emissions. See further at **8.6**.

Affecting or likely to affect the elements of the environment

It is difficult to imagine a factor that is not likely to have an effect on one of the elements since the effect need not be large or adverse and there appears to be no *de minimus* limitation to the effect. As far as 'affecting' is concerned the ICO guidance suggests that this is assessed on a balance of probabilities basis, and 'likely to affect' is a lower threshold, but requires more than a remote possibility. It is enough if there is some probability that an effect on the environment might happen in the future. Even if a public authority is uncertain about the possible effects then they should, in line with contemporary environmental law principles, adopt a precautionary approach.

Practical example

In the *Ofcom* case it was argued that information on radiation from mobile phone masts was not environmental information because there was no evidence as to harm to humans. In light of the precautionary principle, the Tribunal was not prepared to accept such arguments. In assessing whether factors (including radiation) are affecting, or likely to affect, one of the elements of the environment, the Tribunal refused to be drawn into scientific debate about the properties of radio waves and their likely effect on the atmosphere. The Tribunal held that the definition should be given its plain and ordinary meaning and on that basis they 'believe[d] that radio wave emissions that pass through the atmosphere from a base station to any solid component of the natural world are likely to affect one or more elements of the environment'. Even though such a broad approach could potentially catch very low level emissions from domestic sources (such as baby alarms), the Tribunal considered that these would not affect any of the elements of the environment and in any event it would be unlikely that a public authority held any information about such emissions.

3.3.4   EIR 2004, reg.2(1)(c): Measures and activities

The third limb of the definition embraces:

(a)   measures and activities affecting or likely to affect the elements and factors referred to in the first two limbs; and also

(b)   measures or activities designed to protect the elements of the environment.

Measures include:

- administrative measures;
- policies;
- legislation;

- plans and programmes;
- environmental agreements.

The guidance also states that it includes permit schemes, management contracts, land use planning regimes and permits.

Environmental agreements include international, national, regional and local agreements and also agreements between public and private bodies. A contract is an agreement. In *R* v. *Secretary of State for the Environment, Transport and the Regions & Midland Expressway Ltd*, ex parte *Alliance against the Birmingham Northern Relief Road and others* [1999] All ER (D) 318 a concession agreement was held to be information relating to the environment under EIR 1992. A waste management contract falls within this limb (*East Sussex County Council* FER0099394 and *East Riding of Yorkshire Council* FER0066052) as does a PFI contract to outsource waste management services (*Nottinghamshire County Council, Veolia ES Nottinghamshire Ltd and UK Coal Mining Ltd* v. *Information Commissioner* (EA/2010/0142)).

This limb is significantly broadened by the inclusion of the term 'activities'. Activity implies human action and therefore steps taken by an enforcement officer, (i.e. an environmental health officer or a refuse collector) will constitute activities within this limb. Where the Environment Agency or a local authority grants an environmental permit or some other such 'consent', then information about the activity or process that has been authorised will also fall within this limb. (However, information relating to environmental permits is available on public registers – see **Chapter 11**.)

There is little doubt that the Commissioner and the Tribunal place a broad interpretation on the phrases 'measures' and 'activities'. For example, the following have fallen within the limb:

- a copy of a statute (the Land Drainage Act 1991) *Rhondda Cynon Taff County Borough Council* v. *Information Commissioner* (EA/2007/0065));
- legal advice sought by a council in relation to night-time flying policy at Kent International Airport (*Kirkaldie* v. *Information Commissioner & Thanet District Council* (EA/2006/001));
- details about a tender exercise carried out for the provision of wildlife and habitat management at Newquay Cornwall Airport (*Cornwall Airport Ltd* FER0235155).
- details of allotments including the names and addresses of the people keeping the allotments (*Blidworth Parish Council* FS50187166); and
- information about mineral 'reserves' and 'sales'(*Staffordshire County Council* v. *Information Commissioner* (EA 2010/0015)).

Affecting or likely to affect the elements or factors

This limb requires that the measures/activities affect, or are likely to affect, the elements or factors or are designed to protect elements of the environment. The effect need not be detrimental or large scale but there must be more than a remote possibility that there will be an effect. There is no need to engage in semantic discussions about whether a measure/activity is designed to be protective or not because even if it is not then it could still fall within this limb if it affects, or is likely to affect, either the elements or the factors.

Practical example

The Mersey Tunnels Users Association requested all correspondence with the Department of Transport relating to the proposed tolling of a new and existing bridge across the Mersey estuary. Self-evidently, information about the construction of a bridge falls within the definition (a measure/activity affecting land and also factors, such as discharges and emissions from cars).

The issue here was whether information about the proposed tolling was environmental information. The council maintained it was not environmental information since the link between the information and the effect or likely effect was not sufficiently strong (too remote) and also that the information was prepared in contemplation of the taking of measures.

The Commissioner disagreed; the implementation of a toll is likely to impact on volumes of traffic and therefore the environment. In relation to the second argument, the Commissioner took the view that information which would help the public contribute to the preparation of a plan which is likely to have an effect on the environment should be dealt with as environmental information under EIR 2004 (see FER018940). The fact a plan may not come to fruition does not prevent the information from being environmental. The Commissioner's decision was upheld by the Tribunal which considered that the tolling was an integral element of the project and its viability and was therefore environmental information (*Mersey Tunnel User's Association* v. *Information Commissioner and Halton Borough Council* (EA/2009/0001)).

Planning and planning-related activities

Given the sheer volume of decisions relating to planning applications and planning permissions it is worth briefly considering the application of the definition to a range of planning matters. Those authorities which can grant permission to develop on land, particularly local authorities (but see also *Port of London Authority* v. *Information Commissioner* (EA/2006/0083)), should be in no doubt that the granting of planning permission constitutes a measure that affects or is likely to affect the elements of the environment (particularly land and landscape).

Planning authorities are already required to make certain information available to the public under the various provisions of town and country planning legislation (see **Chapter 11**). However, it is clear that EIR 2004 extends this right to information which might not otherwise be available. For example, the Commissioner and Tribunal have ordered disclosure of the following information:

- Information obtained via questionnaires used as part of a consultation process concerning the proposal to build the Thames Gateway Bridge. The outcome of the consultation process would have an important bearing on the decision to proceed with the bridge project (*Transport for London* FS50079628).
- Submissions made to a Minister by his civil servants on a 'called-in' planning enquiry in relation to the Vauxhall tower project (*Lord Baker CH* v. *Information Commissioner and the Department for Communities and Local Government* (EA/2006/0043)).
- Considered view/legal advice obtained by a public authority. See, for example, *Staffordshire Moorlands District Council* FER0069117 where the Commissioner was satisfied that the legal advice given to a council regarding a planning permission 'will inform the council's decision about what, if any, action to take in respect of the planning permission' and is therefore likely to affect one or more of the elements of the environment.
- Legal advice sought by a planning authority in relation to the enforceability of a s.106 planning agreement under the Town and Country Planning Act 1990. The s.106 agreement was an environmental agreement and the legal advice relating to it was a measure likely to affect it (*Kirkaldie* v. *Information Commissioner and Thanet District Council* (EA/2006/001)).
- Information relating to the decision not to take enforcement action in respect of a listed building situated within a national park (*Easter* v. *Information Commissioner and The New Forest National Park Authority* (EA/2009/0092)).

3.3.5 EIR 2004, reg.2(1)(d): Reports on implementation of environmental legislation

This is relatively self-explanatory, which is probably why it receives barely any attention in the guidance or Aarhus Implementation Guide. It would include, for example, the report prepared by Defra on the implementation of Directive 2003/4/EC.

3.3.6 EIR 2004, reg.2(1)(e): Cost-benefit and other economic analyses and assumptions

The 'test' for deciding whether information is environmental information under this limb is as follows:

- the information itself must be on 'cost-benefit and other economic analyses and assumptions'; and
- the 'cost-benefit and other economic analyses and assumptions' must be used within the framework of the measures and activities referred to in EIR 2004, reg.2(1)(c).

In addition, it needs to be recalled that a measure or an activity referred to in reg.2(1)(c) (not the information in question) must affect or be likely to affect the elements and factors in reg.2(1)(a) and (b), or be designed to protect the elements in reg.2(1)(a).

A cost-benefit analysis can generally be defined as a process by which expected costs are weighed against expected benefits to determine the best (or most profitable) course of action. However, the phrase 'other economic analyses' is wider and includes financial analyses and assessments of economic assumptions.

Practical example

The Department for Business, Enterprise and Regulatory Reform (BERR) refused to disclose a copy of a report prepared by independent consulting engineers and submitted to the department by Peninsular Power in support of its application for a bio-energy capital grant towards a proposed biomass project. The report contained a review of the application and comments on whether the technical and commercial claims were achievable; it also included consideration of assumptions and proposed capital costs as well as the estimated output and efficiency of the proposed facility that Peninsular Power had put forward. It was necessary to consider whether the information in the report was used within the framework of a measure as outlined in EIR 2004, reg.2(1)(c) and that there was the necessary link back to reg.2(1)(a). The report was used to enable the department to assess a grant application for a biomass project and such grants constituted a measure which would both be likely to affect the elements and factors referred to in reg.2(1)(a) and (b) and that it had been designed to protect those elements. The Commissioner therefore concluded that the information contained within the report fell comfortably within this limb. See *Department for Business, Enterprise and Regulatory Reform* FER0085500.

Access to this type of information could prove enormously useful to NGOS and groups for a variety of reasons but particularly when they are trying to analyse the assumptions used in environmental decision making. For example, the Environment Act 1995, s.39 requires the Environment Agency, when considering whether and how to exercise any of its statutory powers, to take into account the likely costs and benefits of exercising (or not) its powers and also how it exercises its powers. Information as to how the Agency complies with this duty could fall within this particular limb. This type of information could also be enormously useful to any persons or groups when judicially reviewing decisions taken by public authorities, particularly in cases where it is alleged that the decision maker took irrelevant economic considerations into account (see, for example, *R* v. *Secretary of State for the Environment*, ex parte *Royal Society for the Protection of Birds* [1997] Env LR 431; (1995) (the Lappel Bank case)).

3.3.7   EIR 2004, reg.2(1)(f): The state of human health and safety

For ease this subparagraph can be broken down into three parts:

- information about the state of human health and safety (including contamination of the food chain where relevant to the state of human health and safety);
- information about conditions of human life; and
- information about the state of cultural sites and built structures.

However, the above information only falls within the scope of EIR 2004 in so far as the state of human health and safety to which it relates may be affected by the state of the elements of the environment or through those elements, by any of the factors or measures referred to in reg.2(1)(b) and (c).

In *Stichting Natuur en Milieu, Vereniging Milieudefensie* (Case C-266/09) the ECJ was asked to interpret the corresponding limb of the Directive. A Dutch public authority refused to disclose information provided to it in connection with the authorisation of a plant protection product. The information related to field trials of the product and the residues of the product left on the plant. The information formed part of an authorisation procedure, the purpose of which was to prevent risks and hazards for humans, animals and the environment and on that basis the information concerned the state of human health and safety and the contamination of the food chain. However, this in itself was not sufficient. The information would only fall within the scope of the definition if in so far as the state of human health and safety and the contamination of the food chain to which it relates are, or may be, affected by the state of the elements of the environment or, through those elements, by any of the matters (factors or measures) referred to in art.2(1)(b) and (c) of the Directive. The ECJ considered that although the information did not directly involve an assessment of the consequences of those residues for human health, it concerned elements of the environment which may affect human health if excessive levels of those residues are present, which is precisely what that information is intended to ascertain. The information therefore fell within the definition of 'environmental information'.

The information must refer to the collective health of the public and not the health of an individual, as the latter would be subject to the provisions of DPA 1998. It could, however, include information about the collective health of a group (by type or geographical area) providing it is not possible to identify a living individual.

The ICO guidance refers to the physical, biological and chemical state of human life and also suggests that this may include information on diseases and conditions which may mean that it does not necessarily cover other physical problems such as, for instance, broken limbs. Such an approach is consistent with other 'mainstream' environmental law – notably Part III of the Environmental Protection Act 1990 (which deals with statutory nuisances). In relation to the latter the courts have interpreted the phrase 'prejudicial to health' as injurious, or likely to cause injury, to health and limited to a threat to health in the sense of a threat of disease, vermin or the like (*Coventry City Council* v. *Cartwright* [1975] 1 WLR 845; [1975] 2 All ER 99).

3.4 BOUNDARIES BETWEEN ENVIRONMENTAL INFORMATION UNDER EIR 2004 AND INFORMATION UNDER FOIA 2000

In most instances it should be apparent that a request is for environmental information and public authorities now have the benefit of an increasing number of decisions to draw upon to assist them in the event of any doubt or confusion. However, as was noted earlier, it is not always clear cut and even the Commissioner and Tribunal have been in disagreement. For example, see the difference between the Commissioner's decision in *Department of Trade and Industry* FS50093052 and the Tribunal's in *Department for Business, Enterprise and Regulatory Reform* v. *ICO and Friends of the Earth* (EA/2007/0072). The Commissioner concluded that:

> whilst the information refers to, and can be said to be 'on' energy policy, it is policy in respect of supply, demand and pricing rather than policy affecting or likely to affect the elements of the environment or factors affecting or likely to affect those elements.

In contrast, the Tribunal agreed with the applicant, Friends of the Earth, that policies on energy supply, demand and pricing often will (and are often expressly designed) to affect factors such as energy, waste and emissions which themselves affect, or are likely to affect, elements of the environment both directly and indirectly. In relation to the disputed information, the Tribunal held that where the information related to energy policies or considered climate change then it was covered by EIR 2004.

Inevitably there will be disagreements about the boundaries of the definition, particularly where the link between the information and the environment is remote or where the information only has a slight or tangential association with the elements of the environment. As recalled in the *Glawischnig* case (at **3.2.2**), the mere or tangential association with elements of the environment will not necessarily bring the information within the scope of EIR 2004. An excellent (but rare) example of this can be seen in *Nottinghamshire County Council, Veolia ES Nottinghamshire Ltd and UK Coal Mining Ltd* v. *Information Commissioner* (EA/2010/0142). Here the Tribunal concluded that financial information in a lease for land (which was to be used for waste incineration) was not environmental information. The reality was that the disputed information concerned core financial information which had no bearing on the environment and was particular to the lease contract in terms of pricing and other factors. The Tribunal stated that the 'litmus' test was that the key financial indicators in the lease had no effect on any environmental issues.

Practical example

The very wide scope of the definition of environmental information is demonstrated in the case of *Omagh District Council* v. *Information Commissioner* (EA2010/0163). The request was for the names of the council officials responsible for preparing a draft Equality Impact Assessment (EQIA) in respect of the disposal of land and the correspondence between the council and the Equality Commission for Northern Ireland (ECNI).

The request was made against a background of complaint concerning the council's proposed sale of the land to the Dromore Memorial Committee; the land contained a small memorial to the IRA hunger strikers. Notwithstanding the fact that neither the applicant or the council considered the request was for environmental information the Information Commissioner held that it was and had to be dealt with under EIR 2004.

It was argued before the Tribunal that the request had to be seen within the broader statutory and factual context (i.e. a dispute about an acutely polarised issue in Northern Ireland politics). Despite having some sympathy with this, the Tribunal considered that the obligations under EIR 2004 are not dependent on, or coloured by, the presence or absence of motive for a request. The EQIA concerned the council's decision making relating to the disposal of land and the maintenance of the memorial on the land; as such it was a measure or activity affecting or likely to affect the land or landscape. Even though the memorial itself was very small (a headstone and flagpole with the Irish tricolour) it was still part of the landscape.

3.4.1 Documents which contain environmental information and other information

A practical difficulty inevitably arises when an applicant requests information that falls into the two regimes, i.e. some parts are environmental and others are not. This difficulty can be seen in the BERR case (EA/2007/0072). Although some of the information requested was environmental, the reality was that the Department was faced with many documents which contained both environmental information and non-environmental information and it therefore became necessary to consider which information rights regime to apply to certain information. Neither regime provides a right to 'documents', only to information. Where documents contain a mix of information then the Tribunal has suggested the following approach:

- Where a document divides easily into parts where the subject matter of each part is easily identifiable, this should enable the parts to dealt with under the relevant regime.
- If this is not the case it would be extremely onerous to review the document in exacting detail to decide which parts, paragraphs or even sentences are subject to FOIA 2000 or EIR 2004.
- Public authorities should take a 'pragmatic' approach based on the 'predominant purpose' of the document. Where, for example, the predominant purpose of the document covers environmental information then it may be possible to find the whole document is subject to EIR 2004.
- Failing that, i.e. where it is not possible to discern a predominant purpose, then the public authority has no choice. It must review the contents of the document in detail.
- The public authority cannot take into account the fact that one piece of legislation may be more favourable to it than the other.

3.5 CONCLUSION

The definition of 'environmental information' is broadly drafted and non-exhaustive. In the majority of cases it should be clear that the information requested is environmental. The ICO and Defra offer some considerable guidance to assist public authorities in making a determination and there is an increasing body of decisions which can be used as a guide. However, if there is any doubt a public authority should consider the purpose of the Directive and EIR 2004 which aim to, *inter alia*, encourage environmental awareness and facilitate greater public participation in environmental decision making. Public authorities do not need to cross-reference the terms (such as waste, emissions, radiation) to other legislative acts; they should apply the common sense meaning to the words and phrases used.

CHAPTER 4

Bodies subject to EIR 2004

4.1 INTRODUCTION

An organisation is only subject to the requirements of EIR 2004 if it falls within the definition of 'public authority' provided by the regulations. The definition is intentionally wide, providing as broad coverage as possible. More particularly, its complex structure is designed to prevent access to environmental information being undermined by the privatisation or delegation of public services or activities to other bodies, a point emphasised in the Aarhus Implementation Guide. Despite the use of the word 'public' within the definition, it is clear that EIR 2004 extend their reach to private companies. A private sector environmental consultancy firm, Environmental Resources Management Ltd, was held to be a public authority for the purposes of the specific request for information (*Environmental Resources Management Ltd* FER0090259). Similarly, commercial waste contractors (*South Downs Waste Services Ltd* FS50114241) have also found themselves subject to EIR 2004 in relation to statutory waste functions that they carry out on behalf of local authorities. Although these organisations have a very clear connection with the environment, the definition is wide enough to embrace other organisations which have no obvious involvement with the environment. For example, a consumer protection body associated with regulating the cost of premium rate phone calls and a housing association were both held to be subject to the regulations for the purposes of the information requested (*Phonepay Plus* FER0265609 and *Belfast Improved Housing Association* FER0152607).

Despite the broad approach referred to above, the Commissioner's decision in March 2010 that the private water and sewage companies (and the water supply companies) are not public authorities within the scope of EIR 2004 is without doubt controversial and arguably at odds with the requirements of the Aarhus Convention. The Commissioner's decision was upheld in November 2010 by the Upper Tribunal (*Smartsource Drainage and Water Searches Ltd* v. *Information Commissioner* (GI/2458/2010)). Therefore, at the time of writing, the privatised water and sewage companies that supply drinking water and maintain the public sewers are not public authorities within the scope of EIR 2004. However, in December 2010, Fish Legal (formerly the Angler's Conservation Association) submitted a complaint to the

Aarhus Compliance Committee (ACCC/C/2010/55) which has been accepted as admissible and is now pending further investigation by the committee (see **4.9**).

4.1.1 Functional definition of 'public authority'

Unlike FOIA 2000, which essentially lists the bodies subject to its requirements, EIR 2004 provide a functional definition of bodies falling within its scope, which means that its meaning is open to interpretation. The Defra guidance on who is covered by EIR 2004 states that there can be no comprehensive list of those bodies that are under the control of another body because such relations are dynamic and are prone to frequent change and in consequence 'each body will have to decide for itself whether it is covered by EIR 2004 according to its own circumstances'. However, the Upper Tribunal in the *Smartsource* case (referred to at **4.1**) took the rather unusual step of adding a postscript to its decision in which it considered that it would not be an insuperable problem to produce a list of public authorities subject to EIR 2004 and to keep the list up to date by means of secondary legislation. It remains to be seen whether the Aarhus Compliance Committee will recommend such a step.

In the absence of a list of public authorities, the difficulties in the functional approach are clear. Ultimately, an organisation may only find out it is subject to EIR 2004 when the Commissioner or the Tribunal reaches a decision to that effect.

Practical example

Phonepay Plus, a consumer protection body, received a request for information about any environmental impact assessments and recycling schemes that the organisation was involved in. Although willing to supply a considerable amount of information on a voluntary basis, Phonepay did not consider it was subject to either FOIA 2000 or EIR 2004 and refused to disclose some of the information sought by the applicant. However, in FER0265609 the Information Commissioner decided that although the organisation was not subject to FOIA 2000 it was subject to EIR 2004 and was therefore required to disclose the information. (For further discussion see **4.4**.)

4.2 EIR 2004, REG.2(2): DEFINITION OF 'PUBLIC AUTHORITY'

Public authorities are defined in EIR 2004, reg.2(2). However, EIR 2004, reg.3 specifically excludes any public authority to the extent that it is acting in a judicial or legislative capacity, and either House of Parliament to the extent required for the purpose of avoiding an infringement of the privileges of either House. This limitation is considered more fully below at **4.7**. The definition of 'public authority' can be broken down into three distinct parts. A body need only fall under one of the limbs of the definition to be brought within the scope of EIR 2004.

4.3 EIR 2004, REG.2(2)(A) AND (B): GOVERNMENT DEPARTMENTS AND BODIES SUBJECT TO FOIA 2000

EIR 2004, reg. 2(2)(a) and (b) start by defining 'public authority' by reference to the definition of 'public authority' under FOIA 2000 as follows:

(a) government departments;
(b) any other public authority as defined in section 3(1) of the Act, disregarding for this purpose the exceptions in paragraph 6 of Schedule 1 to the Act, but excluding:

    (i) any body or office-holder listed in Schedule 1 to the Act only in relation to information of a specified description; or
    (ii) any person designated by Order under section 5 of the Act;

Government departments and any bodies which are subject to FOIA 2000 (subject to the limitation discussed below) also fall within the scope of EIR 2004. This appears to present no difficulty since bodies which are subject to FOIA 2000 seem to have readily accepted their additional obligations under EIR 2004, albeit they sometimes appear to default to FOIA 2000 and inappropriately apply it to requests for environmental information.

FOIA 2000, s.3(1) defines a 'public authority' as one which is listed in Sched.1 to the Act, one designated by an Order of the Lord Chancellor or a publically owned company. Schedule 1 is broken down into seven sectoral parts:

- Part I lists the core public authorities such as government departments;
- Part II contains a list of local government authorities;
- Part III covers the NHS, including health authorities, NHS Trusts and individuals providing public medical, dental, ophthalmic and pharmaceutical services;
- Part IV includes schools and institutions providing further and higher education;
- Part V covers the police;
- Parts VI and VII list miscellaneous public authorities and executive agencies such as the British Museum, the Coal Authority and the Commission for Racial Equality.

However, the scope of EIR 2004 under this limb of the definition is both wider and narrower than FOIA 2000:

- It is wider because it also includes (by disregarding the exception granted in FOIA 2000, Sched.1, para.6) the special forces and any unit or part of a unit which is for the time being required by the Secretary of State to assist the Government Communications Headquarters in the exercise of its functions.
- It is narrower because those bodies which are subject to FOIA 2000, but only in relation to the information specified in Sched.1, are excluded from this part of the definition. For example, Sched.1 provides that any person providing general medical, ophthalmic or pharmaceutical services under Part II of the National Health Service Act 1977 is only subject to FOIA 2000 in respect of information relating to the provision of those services. Such a person would not

therefore be subject to EIR 2004 (unless they fall within either of the remaining limbs discussed below).

- It is also narrower because any person designated by order under FOIA 2000, s.5 is also excluded from the definition of 'public authority' in EIR 2004, reg.2(2)(b). Between October 2007 and February 2008, the Ministry of Justice completed a consultation exercise on whether it should use its powers under s.5 to extend the designation of bodies covered by FOIA 2000 but to date no s.5 orders have been made.

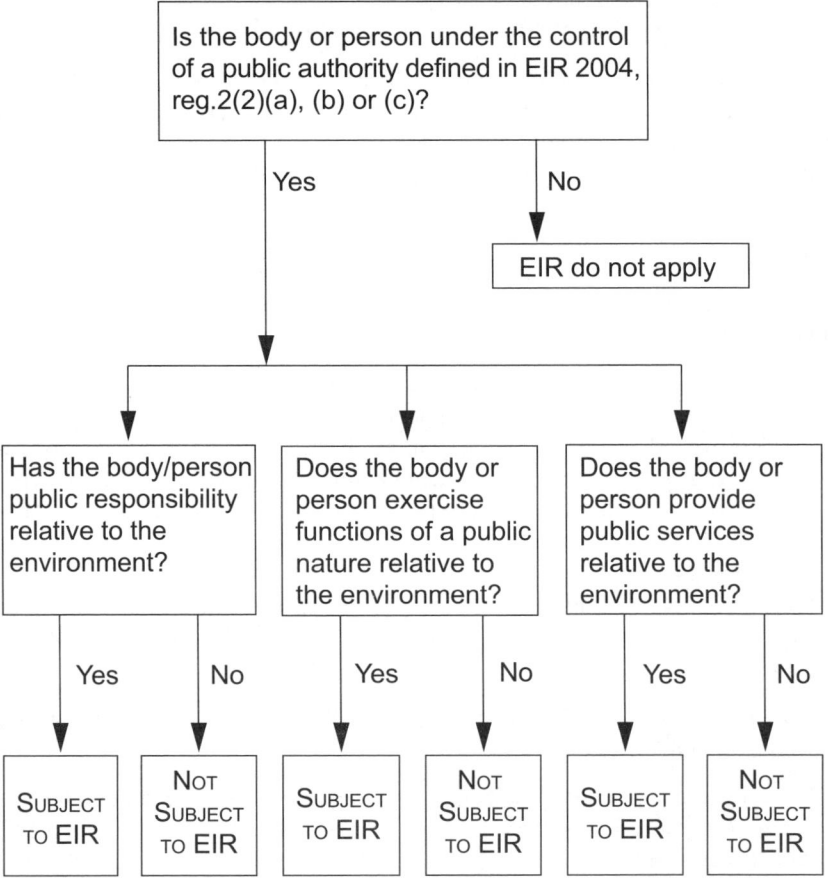

Figure 4.1 Public body/person in relation to EIR 2004

4.4 EIR 2004, REG.2(2)(C): BODIES CARRYING OUT FUNCTIONS OF PUBLIC ADMINISTRATION

To provide the broad coverage required by the Aarhus Convention and Directive 2003/4/EC, EIR 2004 includes two further categories of bodies that fall within the definition of 'public authority'. The first is any other body or other person that carries out functions of public administration (EIR 2004, reg.2(2)(c)). In practice, most authorities that fall within this description are also likely to already be subject to FOIA 2000 and therefore will fall within reg.2(2)(a) or (b). Consequently, the application of this limb is likely to be relatively narrow; however, some surprising organisations have been caught within its scope. To date the Information Commissioner has decided that the following bodies fall within EIR public authorities although none of them are subject to FOIA 2000:

- Port of London Authority (*Port of London Authority* FER0086096 and upheld by the Tribunal in EA/2006/0083) and The Mersey Docks and Harbour Company (*The Mersey Docks and Harbour Company* FER 0195081);
- Housing Associations (*Belfast Improved Housing Association* FER0152607; *Wesley Housing Association Ltd* FER149772); and
- Phonepay Plus, a consumer protection organisation company, limited by guarantee (*Phonepay Plus* FER0265609).

The defining feature of this limb is that the body must carry out functions of public administration; the body does not need to be 'public' and the actual functions need not relate to the environment. The Aarhus Implementation Guide notes that a public administrative function is a 'function normally performed by governmental authorities as determined according to national law' and there needs to be a legal basis for the functions. It has fallen to the Information Commissioner and Tribunal to interpret what this means within a domestic context and their general approach is to first consider whether the body exercises functions that are public in nature and then to ask whether the functions are administrative.

4.4.1 Are the functions public in nature?

There is not a universal test which can be applied to decide whether functions are public in nature, particularly given the diverse nature of government today. (See, for example, in the context of the Human Rights Act 1998, the analysis of Lord Nicholls of Birkenhead in *Parochial Church Council for the Parish of Aston Cantlow and Wilmcote with Billesley* v. *Wallbank and another* [2003] UKHL 37 at para.12.) In considering the question 'are the functions public in nature' it will be necessary to consider the extent to which the body in question is:

- publicly funded, although this is not necessarily conclusive;
- exercising statutory powers;
- taking the place of central government or local authorities;
- providing a public service;
- controlled by government;
- performing a regulatory function.

This will require an examination of the organisation itself, its legal basis and structure. It will also be relevant (but not determinative) if the body is a public authority for the purposes of the Human Rights Act 1998. It should also be noted that the mere fact that a body is subject to an intensive regulatory control regime does not necessarily denote that the provision of the service is a function of a public nature.

4.4.2 Are the functions of public administration?

If it is concluded that the body exercises public functions then a further examination is required to decide whether the functions are functions of public administration. This is a much more difficult question to answer.

Although this limb has yet to be tested by the courts, it appears that the Tribunal considers that the jurisprudence of the courts on what constitutes a public authority for the purposes of the Human Rights Act 1998 is 'helpful' as a starting point. (For example, see *Cameron* v. *Network Rail Infrastructure Ltd (formerly Railtrack plc)* [2006] EWHC 1133 (QB); *YL* v. *Birmingham City Council* [2007] UKHL 27.) However, both the definition of 'public authority' under the Human Rights Act 1998 (persons whose functions are functions of a public nature) and the Civil Procedure Rules, Part 54 (judicial review applies to bodies performing a public function) are wider than the definition under EIR 2004, reg.2(2)(c) since neither of these provisions is limited by reference to functions of public administration. It follows that a body may be a public authority for the purpose of the Human Rights Act 1998, and/or amenable to judicial review under CPR rule 54.1, and yet still fall outside EIR 2004, reg.2(2)(c).

In short, the functions of public administration are a subset of public functions generally. This therefore raises the question 'what are functions of public administration?' The Information Tribunal's decisions in *Network Rail Ltd* v. *Information Commissioner* (EA/2006/0061 and 0062) and *Port of London Authority* v. *Information Commissioner* (EA/2006/0083) provide a checklist of the factors that are 'helpful' in assessing whether functions are functions of public administration. Although the First-tier (Information Rights) Tribunal's decisions do not set any judicial precedent, the Upper Tribunal has 'approved' the multi-factored approach described below (see *Smartsource Drainage and Water Searches Ltd* (EA/2010/0077, GI/2458/2010)). The factors that should be taken into account are:

1. Nature of the functions:

    (a) Are these typically governmental functions? A function is governmental in nature if it involves the authoritative administration, management, control or direction of a function in the public interest or in the interests of society as a whole (see *The Mersey Docks and Harbour Company* FER0195081).

    (b) Do the functions of the body in question form part of a statutory scheme of regulation?

    (c) Are those functions such that if the body did not exist some governmental provision would need to be made for the exercise of these functions?

2.　　Legal structure and legal basis:

(a)　Has the body got a statutory basis (as opposed to existing purely as a matter of contract)? The fact that a body has been established by statute is not determinative but the terms of the statute will be of assistance in defining the nature of the organisation and its powers, functions and levels of accountability.

(b)　Is the body accountable to government in some way? Does the body have to submit annual reports to Ministers? Can the government influence/control the composition of the body's board? In the instance of the Port of London Authority, the Secretary of State appointed the Chair and three other members.

(c)　Has the body got any special powers over and above those that general public and private organisations have? For example, in *Port of London Authority* the Port Authority had the power to compulsorily purchase land in the same way a local authority could. Can the body regulate others?

An assessment of whether a body is carrying out functions of public administration will involve a 'multi-factor' assessment of law and fact. In *Network Rail* the Tribunal concluded that Network Rail did not carry out public functions nor did it carry out functions of public administration. However, in *Port of London Authority* the Tribunal concluded, taking into account the statutory scheme that governed the Port Authority's operations, it was carrying out functions of public administration. In *Belfast Housing Improvement Association* FER0152607 the Commissioner concluded that the Belfast Housing Association, a registered housing association whose role was to build affordable housing, carried out functions of public administration because the allocation of affordable residential accommodation had to be in line with a scheme operated in conjunction with the Northern Ireland Housing Executive and approved by the Department for Social Development. (See also *Wesley Housing Association Ltd* FER149772.) In *Payphone Plus* FER0265609 the Commissioner decided that Payphone Plus was carrying out functions of public administration because: it was tasked with a specific co-regulatory function, namely regulating premium rate telephone service providers; it had the power to issue and enforce a Code of Practice and issue directions; and it was controlled by Ofcom, a public authority under both FOIA 2000 and EIR 2004.

More recently the Upper Tribunal concluded that the reach of EIR 2004, reg.2(2)(c) did not extend to the private water and sewage companies or the water-only companies (*Smartsource Drainage and Water Searches Ltd* v. *Information Commissioner and A group of 19 water companies* (GI/2458/2010)). The water and sewerage industry was privatised in 1989 by the Water Act 1989; some companies provide both water and sewage services (WASCs) and others only supply water (WOCs). They are regulated by the Environment Agency and the Office of Water Services (OFWAT). Despite extensive arguments to the contrary, the Tribunal concluded that neither the WASCs nor the WOCs were public authorities under this limb (or indeed at all). In a lengthy decision the Tribunal considered a range of factors which led to the conclusion that the companies were not performing functions that were public in nature and neither were they carrying out functions of public administration. Amongst the factors that the Tribunal considered relevant were that the companies:

- owned and managed a utility industry which serves paying customers;
- have private shareholders and do not have any government nominees on their boards (in some instances the companies were foreign owned);
- do not receive any public funding;
- have considerable commercial freedom (for example in setting staff salaries);
- are subject to a degree of price regulation;
- do not set or enforce health and safety standards but rather are subject to a regulator;
- although subject to a license supervised by a regulator, their functions were not public in nature;
- are fundamentally private companies incorporated under the Companies Acts and established in the normal way with a Memorandum of Association and Articles of Association. Although they are appointed by statute and licensed under statute they are not created by statute; and
- several of the water companies are foreign owned and can buy each other, subject only to competition legislation.

The cumulative effect of these factors was that the water companies demonstrated few of the characteristics of a public authority. For further discussion of the position regarding the private water and sewage companies and the water only companies, see **4.5.1**.

Ultimately the decision about whether a public authority carries out public administrative functions will have to be made on a case-by-case basis and will therefore be dependent on the facts of what that particular body does. However, organisations should note that the Commissioner and Tribunal will also take into account the way in which the organisation identifies itself. For example, the Port of London Authority referred to itself as a public authority in its contracts with third parties; a point not lost on the Commissioner.

4.5   EIR 2004, REG.2(2)(D): BODIES WITH PUBLIC RESPONSIBILITIES, ETC. RELATING TO THE ENVIRONMENT

EIR 2004, reg.2(2)(d) includes the following within the definition of 'public authority':

> any other body or other person, that is under the control of a person falling within sub-paragraphs (a), (b) or (c) and–
>
> (i)   has public responsibilities relating to the environment;

(ii)   exercises functions of a public nature relating to the environment; or
(iii) provides public services relating to the environment.

This is arguably the most interesting part of the definition, not least because it was deliberately intended to be wide enough to ensure that the trend towards privatisation of essential services should not put public services or activities outside the realm of access to environmental information. This particular limb includes service providers or other companies that fall under the control of either public authorities or other bodies to whom public functions have been delegated by law. Although this limb is wider than the previous limbs, it does differ from them in one key respect. Subparagraphs (a), (b) and (c) define public authorities without limitation to the particular field of activity. However, only persons performing public responsibilities, exercising functions or providing public services in relation to the environment can be public authorities under this subparagraph.

Essentially this subparagraph involves a two-stage test:

- first, the person/body must fall under the control of a public authority; and
- second, the person/body must demonstrate at least one of the following: have responsibilities relating to the environment, exercise functions of a public nature relating to the environment, or provide public services relating to the environment.

The important point about the reg.2(2)(d) limb is that it does *not* require the body to be public; the body may be privately owned but still be a public authority within EIR 2004 if it meets the criteria in both tests. The following organisations have been held to be public authorities by virtue of reg.2(2)(d):

- a private environmental consultancy firm undertaking an environmental impact assessment on behalf of another public authority (*Environmental Resources Management Ltd* FER0090259);
- private waste contractors, i.e. *South Downs Waste Services Ltd* FS50114241;
- *Belfast Improved Housing Association* FER0152607.

Practical example

When the Regional Assembly for the North East of England (RANE) secured the services of Environmental Resources Management Ltd (ERM) to carry out a strategic environmental impact assessment (that RANE was bound by statutory provisions to undertake), it put ERM within the scope of reg.2(2)(d). The Commissioner held that ERM was not simply acting on behalf of RANE; legislation provided RANE with a choice as to whether to carry out the environmental impact assessment itself (which presumably it did not have the requisite skills to do) or to secure another body to do it. The result of this was that the other body (ERM) 'assumed' the public functions relating to the environment whilst carrying out the assessment. The control was achieved via the contract between RANE and ERM (see *Environmental Resources Management Ltd* FER0090259).

4.5.1   Control by a public authority

EIR 2004 provides that for a body or person to be covered by reg.2(2)(d) it must first be shown to be under the control of a public authority as defined under the first three limbs.

According to Defra, the control must be constituted by statute or regulations, rights, license, contracts or other means such as to confer on the controlling body the possibility of directly or indirectly exercising a decisive influence on the 'controlled' body. The Commissioner will look to see whether the controlling public authority has 'the power to direct, manage, oversee and/or restrict the affairs, business or assets of a person or entity'.

As yet 'the scope of regulation 2(2)(d) of EIR 2004 is virgin territory so far as the courts are concerned' (*Smartsource Drainage and Water Searches Ltd* (GI/2458/2010), para.94; [2010] UKUT 415 (AAC)), however, it has been considered at some length by the Upper Tribunal in *Smartsource*. The *Smartsource* case gave the Tribunal the opportunity to review the guidance offered by Defra, the Aarhus Implementation Guide and the analysis in the leading text book on the subject (Philip Coppel QC, *Information Rights: Law and Practice*, 3rd edn, Hart Publishing). In addition the Upper Tribunal considered the way in which the term 'control' had been interpreted by the courts in other contexts. Although these previous judicial decisions were of limited assistance in interpreting EIR 2004, the Upper Tribunal felt the ruling of McKenna J in *Mixed Concrete* v. *Ministry of Pensions* [1968] 1 All ER 433 (at 440C), gave a taste of what control means:

> Control includes the power of deciding the thing to be done, the way in which it shall be done, the means to be employed in doing it, the time when, and the place where it shall be done.

However, for the Upper Tribunal the starting point in interpreting 'control' had to be the plain words of EIR 2004 read against the background of the Convention and the Directive. In the Upper Tribunal's view the focus of both these instruments is on 'capturing governmental and executive functions in the various guises'. An important distinction needs to be drawn between control and regulation. Private commercial activities may be subject to a degree of state regulation (even intensive state regulation) but still remain at 'arm's length from the machinery of the state'.

• Regulation involves a regulator formulating policy and strategy, determining outcomes, making and enforcing rules, and issuing guidance for those bodies it regulates. Regulation may be light touch or heavy handed.
• Control must go further than regulation. Control connotes command and compulsion and the power to determine not just the ends but also the means to achieve those ends. According to the Tribunal, this is reflected in the Defra guidance which refers to 'decisive influence'.

Applying this reasoning, the Upper Tribunal upheld the Information Commissioner's decision that the private water companies operating in England and Wales were not public authorities within the meaning of this limb. Although the water companies are subject to a detailed regulatory regime under the Water Industry Act 1991, the Act provides for a system of regulation rather than control. The Upper Tribunal examined the nature of the regulation under the Act, which they considered was underpinned by free market principles. The Tribunal also noted the important distinction between the regulators (in this case, OFWAT and the Secretary of State for the Environment), which do exercise control and are subject to EIR 2004, and the privatised companies, which enjoy a high degree of commercial freedom and are sufficiently distanced from the public role. (See the postscript at **4.9** below.)

Contractual control

The Defra guidance notes that control may be exercised via a contract. The sub-contracting of essential public 'environmental' services potentially puts private companies within the EIR 2004 radar if the services/functions are environmental in nature, providing the contract enables the controlling body to exert decisive influence. Typically, local authorities sub-contract their statutory waste disposal and collection functions to either arm's length companies or private sector firms. For example, South Downs Waste Services Ltd, a private waste company, was held to be a public authority by virtue of the integrated waste management contract it had entered into with two councils (*South Downs Waste Services Ltd* FS50114241).

The simple existence of a contract does not necessarily provide the degree of control needed; the Commissioner will closely examine the contract terms to discover the nature of the relationship between the public authority and the third party service provider. The factors to take into account are amply demonstrated in the *South Downs Waste Services* case:

- the waste contract required the waste company to provide an annual report to the councils in relation to the effectiveness of its activities in relation to the environment;
- the councils could take action in relation to any part of the services provided by the company if there was an imminent and serious risk to the environment;
- the contract provided that whilst the statutory duties remained the responsibility of the councils they had contracted the provision of the services to meet those duties to the waste contractor (*South Downs Waste Services Ltd* FS50114241).

In *Wesley Housing Association* FER149772 control was exercised by the Department of Social Development for Northern Ireland because the Department had the power to oversee the housing association's affairs by extensively regulating it and perusing its annual accounts.

This clearly has important implications for private sector providers who enter into contracts to carry out the statutory responsibilities of public authorities, and authorities who put such contracts out to tender should make companies aware of this possibility under EIR 2004. It also means that bodies may move in and out of the scope of EIR 2004 depending upon the level of control exerted via a contract.

4.5.2 Public responsibilities and providing services relating to the environment

In relation to public responsibilities, exercising functions of a public nature, and providing public services, it must also be established that the body in question is:

- carrying out public responsibilities in relation to the environment;
- exercising functions of a public nature in relation to the environment; or
- providing a public service in relation to the environment.

The Defra detailed guidance suggests that this includes private companies or public private partnerships with obvious environmental responsibilities such as waste disposal, water, energy or transport regulation. However, there is nothing in the actual definition to suggest that only 'obvious' environmental responsibilities qualify. A private waste services company that is providing waste collection, disposal and recycling services on behalf of a local authority that is under a statutory obligation to provide such services easily fulfils all three of the above (see the discussion of *South Downs Waste Services Ltd* FS50114241 under 'Contractual control' at **4.5.1** above). Given that very many local authorities contract out their waste responsibilities this is likely to bring a considerable number of waste service companies within the scope of EIR 2004. It would also apply to a company that has been contracted to provide land remediation services on behalf of a local authority where the local authority is obliged to undertake the remediation.

Whilst it may be fairly obvious that a waste contractor has public responsibilities relating to the environment, the link with the environment need not be so direct and 'relate' can be taken to mean 'having a connection to'. An excellent example of this can be seen in *Belfast Improved Housing Association Ltd* FER0152607:

- the provision, construction, improvement or management of social housing had significant effects on energy use; and
- energy use is connected to the environment (reducing energy use in housing can have a positive effect in reducing carbon dioxide emissions and therefore the state of the air and atmosphere);
- the funding that the housing association received was conditional on certain strong environmental considerations and environmental standards, supporting the decision that the housing association had specific responsibilities relating to the environment.

4.6 IMPLICATIONS FOR THE PRIVATE SECTOR

It should be clear from the discussion above that private sector organisations may be public authorities for the purposes of EIR 2004 providing they fall within either reg.2(2)(c) or (d). As the discussion earlier reveals, some surprising organisations have been captured by the definition, perhaps the most surprising being Payphone Plus. Conversely, the exclusion of the private water companies, despite the fact that water is one of the essential elements of the environment, is quite controversial. What is clear is that the case-by-case approach that this definition demands will continue to throw up some surprising results and private sector companies cannot assume that they fall outside EIR 2004 simply because they are not traditional public authorities. It is also clear that when a company or private organisation enters into a contract with a public authority to exercise functions or provide services relating to the environment, this may bring that company/organisation within the scope of EIR 2004 depending on the degree of control exerted by the public authority contractor.

Public private partnerships (PPP) may fall under reg.2(2)(d) providing they carry out public responsibilities in relation to the environment; exercise functions of a public nature in relation to the environment; or provide a public service in relation to the environment. In addition, of course, the PPP must be under the control of a public authority; the degree of control will be ascertained along the lines described above. Inevitably this will need to be determined on a case-by-case basis.

The same consideration applies to the privatised utilities. The Defra detailed guidance on who is covered by the regulations recognises that public utilities that are 'involved in the supply of essential public services such as water, sewerage, electricity and gas' may fall within the scope of EIR 2004. At the time of writing there has been no consideration of this beyond the private water companies.

4.6.1   Mixed private and public functions

Prior to the Upper Tribunal's decision in *Smartsource* it appeared that a body could fall within the definition of an EIR public authority in respect of some of its 'public' functions whilst still carrying on private/commercial functions (see *Port of London Authority* (EA/2006/0083)). The term 'hybrid' authorities was coined to describe such bodies which operated a mix of public and private functions. However, the Upper Tribunal robustly rejected this possibility in the *Smartsource* case. The Tribunal pragmatically accepted that it would be too time consuming if a body was an EIR public authority for some purposes of EIR 2004 but not for others. More significantly the Upper Tribunal did not accept that the language of EIR 2004, reg.2 supported the possibility that an organisation could be simultaneously within and without the ambit of EIR 2004. The author is of the view that this a very restrictive and literal approach to interpretation and is at odds with the need to provide the widest possible access to environmental information as demanded by the Convention.

4.7   EIR 2004, REG.3(3) AND (4): EXCEPTIONS TO DEFINITION OF 'PUBLIC AUTHORITY'

As noted earlier the definition of 'public authority' under EIR 2004 excludes:

- any public authority to the extent that it is acting in a judicial or legislative capacity (EIR 2004, reg.3(3));
- either House of Parliament to the extent required for the purpose of avoiding an infringement of the privileges of either House (EIR 2004, reg.3(4)).

The exclusion of public authorities acting in a judicial or legislative capacity exactly mirrors the provisions of the Aarhus Convention. The effect of this is that when a public authority acts in either a judicial or legislative capacity, it is excluded. This does not mean that the body per se is excluded. Courts and tribunals are subject to EIR 2004 in respect of information that they keep in respect of their non-judicial functions or after the completion of any relevant judicial procedure or appeal period. So, for example, a request to a court about its recycling facilities should be dealt with by the court in compliance with EIR 2004 requirements. Similarly, the House of Commons may be subject to a request for information which is not related to the exercise of its legislative functions (such as the amount of expenses payable to MPs). A German court has sought a preliminary ruling from the ECJ in relation to the corresponding provision of the Directive (*Flachglas Torgau GmbH* v. *Federal Republic of Germany* (Case C-204/09)). The ECJ has been asked, *inter alia*, whether the exception only covers bodies and institutions which take the final decision in the legislative process and also whether bodies are excluded from the definition only for the period until the conclusion of the legislative process. At the time of writing the ECJ has not given its ruling on these questions.

The second limitation is also contained within FOIA 2000, s.34. The purpose of this exception (and corresponding FOIA exemption) is to enable either the House of Commons or the House of Lords to avoid having to disclose any information which would result in an infringement of the privileges of either House. There does not appear to be any decision notices regarding this EIR 2004 exception.

4.7.1   Scottish public authorities

EIR 2004 do not extend to Scottish public authorities which are subject to the Environmental Information (Scotland) Regulations 2004, SSI 2004/520. Scottish public authorities are defined by reference to FOIA 2000, s.84 and the Freedom of Information (Scotland) Act 2002, s.3. Essentially this includes:

- the Scottish Parliament;
- any part of the Scottish administration;
- the Scottish Parliamentary Corporate Body;
- any Scottish public authority with mixed functions or no reserved functions within the meaning of the Scotland Act 1998;

- any body defined as a 'public authority' by the Freedom of Information (Scotland) Act 2002, s.3.

However, where an English or Welsh public authority under EIR 2004 exercises functions in relation to Scotland, or is located in Scotland, it will be subject to EIR 2004. It should also be noted that an EIR public authority may transfer a request to a Scottish public authority.

4.8 CONCLUSIONS

EIR 2004 apply to public authorities. The definition of 'public authority' is wider than that in FOIA 2000 in order to comply with the requirements of the Aarhus Convention and Directive 2004/3/ EC. The definition is capable of including private sector companies and public private partnerships.

The Information Commissioner's Office has indicated that its general approach will be to adopt a broad interpretation of the definition of 'public authority' in EIR 2004 in order to bring it in line with the Directive. This broad approach avoids the problem of public sector bodies contracting out public services in order that legal obligations to disclose environmental information may be avoided. This approach is consistent with the approach adopted by the ECJ.

4.9 POSTSCRIPT

The *Smartsource* decision of the Upper Tribunal (GI/2458/2010) remains the most authoritative interpretation of this aspect of EIR 2004 to date. However, as noted at **4.1**, the Aarhus Compliance Committee is (at the time of writing) investigating a complaint lodged by Fish Legal in December 2010. The essence of the complaint is that the approach adopted by the Upper Tribunal was narrow, that the Tribunal failed to adopt a purposive approach and that it cannot have been the intention of the Aarhus Convention that the water companies should be above the scrutiny of the public. It remains to be seen how the Compliance Committee will decide this issue.

CHAPTER 5

The active dissemination of environmental information

5.1 INTRODUCTION

The public increasingly expects to be able access an enormous amount of information via the Web and this includes information about the public authorities that 'regulate' their daily lives. People want to know which are good and bad hospitals, which schools are performing well and how public services are run. If the only way in which people could access this information was by way of a request, public authorities might soon grind to a halt. The objective of the active dissemination provisions can therefore be considered to be both principled and pragmatic. On the one hand, the aim is to promote openness and transparency and to facilitate informed public participation in decision making. In addition, there are obvious practical advantages to be gained by actively disseminating information. A public authority that makes information available in an easily accessible fashion can significantly reduce the number of requests it receives for information, enabling it to focus on delivery of front-line services.

Both FOIA 2000 and EIR 2004 impose a dual obligation on public authorities: to make information available on request and to routinely and progressively make information available to the public so that they can access it without having to make a request. The active dissemination provisions of EIR 2004 are to be found in EIR 2004, reg.4 which, *inter alia*, requires public authorities to progressively make information available to the public by electronic means.

The vast majority of public authorities subject to EIR 2004 are also subject to FOIA 2000 and will therefore already be familiar with the active dissemination obligations under the Act, which require public authorities to produce and maintain publication schemes (FOIA 2000, s.19). Although EIR 2004 does not require public authorities to have publication schemes it is clear (from both the ICO and Defra guidance) that a public authority that actively updates and expands its FOIA publication scheme is likely to fulfil its obligation under EIR 2004 at the same time, if the publication scheme includes environmental information. The active dissemination requirements of EIR 2004 should not therefore impose any additional burdens and duties on a public authority over and above the requirements of FOIA 2000. However, not all EIR public authorities are subject to FOIA 2000 (for example, the Port of London Authority or private waste companies). The 'EIR only' public authorities will need to consider what steps they need to take to ensure compliance with EIR 2004, reg.4.

This chapter will consider what the obligations under EIR 2004, reg.4 entail from the point of view of public authorities, and to this end will include an examination of publication schemes under FOIA 2000. The chapter will also include a brief examination of the impact of the European Convention on Human Rights (ECHR) and the Human Rights Act 1998 on the duty to actively provide environmental information.

5.2 BACKGROUND: THE CONVENTION AND DIRECTIVE

Article 5 of the Convention implicitly recognises that improving public awareness about the environment requires more than simply giving the public the right to request environmental information. It additionally provides for the collection and active dissemination of environmental information without a request having to be made. Article 5 requires that public authorities possess and update environmental information which is relevant to their functions and make it available in a manner that is transparent and effectively accessible. Article 5 of the Convention is transposed by art.7 of Directive 2003/4/EC. Under both the Convention and the Directive the detailed arrangements are to be determined by national legislation and the discussion that follows is largely about EIR 2004. However, the active dissemination requirements of the Convention are wider than those imposed by EIR 2004 and not all have been translated under EIR 2004 as legally binding obligations on public authorities. This does not mean that the UK is in breach of the Convention since the obligations may be fulfilled by other measures, some of which are referred to in this chapter. Under art.5, signatory states must:

- ensure that mandatory systems are established so that there is an adequate flow of information to public authorities about proposed and existing activities which may significantly affect the environment. This much generalised obligation is not repeated in Directive 2003/4/EC but is largely fulfilled by other measures outside the scope of EIR 2004. For example, detailed information in planning applications and associated environmental impact assessments, as well as monitoring requirements attached to environmental permits;
- ensure that in the event of any imminent threat to human health or the environment, whether caused by human activities or due to natural causes, all information which could enable the public to take measures to prevent or mitigate harm arising from the threat and is held by a public authority is disseminated immediately and without delay to members of the public who may be affected. This in turn is transposed by art.7(4) of the Directive but does not appear within EIR 2004;
- publish and disseminate at regular intervals (not exceeding three or four years) a national report on the state of the environment including the quality of, and

pressures on, the environment. Directive 2003/4/EC transposes this into art. 7(3) which in turn also refers to regional or local reports, where appropriate. This requirement is not translated into EIR 2004. In the main (although not exclusively) such reports will be published by Defra, the Environment Agency and local authorities in fulfilment of other statutory obligations;

- encourage operators whose activities have a significant impact on the environment to inform the public regularly of the environmental impact of their activities and products, where appropriate within the framework of voluntary eco-labelling or eco-auditing schemes or by other means;
- develop mechanisms with a view to ensuring that sufficient product information is made available to the public in a manner which enables consumers to make informed environmental choices;
- take steps to progressively establish a coherent, nationwide system of pollution inventories or registers on a structured, computerised and publicly accessible database compiled through standardised reporting. Such a system may include inputs, releases and transfers of a specified range of substances and products, including water, energy and resource use, from a specified range of activities to environmental media and to on-site and off-site treatment and disposal sites. (art.5(9) of the Aarhus Convention). For further discussion see **11.8** in relation to the Protocol on Pollutant Release and Transfer Registers.

A discussion of whether, and to what extent, the UK complies with all of the above requirements is largely outside the scope of this handbook. The Defra 2008 Aarhus Compliance Report claims there were no obstacles to achieving the requirements of art.5, however the Report's comments on the steps taken is very generalised.

5.2.1   Requirement that information must be up to date

In addition to art.7 of the Directive, art.8 requires that Member States must, as far as is within their power, ensure that any environmental information compiled by them or on their behalf is up to date, accurate and comparable. EIR 2004 does not transpose this requirement to the provisions of reg.4 but does apply it to information supplied in response to a request under reg.5(1).

5.3   EIR 2004, REG.4: REQUIREMENTS

EIR 2004, reg.4(1) requires public authorities to do two things in relation to the environmental information that they hold:

1.   progressively make the environmental information available to the public by electronic means which are easily accessible; and also
2.   take reasonable steps to organise the information relevant to its functions with a view to the active and systematic dissemination to the public of the information.

Essentially this requires that:

(a)   the dissemination of environmental information is active and systematic;
(b)   the dissemination is progressive and is by electronic means;
(c)   information must be easily accessible;
(d)   steps are taken to organise the information to best achieve these aims.

The dissemination requirements discussed below are subject to the same exceptions that apply to requests for environmental information under EIR 2004, reg.5. The exceptions to disclosure are examined in **Chapters 7–9**.

5.3.1   Progressive dissemination

The obligations imposed under EIR 2004, reg.4(1) can be characterised as ongoing, requiring an active consideration of any new information for dissemination. Although EIR 2004 does not explicitly state whether any particular information should be 'prioritised' in this progressive dissemination, it makes sense to start with the information identified in EIR 2004, reg.4(4) (see **5.4.1**). Beyond this it also makes sense to prioritise that information which is most likely to be of interest to the public, for example, information about waste streams and the quality of the environment. A public authority that logs requests for environmental information should soon get a feel for the issues that the public are interested in. See also discussion of disclosure logs at **5.6.1**.

5.3.2   By electronic means that are easily accessible

It is not sufficient for a public authority to make the information available on its website if it is difficult to navigate or use; EIR 2004 requires that the information is easily accessible. Whether information is easily accessible will often be determined by the skill and experience of the person conducting the search. There is little doubt that if information is difficult to locate, it is likely that members of the public will resort to making requests for information. If a public authority is receiving requests for information which it has made available via its website this may lead to the conclusion that the site is not easily accessible or further guidance needs to be provided about the way information is organised.

5.3.3   Organising information relevant to functions

Under EIR 2004, reg.4(1)(b), public authorities are required to take reasonable steps to organise environmental information relevant to their functions, with a view to the active and systematic dissemination of the information to the public. This provision should be read with care; it requires that the authority organises the environmental information relevant to its functions; it does not limit this to any specific environmental functions that the authority carries out. It is for each public authority to decide how it is going to do this.

Reasonable steps

The requirement is not absolute; public authorities are only required to take reasonable steps. What is reasonable will clearly depend on the size, nature, activities and resources of the authority concerned and the type of information that it holds. In the current economic climate with many public authorities facing significant cut-backs the question of resources is likely to play a key role in deciding what is reasonable.

In order to fulfil this obligation it is recommended that each public authority:

- prepares a plan of how it is going to organise its information so as to enable the active and systematic dissemination to the public. The authority should consider whether the information that it holds is already well organised and readily retrievable so that it can be made available to the public;
- considers drafting a written policy for the consideration of any new environmental information that the public authority produces or holds;
- informs the public, preferably on the authority's website, about the steps the authority is taking or proposes to take to fulfil this obligation;
- encourages members of the public to check its website to see whether the information is in the public domain before making a request.

Breach of EIR 2004, reg.4

Public authorities must comply with EIR 2004, reg.4. However, at the time of writing there were no decision notices in relation to this provision. This either means that all public authorities are complying with the requirement or there have been no complaints in relation to active dissemination. In all likelihood, anyone who has found it difficult to navigate a public authority's website (or publication scheme) to find information has followed this up with a request for the particular information. If the information has been refused this is more likely to have resulted in a complaint against the refusal rather than against the publication scheme per se. In any event, information which is 'exempt' from disclosure under EIR 2004 does not need to be actively disseminated under EIR 2004, reg.4.

5.4 INFORMATION THAT MUST BE INCLUDED

Although EIR 2004, reg.4 does not prescribe which information should be prioritised for electronic publication, it does state that as a minimum the information must include:

(a) the information referred to in art.7(2) of Directive 2003/4/EC; and
(b) the facts and analyses of facts which the public authority considers relevant and important in framing major environmental policy proposals.

5.4.1 Information referred to in art.7 of Directive 2003/4/EC

Article 7(2) of Directive 2003/4/EC requires that as a minimum the information set out in **Table 5.1** is made available and disseminated must include the following:

** Column 3 lists the suggestions provided in the Defra guidance on using the ICO model publication scheme to disseminate environmental information (March 2009).

5.4.2 Relevant facts and analyses in framing major environmental policy proposals

With regard to the facts and analyses of facts which the public authority considers relevant and important in framing major environmental policy proposals, it is entirely possible that a public authority not involved in framing such policy proposals will not hold this type of information. On the other hand, it is self-evident that some organisations, particularly those involved in environmental regulation and planning, will. However, EIR 2004, reg.4(4)(b) is capable of including information held by one public authority (for example, information held by a local authority in relation to local air pollution control) which is considered to be relevant when another body (i.e. the Environment Agency or a government department) frames major environmental proposals.

5.5 LIMITS ON DUTY TO ACTIVELY DISSEMINATE INFORMATION

There are two caveats to the requirements of EIR 2004, reg.4(1).

- First, reg.4(3) states that the duty does not extend to any information which the public authority would be entitled to refuse to disclose under EIR 2004, reg.12 (see **Chapters 7–9**).
- Second, by reg.4(2) the requirement does not apply to information collected before 1 January 2005 in non-electronic form. Although not expressly stated, this implies that if environmental information was collected before this date and is held electronically then it should be made available. There is nothing to prevent a public authority making information that it collated before 1 January 2005 in a non-electronic form available electronically. In fact, the ICO guidance on proactive dissemination recommends this course of action because such information could be caught by a general request for information under EIR 2004. It may be sensible to make it available on the public authority's website if it is anticipated that it is likely to be requested in any event. The Defra guidance also suggests that in the interests of coherence and transparency public authorities may choose to convert some of their paper-based environmental information into an electronic format, particularly those pieces of information which are likely to be of public interest. It has been argued (Jean-Jacques Paradissis, *The Right to Access Environmental Information: An*

Table 5.1 Information required in Directive 2003/4/EC

Information required	Comment/observation	Possible location in a Publication Scheme**
Texts of international treaties, conventions or agreements, and of (EU), national, regional or local legislation, on the environment or relating to it.	Not all public authorities will hold the texts of international treaties. All public authorities will be subject to some form of environmental legislation and they should consider either making the text of such legislation available on their website or providing a link to a website that contains this information, such as **www.legislation.gov.uk** or Eurlex: **www.eur-lex.europa.eu/en**.	• Who we are and what we do – organisational information, locations and contacts, constitutional and legal governance. • Our policies and procedures – current written protocols for delivering our functions and responsibilities.
Policies, plans and programmes relating to the environment.	This is not limited to governmental policies or plans directly relating to the environment. For bodies with specific environmental functions much of the information they hold is likely to fall into this category. However, all public authorities are likely to have some form of policy or plan which affects the environment, for example a policy or plan relating to a cycle-to-work scheme may fall within this sub-category.	• Who we are and what we do – organisational information, locations and contacts, constitutional and legal governance. • What our priorities are and how we are doing – strategy and performance information, plans, assessments, inspections and reviews. • How we make decisions – policy proposals and decisions. Decision-making processes, internal criteria and procedures, consultations. • Our policies and procedures – current written protocols for delivering our functions and responsibilities.

Information required	Comment/observation	Possible location in a Publication Scheme**
		• The services we offer – advice and guidance, booklets and leaflets, transactions and media releases. A description of the services offered.
Progress reports on the implementation of the items referred to in (a) and (b) when prepared or held in electronic form by public authorities.	Certain legislation requires public authorities to report on the implementation of legislation, e.g. Defra is under a duty by art.9 of Directive 2003/4/EC to report on the experience gained in implementing the Directive by EIR 2004. A public authority may report on the implementation of a policy or plan, e.g. a local authority policy on recycling may set targets and require regular implementation reports. Most public authorities will produce annual reports which consider performance against targets.	• What our priorities are and how we are doing – strategy and performance information, plans, assessments, inspections and reviews. • What we spend and how we spend it – financial information relating to projected and actual income and expenditure, tendering, procurement and contracts. • Lists and registers – information held in registers required by law and other lists and registers relating to the functions of the authority.
Reports on the state of the environment.	The Directive requires Member States to ensure that national (and, where appropriate, regional and local) reports on the state of the environment are published at regular intervals (at least every four years). Such reports must include information on the quality of, and pressures on, the environment. This latter requirement (to publish regular reports on the state of the environment) is not directly translated into EIR 2004 but is likely to arise from reporting requirements under other EU Directives and corresponding domestic legislation.	• What our priorities are and how we are doing – strategy and performance information, plans, assessments, inspections and reviews.

65

Information required	Comment/observation	Possible location in a Publication Scheme**
Data or summaries of data derived from the monitoring of activities affecting, or likely to affect, the environment.	In the main (although certainly not exclusively) such activities will require planning permission and/or an environmental permit. Other regulated activities may be required to supply monitoring data to the regulator as part of the licensing/ authorisation agreement. This information may be included within the body of reports or held separately as databases, spreadsheets, or in public registers, etc.	• What our priorities are and how we are doing – strategy and performance information, plans, assessments, inspections and reviews. • How we make decisions – in particular background information for major policy decisions. • Lists and registers – information held in registers required by law and other lists and registers relating to the functions of the authority.
Authorisations with a significant impact on the environment and environmental agreements or a reference to the place where such information can be requested or found.	This is likely to be most relevant to the Environment Agency and local authorities who grant environmental permits, but it will extend to a range of other bodies that authorise polluting activities. It will also apply to local planning authorities which enter into environmental agreements. The information may be included within the body of reports or held separately as databases, spreadsheets, or in public registers.	• Who we are and what we do – organisational information, locations and contacts, constitutional and legal governance. • How we make decisions – policy proposals and decisions. Decision-making processes, internal criteria and procedures, consultations. • Lists and registers – information held in registers required by law and other lists and registers relating to the functions of the authority.

Information required	Comment/observation	Possible location in a Publication Scheme**
Environmental impact studies and risk assessments concerning the environmental elements referred to in the definition of 'environmental information' or a reference to the place where the information can be requested or found.	Environmental impact assessments within the meaning of Directive 85/337/EEC, as amended, must be within the public domain to enable public participation in environmental decision making. However, this category of information is wider than environmental impact assessments.	• What our priorities are and how we are doing – strategy and performance information, plans, assessments, inspections and reviews. • How we make decisions – policy proposals and decisions. • Decision-making processes, internal criteria and procedures, consultations.

Analysis of UK Law in the Context of European, International and Human Rights Law (2009, VDM Verland)) that the date of 1 January 2005 breaches Directive 2003/4/EC, which limits the requirement to information collected before the Directive came in to force, which was 14 February 2003.

5.6   EIR 2004 AND PUBLICATION SCHEMES

As previously stated, EIR 2004, in contrast to FOIA 2000, do not require public authorities to establish approved publication schemes. However, the vast majority of public authorities subject to EIR 2004 should already have their approved publication schemes in place. According to the ICO, EIR 2004, reg.4 does not impose any additional responsibilities on those public authorities that are already compliant with FOIA 2000 requirements for maintaining their records, and are taking a proactive and transparent approach towards keeping their publication schemes up to date and progressively expanding their coverage.

5.6.1   FOIA 2000 publication schemes

Every public authority subject to FOIA 2000 is required to adopt, maintain and review a 'publication scheme'. The public authority must publish information in accordance with that scheme (FOIA 2000, s.19). Like EIR 2004, reg.4, the aim of s.19 is to ensure that public authorities take proactive steps in releasing information to the public. The requirements of a publication scheme are set out in s.19(2). The publication scheme must:

- specify classes of information which the public authority publishes or intends to publish;
- specify the manner in which each class of information is, or is intended to be, published; and
- specify whether the material is, or is intended to be, available to the public free of charge or on payment.

It must be easy for members of the public to find out what information is available and where they can find it.

When a public authority adopts and reviews its publication scheme it is required to have regard to the public interest in allowing the public access to the information it holds and also the reasons for the decisions it makes. The scheme must be approved by the Information Commissioner and he may give approval for a specific period of time. The Commissioner may also revoke his approval. However, a public authority does not need to seek the Commissioner's approval where it adopts the model publication scheme published by the Commissioner.

Model publication schemes

To assist public authorities, the Commissioner has published a single model publication scheme that is suitable for every public authority to adopt; the scheme was effective from 1 January 2009 and was developed in conjunction with representatives from a wide range of public authorities. A public authority that adopts this model publication scheme does not need to seek the approval of the Commissioner, nor indeed does it need to notify the Commissioner that it is adopting the model scheme. FOIA 2000, s.20 suggests that a public authority may be able to adopt the model scheme with modifications, but such modifications must be approved by the Commissioner. However, the Commissioner's guidance states unequivocally that public authorities must not alter or amend the model scheme.

What is a publication scheme and what must it include?

A publication scheme is not a list of everything that is published. The intention is that the publication scheme provides:

- a guide to the different types of information that a public authority routinely publishes and intends to publish;
- details of how the information is published (for example, the format);
- whether there are any charges for the information.

FOIA 2000 does not actually specify what must be included in the publication scheme, nor does the Information Commissioner's model publication scheme. Instead the latter identifies seven broad classes of information. Public authorities should arrange the information as follows:

1. Who we are and what we do.
2. What we spend and how we spend it.
3. What our priorities are and how we are doing.
4. How we make decisions.
5. Our policies and procedures.
6. Lists and registers.
7. The services we offer.

Beyond these core categories the information may be further divided into more specific sub-categories. For example, the first category may be broken down to provide information about the public authority's organisational structure and its roles and responsibilities, contact details and the legislation that governs the organisation.

Definition documents

The ICO has produced guidance to show the types of information it expects different types of authority to publish; these are referred to as 'definition documents'. Public authorities are required to publish everything which is listed in the definition document for the particular type of authority except for, of course, information which the public authority does not hold and:

- information which is exempt from disclosure under FOIA 2000, EIR 2004 or any other statute;
- information which is archived, out of date or otherwise inaccessible; or
- material which would be impractical or resource intensive to prepare for routine release.

Disclosure logs

Some public authorities publish the information they have made available on request via a disclosure log. Essentially this enables the public to access, via the public authority's website, information it has disclosed. The value of the disclosure log is that it enables the public authority concerned to release the requested information to the public at large (as well as to the individual applicant). FOIA 2000 does not require disclosure logs and nor does EIR 2004, but it is suggested that they provide a valuable way of ensuring the progressive dissemination of information required by EIR 2004, reg.4(1).

Publication schemes and environmental information

Strictly speaking, environmental information is exempt from FOIA 2000 and therefore there is no need to include environmental information on a FOIA publication scheme; however, it really does not make sense for a public authority to exclude environmental information from its publication scheme given the demands of EIR 2004, reg.4. The Commissioner's guidance suggests that environmental information should be included in a publication scheme, as well as information which a public authority is required to make available for inspection under another enactment. The latter includes information on the various public registers discussed in **Chapter 11**.

5.6.2   Bodies subject to EIR 2004 only

There are a small number of organisations that fall within the definition of an EIR 'public authority' but are not subject to FOIA 2000 (see **Chapter 4**). Such organisations are not under any obligation to publish a publication scheme, however, the Defra guidance suggests that they may find it useful to consult the guidance on publication schemes and record keeping to form a view on how this would assist them with complying with EIR 2004, reg.4.

5.7 CHARGING FOR INFORMATION THAT IS PROACTIVELY DISSEMINATED

Where information is published on a public website, access is usually free of charge (see **5.7.1** for discussion of copyright issues). In addition to making information available electronically, a public authority may choose to provide a hard-copy version of material for which it may make a reasonable charge under EIR 2004, reg.8 (see **6.5** on charging).

5.7.1 Re-use of information

The supply of information via a public authority's website or publication scheme does not give the person who accesses the information an automatic right to re-use the material in a way that would infringe copyright. If the public authority specifies that approval is required to re-use information available on its website then the burden falls on the user to obtain the necessary copyright approval or licence under the Re-use of Public Sector Information Regulations 2005, SI 2005/1515 (see **11.10**).

5.8 INFORMATION NOT AVAILABLE ELECTRONICALLY

Article 3(5) of Directive 2003/4/EC requires that as far as requests for information are concerned Member States must make practical arrangements for ensuring that rights of access to environmental information can be effectively exercised. This includes the establishment and maintenance of facilities for the examination of information. The Directive does not say anything about making such facilities available to support the active dissemination of environmental information and nor does EIR 2004. However, not all available information will be via a website, for example, large maps or archived documents. Public authorities may wish to consider how such information can be actively disseminated. Where a public authority is relying on a publication scheme to comply with EIR 2004, reg.4, the scheme should inform the public where, when and how they can access information that is not available electronically. It should also be recalled that a public authority is not permitted to levy any charge for in situ inspections of information (see **6.5**).

5.9 RELATIONSHIP BETWEEN ACTIVE DISSEMINATION AND DUTY TO RESPOND TO REQUESTS

Compliance with EIR 2004, reg.4 does not remove the obligation to respond to requests for environmental information. However, where a public authority has made the requested information available via its website then it may, under EIR 2004, reg.6(1), refuse to provide the information in a particular form or format requested. EIR 2004, reg.6(1) is only triggered when an applicant requests information in a particular form or format. So, for example, an applicant who asks to inspect original documents or who requests a hard copy of information engages EIR 2004, reg.6(1). The public authority may refuse to supply the information in the form/format requested if the information is already publicly available and easily accessible to the applicant in another form or format (for example, a PDF copy on the authority's website) (EIR 2004, reg.6(1)(b)). However, the mere fact that the information is available online does not necessarily mean the authority can rely on EIR 2004, reg.6(1)(b), because the information must be easily accessible to the applicant. (For further discussion of EIR 2004, reg.6, see **Chapter 6**.)

5.10   INFORMATION ON THE IMMINENT THREAT TO HUMAN HEALTH OR THE ENVIRONMENT

Directive 2003/4/EC requires that Member States must take the necessary measures to ensure that in the event of an imminent threat to human health or the environment, whether caused by human activities or due to natural causes, all information held by, or for, public authorities which could enable the public likely to be affected to take measures to prevent or mitigate harm arising from the threat is disseminated, immediately and without delay.

5.10.1   EU Directives

The above obligation is without prejudice to any other specific obligation laid down by any other EU legislation such as the so-called Seveso II Directive. Council Directive 96/82/EC (Seveso II) on the control of major-accident hazards involving dangerous substances (as amended) requires Member States to ensure that information on safety measures and on the requisite behaviour in the event of an accident is supplied regularly, and in the most appropriate form, to all persons and all establishments serving the public (such as schools and hospitals) liable to be affected by a major accident caused by an establishment where dangerous substances are present. The requirement is for proactive dissemination of this information without there having to be a request. Proactive dissemination in these instances may be achieved through the distribution of leaflets or brochures informing the public about behaviour in the event of an accident.

5.10.2   Impact of the ECHR

ECHR, art.8

At first glance, art.8 of the ECHR, which provides that everyone has a right to respect for his private and family life, his home and his correspondence, would appear to have no direct relevance to access to environmental information. Its aim is to protect individuals from an arbitrary interference with these rights. However, in *Guerra* v. *Italy* (Application No.14967/89) (2001) 34 EHRR 42, the European

Court of Human Rights interpreted art.8 as imposing a positive obligation to provide information regarding environmental hazards to enable families to assess risks posed by living in particular localities. Reliance was placed on an earlier case, *López Ostra* v. *Spain* (Application No.16798/90) (1995) 20 EHRR 27, in which the Court had held that severe environmental pollution can affect the well being of individuals and prevent them from enjoying their homes in a way that interferes with their art.8 rights. In *Guerra* the Court went a step further when it decided that the failure to provide information to local residents about the dangers of a local chemical factory so that they could assess the risks to their families if they continued to live in the locality constituted a breach of the applicant's art.8 rights. In *Guerra* the Court expressly stated that the duty to provide information exists whether or not people have requested such information; in short the Court required the positive dissemination of the information held. However, such a positive obligation must be seen in context. Only a severe threat to art.8 rights, such as existed here where the emissions from the chemical company were particularly hazardous, will trigger the application of art.8. This is evident in *R (on the application of Furness)* v. *The Environment Agency* [2002] Env LR 26; [2001] All ER (D) 242 (Dec) where the High Court rejected a claim that the Agency should make monitoring information relating to a municipal waste incinerator available prior to it being made available via the relevant public registers. The High Court considered that the risks posed by the waste incinerator were not of the substantial kind evident in *Guerra*.

CHAPTER 6

Handling requests for environmental information

6.1 INTRODUCTION

This chapter aims to provide practical guidance to public authorities on how to respond to requests for environmental information. Additionally, it is hoped that the chapter will enable members of the public to know what they can expect when they make a request for environmental information from a public authority. The chapter considers the procedural requirements where a public authority decides to disclose the information requested. The chapter considers, *inter alia*, the following issues:

- who can make a request;
- what information can be requested;
- the 'holding' requirement;
- dealing with oral requests and logging requests;
- advising and assisting applicants;
- making information available;
- form and format of the response;
- time limits;
- charges;
- transferring requests;
- public records; and
- refusal notices.

Chapter 7 examines the procedures that must be followed where the authority decides on partial disclosure or to withhold information.

6.2 THE RIGHT OF ACCESS TO INFORMATION

6.2.1 Who can make a request?

Anybody can make a request for environmental information; individuals, companies and pressure groups are all equally entitled to make requests for environmental information. EIR 2004 refers only to the 'applicant' as the person who makes the request and to information being progressively made available to 'the public'. The Aarhus Convention and Directive 2003/4/EC are unequivocal about the necessity to ensure 'that any natural and legal person has a right of access to environmental information held by or for public authorities without his having to state an interest'. There does not appear to be any jurisdictional limit either, so the applicant may live in China or the USA, and that would not be a bar to receiving the information. Applicants are not required to explain why they want the information and nor are they required to cite EIR 2004 as the basis of their request. (See, for example, *North East Lincolnshire Borough Council* FER0326629.)

6.2.2   EIR 2004 are purpose blind

A public authority cannot enquire why an applicant wants the information; to that extent EIR 2004 are said to be both applicant and purpose blind. Applicants should not be forced to explain why they want the information; although as noted below (at **6.3.2**), some explanation may help a public authority to discharge its duty to advise and assist applicants.

However, if the applicant intends to publish or use the information for another commercial purpose, this is relevant. Such requests should be dealt with under the Re-use of Public Sector Information Regulations 2005, SI 2005/1515. (For further discussion, see **11.10**.)

6.2.3   Who can a request be made to?

EIR 2004 are only binding on public authorities as defined by reg.2(2). The definition is considered fully in **Chapter 4**. If a request is declined by a body which claims that it is not subject to EIR 2004, then the applicant may request an internal review of that decision. If the body is claiming it is not subject to EIR 2004, it is unlikely to have an internal review procedure process, but the complaint should still be considered by the authority under its existing complaints procedures. If the body still maintains it is not subject to EIR 2004, the applicant can (if minded) complain to the Information Commissioner. It is not the applicant's responsibility to prove that the body is subject to EIR 2004, but if applicants have any doubt then they could consider asking the ICO for some advice prior to making the request.

6.2.4   What information can be accessed? The holding requirement

Members of the public only have a right to access environmental information that is 'held' by a public authority. Under EIR 2004, reg.3(2) a public authority holds environmental information if the information:

(a)   is in the authority's possession and it has either been produced (either in whole or in part) by the authority or received by the authority. The effect of this is that any information that is in the authority's possession is held by the public authority irrespective of whether the public authority produced it itself or it was provided to the authority by a third party. For example, information supplied by a private firm, an individual or an external legal advisor is held by the public authority even if the person who provided the information was not aware that this could make it potentially discloseable. This means that a private contractor supplying information to a public authority as part of a tender exercise could find that the information, now in the possession of the authority, is subject to the scope of EIR 2004.

(b)   is held by another person on behalf of the authority. If the information is held by another person on behalf of a public authority, the public authority holds that information for the purposes of EIR 2004. On the other hand, information would not be held under this provision where the information is held on behalf of another person, and is not held at all for that public authority's own purposes. (See *Kirkby Malzeard, Laverton and Dallowgill Parish Council* FS50294322.) Public authorities will need to consider information they have placed on external facilities such as 'Cloud' computing and other online storage platforms.

No duty to create new information

EIR 2004 do not require public authorities to create new records in order to deal with requests. A case which merits some attention is *Fowler* v. *Information Commissioner & Brighton & Hove City Council* (EA/2006/0071). The applicant made numerous requests for information relating to waste and waste collection including the council's views on the merits of a change in its operational practices. It was only possible to answer this type of question by preparing an individual reply and the Tribunal unequivocally noted that:

> The EIR does not require public authorities to go to such lengths. The obligation is to provide recorded information, not to create a record so that an answer may be given … If the public authority does hold information in recorded form which answers the question, it should provide it; if it does not hold the information in recorded form, it should say so.

The form of the information

Environmental information may be in various forms; for example, photos, maps, information which is stored electronically, handwritten notes and emails. However, it is important to note that the right is to 'information' rather than documentation. Consequently, the public authority may need to collate the information from a document or documents, but it is not required to create or assemble new documentation in order to respond to a request.

6.3 THE REQUEST

6.3.1 Making the request: oral requests

Unlike FOIA 2000, there is no requirement on the part of the person requesting environmental information to make the request in writing or to provide his or her name or address. From the requestor's point of view this makes requesting information a good deal simpler and easier. However, it can create some practical difficulties for public authorities because requests for environmental information may be made orally in conversation or over the phone and technically the public authority is bound to deal with them under EIR 2004. This does not mean that every member of staff who is likely to come into contact with the general public should be trained in the details of EIR 2004. But public authorities must comply with the Code of Practice and this requires them to provide proper training on EIR 2004. A public authority needs to ensure that staff are at least aware of the authority's obligations under EIR 2004. This may be at a basic level but one would expect such staff to know who to pass requests on to and/or how to log requests so that they are properly dealt with.

Where members of staff routinely deal with public enquiries (for example, receptionists or telephone operatives), they must be familiar with the basic requirements of EIR 2004 and the Code of Practice.

Practical example

A member of the public approaches a porter at a hospital and asks what is going to happen to the waste he collects. This is a request for environmental information. There are various possible outcomes, some more plausible than others, but each reveals the issues involved:

- The porter says he doesn't know. The requestor may leave it at that or may get in contact with somebody more senior to find out.
- The porter answers and the requestor is happy. This is likely to be regarded by most public authorities as a routine 'business as usual' type question, not raising any specific information rights issues.
- The porter says he doesn't know and isn't obliged to answer because the request should be in writing. Under FOIA 2000 requests must be in writing but this is not the case under EIR 2004.
- The porter says he doesn't know but he logs the question and says he will pass it on to somebody else. In this scenario the requestor would almost certainly have to provide some contact details, even if they do not wish to provide their name.

A public authority needs to establish a system for logging/recording oral requests for environmental information. The ICO has published a form that authorities may use or adapt for this purpose.

Supplying a name and an address

There is no legal requirement for an applicant to supply his name or address and he may remain wholly anonymous, unless the information request includes a request for personal data and the public authority needs to establish whether the applicant is the data subject. However, in practice, it may be necessary for the applicant to provide contact details where the request cannot be answered immediately. There is nothing to prevent a public authority asking for such details so that the public authority can communicate the information to the applicant at a later date. Despite this very practical consideration, there is absolutely no legal obligation on the part of the applicant to supply his name or address.

6.3.2 Advice and assistance

Applicants have the right to receive reasonable advice and assistance in formulating their requests for environmental information (EIR 2004, reg.9). Ultimately it is for each public authority to decide how it is going to provide this. Conforming with the practices recommended in the Code of Practice will secure compliance with the requirements of reg.9 and so this seems a very good starting point for any public authority.

The Code of Practice aims to protect the interests of applicants by setting out the minimum standards of advice and assistance that should be followed as a matter of good practice. It is always open to a public authority to provide further support mechanisms for applicants and would-be applicants, but the public authority's duty to help applicants is only to a standard that it would be reasonable to expect from a reasonable authority. Essentially, EIR 2004, reg.9 is concerned with the provision of good customer service. Nevertheless, it also clearly makes good business sense for a public authority to try to find out exactly what the applicant wants in order to narrow down the search and avoid unnecessary costs in retrieving information that the applicant does not actually want.

The type of assistance that a public authority may provide includes:

- Helping the applicant to clarify what information he or she is looking for. The applicant should be contacted as quickly as possible, preferably by telephone or email, where more information is required to help clarify the request.
- Providing an outline of the different kinds of information that meet the terms of the request.
- Providing access to detailed catalogues and indexes (if they are available) so that applicants can see the nature and extent of the information held by the public authority.
- Providing a general response to the request which sets out options for further information that could be provided on request.
- Advising applicants about where they can get additional help and assistance in framing their request (for example, the Citizens Advice Bureau).

As noted at **6.2.2** above, EIR 2004 are said to be 'purpose blind', meaning that the applicant's reasons for requesting the information are wholly irrelevant. Even if the public authority is aware that the applicant wants to use the information to embarrass the authority, this is not a relevant consideration. However, in terms of delivering good customer service it may help to know why a person is making a request. For example, if the applicant is requesting information in order to submit his or her views about a planning application, it would be helpful to know this as the likelihood is that the applicant will be operating within a tight time frame to make his or her representations. Knowing why the applicant wants the information may also help the public authority provide appropriate advice and assistance in framing the request. Applicants should be aware, however, that they are not required to supply this information unless they want to. The Code of Practice is emphatic that the duty to advise and assist is targeted at the applicant and cannot be used by authorities to conduct fishing expeditions into the motives of the applicant. The duty to advise and assist is enforceable by the Information Commissioner and if a public authority fails in its statutory duty, the Commissioner may issue a decision notice or an enforcement notice against the public authority (see **Chapter 10**).

Advising prospective applicants

The duty not only applies to applicants; it also extends to prospective applicants. Although not specifically required by EIR 2004, the Code of Practice recommends that public authorities may satisfy this aspect of the duty by publishing information about their procedures for dealing with requests for environmental information. This should, amongst other things, alert applicants to the authority's usual procedures for transferring requests (see **6.7**) and must also include contact details so that prospective applicants can find out where and how they can receive further advice and assistance. If the public authority operates a publication scheme (see **5.6**) then this information should be included in it. In any event, this information must be in the public domain, the public authority's website is the obvious place, but authorities may want to consider other forms of publication, such as posters and/or leaflets.

6.4   THE RESPONSE

Public authorities subject to FOIA 2000 should have a system in place to ensure the efficient processing of requests for information. The same is true of EIR 2004 and invariably where a public authority has a nominated information rights officer, he or she has responsibility for dealing with requests under both regimes. Those bodies that are only subject to EIR 2004 will not necessarily have a dedicated information rights officer but they are well advised to nominate a person with responsibility for processing requests for environmental information. In the light of what was said earlier about oral requests being acceptable under EIR 2004 (at **6.3.1**), public authorities will need to make front-line staff aware of the procedures that have been put in place in the authority for dealing with requests.

6.4.1 Dealing with a request – initial considerations

Although there is no specific statutory requirement, it makes good sense if all requests for information (including oral requests) are logged on receipt. Logging involves noting the details of the request, the date and time of the request and any address supplied for the information to be communicated to the applicant. Logging requests will also facilitate better tracking to ensure that information is supplied within prescribed time frames. As noted at **6.3.1**, the ICO has published a form that may be used by authorities for logging requests for environmental information.

Good customer service practice would also dictate that the authority acknowledges receipt of the request and informs applicants that the request is being dealt with.

On receipt of the request, the public authority will need to consider whether the request:

- is for environmental information:
    - if it is, then it should deal with the request under EIR 2004;
    - if not, then it should deal with the request under FOIA 2000 if the public authority is also subject to FOIA 2000;
    - if the request involves both environmental information and non-environmental information, both FOIA 2000 and EIR 2004 may need to be applied.

- includes a request for personal data (see **Chapter 9**).

Once it has been established that the request *is* for environmental information then the public authority will need to consider:

- whether the request is specific enough to enable it to respond. If the public authority thinks that the request has been formulated in too general a manner (for example, it is not clear what the applicant wants or the request is ambiguous) then the authority is required (by EIR 2004, reg.9(2)) to ask the applicant to provide more particulars and should also assist the applicant in providing these particulars. This has to be done as soon as possible and in any event within 20 working days;
- whether the request is manifestly unreasonable. Even where the request is manifestly unreasonable, the public authority should consider whether it has provided advice and assistance to the applicant.
- whether the request is particularly complex or voluminous (in which case the timescale may be extended from 20 to 40 working days (see **6.6.3**);

- whether it holds the information requested. If not, then the public authority should consider whether the request needs to be transferred to another public authority;
- how the information is to be made available and whether any charges may be levied;
- whether the applicant has requested the information in a particular form or format and whether any charges are to be levied; and
- whether the information can be disclosed in full or whether some or all of the information should be withheld because of the application of an exception(s).

6.4.2 Nature of the response: duty to make information available

EIR 2004, reg.5(1) provides that subject to the exceptions to disclosure (see **Chapters 7–9**) a public authority that holds environmental information should make it available on request. This contrasts with the provisions of FOIA 2000, s.1(1) which provides that the applicant be informed in writing by the public authority whether or not it holds the information requested and to have that information communicated to him. In *Rhondda Cynon Taff County Borough Council* (EA/2007/0065), the Tribunal sought to distinguish these provisions but was unable to say unequivocally what that difference was. In a rather guarded statement, the Tribunal concluded that the obligation to make information available under EIR 2004 'may not mean physically providing an applicant with a copy of the information'. It concluded that the obligation under EIR 2004 could be met by allowing inspection of the information held by the public authority. However, more recently (in *East Riding of Yorkshire Council* v. *Information Commissioner* (EA/2009/0069)) the Tribunal confirmed that EIR 2004, reg.5(1) sets out a broad obligation to make environmental information available; it does so in general terms without specifying the means by which it should be made available or whether conditions may be imposed on those requesting it. In the latter case, the Tribunal refuted the argument that EIR 2004 imposes a duty on public authorities to permit in situ inspection of information held by the public authority.

   In practice, public authorities can make information available in a variety of ways, for example:

- Where information is readily available it may be possible to provide a quick verbal or written response or information could be attached to an email. Ideally, a public authority should keep a record of any oral replies or communication in the event of any subsequent complaints.
- The applicant may be advised that he or she can inspect the information in situ at the public authority's offices or a designated place (for example, a library). A public authority may consider it an efficient option to set aside reception facilities specifically to allow members of the public to inspect information. Consideration should also be given to providing access to a printer and photocopier for applicants to use.

- The information may already be available on the public authority's website and the applicant may be advised of this.
- The information may be communicated to the applicant in hard copy form (i.e. photocopies sent in the post) or electronically.

However, as will be discussed below, the applicant may ask for the information to be made available in a particular format, or may request inspection of the information.

Where the public authority is making information available to an applicant and the information is about factors affecting or likely to affect the elements of the environment (see **3.3.3**), then EIR 2004, reg.5(5) comes into play. This provides that if the applicant requests it, the public authority should (if it is able to):

(a) inform the applicant of the place where he or she can obtain information on the measurement procedures used in compiling the information (this includes information about the methods of analysis and sampling); or

(b) refer the applicant to the standardised procedures used.

6.4.3   Form and format of the response

The applicant can ask that the information be made available in a specific form or format (EIR 2004, reg.6(1)) and if such a request is made then the public authority should comply with the applicant's request unless:

(a) it is reasonable for the authority to make the information available in another form or format; or

(b) the information is already publicly available and easily accessible to the applicant in another form or format.

If EIR 2004, reg.6(1) is triggered by the applicant asking for the information to be made available in a particular form or format, then the public authority may only refuse if one of the conditions in reg.6(1)(a) or (b) is satisfied.

The Defra guidance and Code of Practice both recommend that public authorities try to be as flexible, as far as is reasonable, in responding to requests for information to be supplied in a specific format. For example, if a person requests information in hard copy format, the public authority should not refuse this request simply because the information is otherwise easily accessible via the Internet. Not all applicants have access to a computer or the Internet and public authorities should bear that in mind. Public authorities will need to consider their obligations under other legislative provisions such as the Equality Act 2010 (for example, in relation to access to buildings for disabled people to allow for the inspection of documents, documents supplied in Braille, etc.).

Although a public authority should be flexible when responding to requests for information in electronic form (i.e. a Word document or a PDF file), they are not required to supply the information in a specific software format. The Commissioner's view is that there is a distinction between the form in which the information is communicated and how the data is arranged within that form (i.e. the specific software format). See *Bath and North East Somerset Council* FS50094281. Although this case concerned the application of FOIA 2000, s.11(1)(a), it would appear to be equally applicable to EIR 2004 requests. In the same case the Commissioner also noted that when an applicant is requesting information in a particular form, he or she should ask for it at the outset when making the request.

Requesting inspection of information

Although EIR 2004, reg.6 appears to cover requests in a particular format, it has been interpreted broadly to include the right to request in situ inspection of the information at a public authority's premises (or designated place for inspection). Where a person requests in situ inspection, this will trigger reg.6, in which case the public authority should allow the applicant to inspect the information, unless one of the conditions in reg.6(1)(a) or (b) apply. This has been a particularly contentious issue for local authorities in relation to requests from property search companies to inspect information held by the authorities. In a number of instances, local authorities have refused to allow inspection but have offered to make the information available by way of a checked, collated and redacted document or report. This has given rise to a number of challenges which are considered more fully in **Chapter 11**.

It is reasonable for the authority to make the information available in another form

Where an applicant expresses a preference for information to be provided in a particular form or format (including inspection), the onus falls on the public authority concerned to demonstrate that it is reasonable to provide the information in another form. An examination of the cases considered by the Information Commissioner and the Tribunal reveal that:

- Public authorities need to adduce evidence as to why it is unreasonable to comply with the request to provide information in a particular manner. They cannot make assertions which are not backed up by evidence (see in particular the Tribunal's scathing remarks about witness statements in *East Riding of Yorkshire Council* v. *Information Commissioner* (EA/2009/0069)).
- The fact that a public authority cannot charge for any in situ inspection is not a good reason for refusing to allow inspection.
- Each request for information should be considered on an individual basis. The Commissioner will not accept that it is appropriate to consider the impact of complying with a large range of similar requests when assessing whether EIR 2004, reg.6(1)(a) applies.

Practical examples

See *East Riding of Yorkshire Council* v. *Information Commissioner* (EA/2009/0069) and *New Forest District Council* FER0308439. In both cases the respective councils refused to allow an in situ inspection by a property search company. Both local authorities raised several arguments about why in situ inspection would not be reasonable and that it was reasonable to provide the information in a collated report. In particular, it was argued that allowing an applicant to search information in situ (using the authority's computer system) could result in:

- access to personal data, which could result in a breach of the DPA 1998;
- the corruption or deletion of unlocked information;
- breach of any licenses held by an authority (for example, a software licence for 10 users);
- increased costs of purchasing additional licences to accommodate in situ inspections;
- security risks of using back office terminals;
- time spent explaining to applicants how to search information;
- cost implications for the public authority.

In *East Riding of Yorkshire Council* v. *Information Commissioner* the Tribunal did not accept that the council had either adduced evidence of these risks or taken reasonable steps to see what it could do to mitigate such risks. In *New Forest District Council* FER0308439 the Commissioner suggested that if the difficulties were real the authority could copy the information from the computer systems, redact any information subject to the DPA 1998 or an exception, and make the complied information available for inspection. In both cases the councils had breached EIR 2004, reg.6(1). It appears that the threshold for proving that it is unreasonable to allow in situ inspection, although not impossible, is particularly high.

The information is already publicly available and easily accessible to the applicant in another format

This provision allows a public authority to refuse to supply information as per the applicant's preferred form or format if the information is:

- already publicly available; and
- the information is easily accessible to the applicant in another format.

This necessarily involves a subjective assessment about whether the particular applicant can easily access the information. For example, if a person requests a hard copy of a document that is already available on a public authority's website, then the applicant could be directed to the website. However, if the applicant indicates that he or she has no access to a computer or does not know how to use the Internet, then the second condition might not be satisfied and the authority should consider providing the hard copy. As noted earlier, the authority must ensure that when it responds to a request it complies with its duties under the Equality Act 2010.

Information is not easily accessible to an applicant in another format if the public authority imposes a charge for supplying the information in that alternative format.

The duty to provide advice and assistance (EIR 2004, reg.9) is also relevant in relation to form and format and good customer service practice would suggest that the person dealing with the request asks the applicant how he or she would like the information to be made available, unless it is very obvious or there is only one method of communication.

Procedural requirements

Where the authority determines not to make the information available in the format requested, then the authority is under a duty to:

(a) provide reasons for its decision. It must provide these as soon as possible and no later than 20 days after the receipt of the request (EIR 2004, reg.6(2)(a));
(b) provide the explanation in writing if the applicant requests; *and*
(c) inform the applicant of his or her rights to make representations under EIR 2004, reg.11 and the enforcement and appeals procedures under EIR 2004, reg.18.

A failure to comply with the above requirements will constitute a breach of EIR 2004.

6.5 CHARGES

6.5.1 General considerations

Public authorities are permitted under EIR 2004, reg.8 to charge applicants for making information available. Before examining this in any detail, a number of general observations can be made:

- It is possible to charge for making environmental information available, but charging is discretionary and must be reasonable.
- Recital 18 of Directive 2003/4/EC provides that any charges should be reasonable and this implies that, as a general rule, charges may not exceed actual costs of producing the material in question.
- Public authorities can only levy charges to cover disbursements; they cannot charge for retrieving and collating information or for the time spent considering whether any information is exempt from disclosure.
- Where a charge is permitted, the charge must be reasonable. This is assessed objectively. The leading case on charges is *Markinson* v. *Information* (EA/2005/0014).
- The decision to impose a charge ultimately rests with the public authority and if a public authority decides that it intends to make charges it must do so only after taking into account relevant considerations. Additionally, there must be proper authorisation for the decision to charge and the public authority must publicise its schedule of charges.

- No charge can be made for in-situ inspection of information or for accessing public registers or lists of environmental information (see **6.5.2**).
- If an authority is entitled to charge a fee based on another statutory provision, such a fee will be considered to be reasonable. (However, see **6.5.3** and also **Chapter 5**).
- Some public authorities can levy a market-based charge for the information when the information is supplied on a commercial basis.

6.5.2 Circumstances where there can be no charges

Although public authorities are permitted to levy reasonable charges for supplying information, EIR 2004, reg.8(2) prohibits authorities for making any charges for the following:

1. Allowing the applicant to access any public registers or list of environmental information held by a public authority.

    – Although not specifically defined by EIR 2004, public registers are files of information maintained under particular pieces of legislation. Typically the legislation will specify the exact nature of the information which is to be made available to the public and usually where it is located. For example, local authorities are required to maintain a public register of contaminated land within their authority area (Environmental Protection Act 1990, s.78R). Public registers are defined by Directive 95/46/EC (the Data Protection Directive) as registers which according to laws or regulations are intended to provide information to the public and which are open to consultation either by the public in general or by any person demonstrating a legitimate interest. The range of information covered by public registers is considered more fully in **Chapter 11**.

    – EIR 2004 do not define 'lists of environmental information'. Defra guidance suggests such lists are non-statutory lists which may or may not be publicly accessible but which would help requestors in identifying the information they are particularly interested in accessing. By way of example, Defra cites the data.gov.uk website (at **http://data.gov.uk/**) which lists datasets uploaded to the site, many of which will consist of environmental information. Not all public authorities will have public registers or lists; however, the Commissioner suggests that providing easily accessible lists of the environmental information that a public authority holds will help to discharge the obligation under EIR 2004, reg.4 to proactively and progressively disseminate environmental information (see **Chapter 5**).

2.   Allowing the applicant to examine the information requested at the place which the authority makes available for that examination (in other words, in situ).

  –   If an applicant is willing to attend the offices of the public authority (or any other such place as directed, for instance, a public library) and examine the information at that place, then no charge may be levied. If, however, the applicant then wants a photocopy, a reasonable charge for copying can be made (see below).
  –   A number of local authorities have tried to make the 'right' to inspect information in situ subject to payment of a fee. (See in particular *Wrexham County Borough Council* FER0276442 and *Cheshire West and Chester Council* FER0276228 which are discussed further in **Chapter 11** at **11.7.3**.) However, this is not permitted and any charges levied for inspection will result in a breach of EIR 2004.

During the inspection the applicant may make notes. If the applicant wishes to obtain a photocopy then a charge may be levied for the photocopy. In addition to these specific statutory prohibitions on charging the Defra guidance suggests that public authorities do not seek to impose any charge for:

- explaining where information is made publicly available;
- oral queries answered on the spot;
- many requests dealt with by local authorities, such as planning queries.

6.5.3   What can a public authority charge for and what is reasonable?

Other than saying when charges cannot be made (see **6.5.2**) EIR 2004, reg.8 fails to specify exactly what a public authority can charge for other than for 'making the information available' in response to a request. Both the Directive (albeit in Recital 18, which is not technically binding) and the Code of Practice state that a reasonable charge only covers the actual costs incurred by the public authority in 'producing' the information and charges must not exceed this amount unless the public authority is entitled to levy a market-based charge for the information (see below).

A public authority can impose a charge to cover disbursements

A public authority can charge for making the information available and this includes covering the costs of any disbursements, such as photocopying and postage costs. The charges must be reasonable. The leading case on charges is *Markinson v. Information Commissioner* (EA/2005/0014).

Practical example

Markinson v. Information Commissioner

M inspected planning information held by the Kings Lynn and West Norfolk Borough Council at the council's offices. The council could not impose any charge to cover its costs of locating and retrieving the information for this in situ inspection (EIR 2004, reg.8(2)(b)).

However, M found the information complex and difficult to follow and so asked for photocopies. The council wanted to charge £6.00 for a copy of each building control or planning decision and 50p for each photocopied sheet contained in a planning file. The council sought to justify the charges in various ways but noted that the charge was calculated to take into account the officer's time in locating and retrieving the documentation as well as the officer's time in copying the information and other costs such as paper and toner. The Tribunal concluded that since the costs of locating and retrieving a piece of information should be disregarded for the purpose of in-situ inspection (see **6.4.1**), the council could not regard it as reasonable to include these costs in calculating the cost of copying the same material. The Tribunal reiterated that only the actual costs in 'producing' the material should be taken into account in considering what a reasonable charge should be.

Charges for disbursements must be reasonable

Charges for any disbursements must be reasonable. The *Markinson* case also gave the Tribunal the opportunity to make some observations about the factors that are relevant or irrelevant in assessing whether charges are reasonable:

- Reasonableness is assessed objectively; it is not sufficient that a public authority honestly considers its charges are reasonable. It is also necessary to consider whether a reasonable authority, properly directing itself to the relevant law and facts, would conclude the charges were reasonable. In assessing this, the public authority must ignore irrelevant considerations.
- The authority must be able to justify its own costs; it is not sufficient to say that costs are similar to those imposed by other public authorities.
- Assessment of costs must be current, taking into account changes in the costs of, *inter alia*, photocopying.
- The impact on revenue is wholly irrelevant. A public authority cannot factor the impact on workload and income streams into the equation. Charges cannot be used to make a profit and charges cannot exceed actual costs
- Public authorities must have regard to the Code of Practice and the Defra guidance when setting charges. In addition, public authorities should have regard to guidance issued by the Information Commissioner and other relevant bodies. For example, where the information relates to planning issues then it is appropriate to consider any guidance issued by the Department for Communities and Local Government.

- Charges set by ministers and many other public bodies (such as departments, trading funds, the NHS, non-devolved services in Scotland, Wales and Northern Ireland, and most public corporations) are also subject to the guidance in the Treasury publication 'Managing Public Money'. The guidance and principles in 'Managing Public Money' will also be relevant to other bodies such as local authorities in coming to a judgement on what amounts to a reasonable charge.

Reasonable photocopying charges

Where a charge is made to cover photocopying this must be reasonable. A public authority may take into account the number and size of the sheets and also the lease charge on the photocopier. In *Markinson* the Tribunal considered that a cost of 10p per A4 sheet of paper was reasonable but, of course, this may change over time if the costs of reprographics increase. Although there has not been a decision to this effect, the costs of any other disbursements (i.e. postage) should also be reasonable.

Charges for locating and retrieving information

Given that a public authority cannot impose any charges for allowing a person to inspect information in situ, can it ever impose a charge to cover the costs of locating and retrieving information? For example, if a person requests information and asks that it be sent electronically or via the post, can the public authority, as well as charging for any disbursements, charge for the costs of locating, retrieving and extracting the information? The Defra guidance concedes that the answer is yes, depending on the circumstances; unfortunately, it does not explain what type of circumstances would make this acceptable. However, and despite what has just been said, both Defra and the ICO suggest that public authorities should not seek to recover the costs of locating, retrieving or extracting information, precisely to bring EIR 2004 regime in line with FOIA 2000 regime. Under FOIA 2000, public authorities cannot charge for the cost of locating, retrieving or extracting the information, but can only cover disbursements such as the costs of photocopying, printing and postage. The Defra guidance recommends that public authorities providing information under EIR 2004 adopt a similar approach to that under FOIA 2000 and do not impose any charges for requests which fall below FOIA 2000 appropriate limits.

Difference between EIR and FOIA charging regimes

Under FOIA 2000, public authorities need to consider/estimate how much it is going to cost to supply the information; that includes the costs involved in determining whether the information is held, locating and retrieving the information and where necessary editing or redacting it. FOIA public authorities cannot take into account any costs incurred in considering whether the exemptions under the Act apply. If the cost falls below the so-called 'appropriate limits' (defined by secondary legislation and currently £450 or £600 for local and central government respectively), then the public authority should provide the information free of charge, although charges may be levied to cover disbursement costs (photocopying, postage, etc). If, on the other hand, the public authority estimates that it will spend more than these limits then the authority is not required to comply with the request (FOIA 2000, s.12).

EIR 2004 do not include any such limitation, and as noted earlier, EIR 2004 simply allow the public authority to levy a reasonable charge for requests, albeit that the Defra guidance on fees suggests that public authorities adopt a similar approach and do not impose any charges for requests which fall below FOIA 2000 appropriate limits. Defra justify this approach on the grounds that it provides a more transparent and unified approach and is likely to be simpler for authorities to manage. However, public authorities are not bound by this and can, if they wish, charge for providing information where the cost falls below FOIA 2000 appropriate limits. More significantly, a public authority cannot refuse an EIR request solely on costs since the regulations do not prescribe an appropriate limit.

In the light of the above, applicants should consider asking the public authority what its charges are at the outset, although the public authority should publish a schedule of charges in any event (see **6.5.7**).

6.5.4   Market-based charges

Some public authorities are allowed to levy a market-based charge (i.e. on a commercial basis) where this is necessary in order to guarantee the continuation of collecting and publishing such information. There is not a list of which public authorities fall into this category; the Defra guidance only cites trading funds as an example. The Ordnance Survey, as a trading fund, is an organisation that can make commercial charges. In such cases, a 'reasonable amount' is (according to the detailed Defra guidance) understood to include a real rate of return in line with rates achieved by comparable businesses facing a similar level of risk. This provision does not cover information that is collected in order to fulfil statutory obligations or for other normal functions of the public authority.

6.5.5   Information available under other legislation: the impact on charging

It has become very apparent that the broad scope of 'environmental information' means that information may be accessible under EIR 2004 as well as being accessible under other statutory regimes. A problem has arisen in circumstances where the other regime imposes a charge and applicants have used EIR 2004 to effectively bypass the charge by accessing information, freely, under EIR 2004. This has been a big issue in relation to local authority property searches and will be considered more fully in **Chapter 11**. As a general rule, if a public authority is entitled to make a charge under another statutory regime, then such charge shall be considered as reasonable under EIR 2004. However, the fact that the charge has been laid down in another statutory provision does not of itself make the charge reasonable. If the charging provisions in other legislation have been framed on the basis of the principles in 'Managing Public Money' it is likely (but not conclusive) they will be reasonable for EIR 2004 purposes.

6.5.6 Advance payments

A public authority is entitled (under EIR 2004, reg.8(4)) to ask the applicant to make an advance payment, but if it does this then it must notify the applicant within 20 working days after the date of receipt of the request. Somewhat oddly, the regulation does not require this notification as soon as possible, presumably because it may not be immediately apparent to the public authority that it will require an advance payment. If the public authority has notified an applicant that advance payment is required, then the authority is not required to respond to the request (or respond to a request for a specific form/format or issue a refusal notice) until the payment is made. There is a time limit of 60 working days for the payment to be made, starting with the date of notification. Once the payment has been made then the public authority should deal with the request but will disregard the time spent waiting for the payment when determining the time period for dealing with the request.

6.5.7 Schedule of charges

Where a public authority has taken the decision that it intends to impose charges, then it must publish a schedule of charges and make this available to applicants. The schedule should set out what the charges are for, how much will be charged, where charges are discretionary, circumstances in which charges may be waived and where any advance payments apply. Public authorities can publish this information via their publication schemes (see **5.6**) or, where appropriate, at another place on their websites.

6.6   DEALING WITH THE REQUEST: TIMESCALES

6.6.1   EIR 2004, reg.5(2): Duty to respond as soon as possible and within 20 working days

Public authorities must respond to requests 'as soon as possible' and no later than 20 working days after the date of receipt of the request (EIR 2004, reg.5(2)). The 20-day limit allows the authority to fulfil its obligation to provide advice and assistance and to locate/collate the information.

- It is essential that public authorities log receipt of all requests in order to comply with these deadlines.

- As far as oral requests are concerned, the date of the telephone call/ conversation is the date the request is made. This raises problems when applicants leave messages on voicemail systems and public authorities need to consider how to deal with this, at least for those officials likely to receive such requests.
- Public authorities need to put procedures in place which enable officials with responsibility for responding to requests to be able to process requests (and consider exceptions) within the timescales allowed.

Much will depend on the nature of the information that has been requested and also whether the applicant has requested the information in a particular form or format. However, if the information is reasonably accessible then it should be provided as soon as possible and a public authority would be ill advised to delay responding for 20 days simply because they have a 20-day 'window'. See, for example, *R. (on the application of Rockware Glass Ltd)* v. *Chester City Council* [2005] EWHC 2250; [2006] Env LR 30; where the High Court was highly critical of Chester City Council's apparent 'stonewalling' in not disclosing the information promptly, particularly when the information was immediately to hand.

If an applicant wants the information quickly then they should consider telling the public authority; it may also be advisable to suggest a relatively quick form of communication, such as fax or email. For example, if the applicant needs the information in order to make his or her views known during a statutory consultation period, or in order to litigate within a specified period, the applicant should advise the public authority that the information is needed promptly.

6.6.2 Interruptions to the 20-day time frame

The 20-day clock will stop running if the public authority:

1. has asked the applicant for further information because it considers the request is too general (EIR 2004, reg.9(2) and (4)). The date when the applicant provides this further information is then treated as the date after which the period of 20 working days referred to in EIR 2004, reg.5(1) is calculated. If the applicant fails to supply this extra information and the public authority is consequently unable to process the request, then it can rely on the exception in EIR 2004, reg.12(4) (see **7.5.3**);
2. requires the advance payment of a charge (see 6.5.6). The clock will stop from the date of notification of the advance payment to the date the payment is received by the public authority (EIR 2004, reg.8(6)).

6.6.3 Extending the time limits (EIR 2004, reg.7)

Where a person has requested information under EIR 2004, reg.5(1), the only circumstances when the 20-day period can be extended is when the public authority reasonably believes that the complexity and volume of the information requested means that it is impracticable either to:

(a) comply with the request within the 20-day period (this includes complying with the request for the information to be supplied in a particular form or format); or

(b) serve a refusal notice within the specified period under EIR 2004, reg.14(2).

In circumstances where the public authority needs to extend the time period to either comply with the request or to serve a refusal notice, it must notify the applicant as soon as possible and no later than 20 working days after the date of receipt of the request. The authority can only extend the time period to 40 days.

Extensions under EIR 2004, reg.7 should be exceptional and in order for the extension to be utilised by the public authority the request for information must be both complex and voluminous. For example, where the public authority needs to undertake an extensive search to find and retrieve a large amount of information. The time period cannot be extended simply because the applicant requests a lot of information.

6.6.4 Failure to comply with time limits

If a public authority fails to comply with the time limit then it is in breach of its obligations under EIR 2004. The Information Commissioner has issued several decision notices against public authorities for failing to meet the deadlines specified in EIR 2004, for example, *Nottingham City Council* FER0091004.

6.7 EIR 2004, REG.10: TRANSFER OF REQUESTS

Obviously, if a public authority does not hold the information requested then it is not able to make it available; however, the public authority must bear in mind that the information requested may be held by another person on behalf of the authority. Alternatively, there may be circumstances where the public authority holds some, but not all, of the information requested. In these circumstances the public authority should deal with the part of the request that it is able to deal with and advise the applicant that it does not hold all of the information requested, in which case the provisions on transfers of request operate.

If a public authority concludes it does not hold all or some of the requested information it needs to consider whether the information is held by another public authority (including a Scottish public authority). If the public authority believes that the information is held by another public authority it must do one of two things (EIR 2004, reg.10):

1. transfer the request to the other public authority (or Scottish public authority); or

2. supply the applicant with the name and address of that authority.

In either case the authority must notify the applicant by serving a refusal notice on the applicant which should state that the public authority does not hold the information requested.

In relation to the transfer of requests, the following points should be considered:

- Public authorities should publicise their procedures for handling EIR requests and ideally this should include information about the authority's usual procedure when it does not hold information.
- If the authority's usual procedure is to transfer the request then the publicity should say so as the applicant may not want the request to be transferred. The Code of Practice suggests that in some circumstances the authority that received the original request may consider it more appropriate to simply transfer the request without consulting the applicant. It is not clear what these circumstances might be. However, the Defra guidance seems to contradict this when it states that the applicant should always be asked before a request is transferred (para.6.18 of the Defra guidance). On balance it would be advisable for a public authority to contact the applicant as soon as possible to see whether he or she is happy for the request to be transferred or whether the applicant prefers to make a new request to the other public authority.
- Before transferring a request the original public authority should always consult with the other public authority with a view to ascertaining whether it really does hold the information. If there is any doubt then the original public authority should not transfer the request.

When the request is transferred, the second or receiving authority is required to process the request in compliance with EIR 2004 in exactly the same way it would deal with the request had it been made directly by the applicant.

6.8 HISTORICAL AND TRANSFERRED PUBLIC RECORDS

Special provisions apply to historical and transferred public records (see Table 6.1). EIR 2004, reg.17(5) applies the process to records for which the 'responsible authority' is not a public authority.

6.9 EIR 2004, REG.14: REFUSAL NOTICES

If a public authority, having considered the request for environmental information, decides that it is not going to disclose some or all of the information, then it must issue a refusal notice as soon as possible and no later than 20 working days after the date of receipt of the request (unless the time period has been extended by virtue of EIR 2004, reg.7 (see **6.6.3**).

Table 6.1 Historical and transferred public records

Type of information	Special provision
Historical records (records which are over 30 years old but have been retained by the originating authority with the approval of the Secretary of State for Justice under the Public Records Act 1958, s.3(4)).	Where a request relates to information contained in a historical record (except a transferred public record), the public authority may refuse to disclose the information if it considers that it may be in the public interest to refuse disclosure. However, if historical record is a public record within the meaning of the Public Records Act 1958, then the public authority must first consult either the Lord Chancellor or the appropriate Northern Ireland Minister before it decides whether to disclose or withhold the information.
Transferred public records. Public records are the records of bodies that are subject to the Public Records Act 1958 or the Public Records Act (Northern Ireland) 1923. Transferred public records are records that have been transferred to an appropriate records authority, being either the National Archives, the Public Records Office of Northern Ireland or to another records office appointed by the Lord Chancellor under the Public Records Act 1958.	Unless the information has been designated by the responsible authority as open information for the purposes of EIR 2004, the appropriate records authority is required to consult the responsible authority on whether there may be an exception to disclosure under EIR 2004, reg.12(5) (see **Chapter 8**). If the appropriate records authority decides that an exception under reg.12(5) applies, it needs to consult with the responsible authority who will decide whether the public interest favours withholding or disclosing the information. ('The responsible authority' has the same meaning as FOIA 2000, s.15 and is a Minister appointed by the Lord Chancellor.) The responsible authority must communicate his determination within a reasonable time (not defined) and the appropriate records authority must comply with the request under EIR 2004, reg.5 in accordance with that determination. If the transferred public record is a public record within the meaning of the Public Records Act 1958, the appropriate records authority must also consult with the Lord Chancellor before it reaches any decision to withhold or disclose the information.

The refusal notice must specify in writing:

- the reasons why the information is not being disclosed (EIR 2004, reg.14(3));
- the exceptions relied on under EIR 2004, regs.12(4), (5) and 13;
- the issues which the public authority took into account when it conducted the public interest balancing exercise. This is a very important provision designed to serve the interests of the applicant who may wish to challenge the decision at a later stage;
- where the request involves a request for personal data, then, where they apply, any data protection conditions;
- where the authority refuses to provide the information on the basis that the request relates to material which is still in the course of completion, to unfinished documents or to incomplete data (under EIR 2004, reg.12(4)(d)), then the refusal notice must also specify (where it is known) the name of any other public authority preparing the information and the estimated time in which the information will be finished or completed.

In addition, the refusal notice must also provide the applicant with clear details about the procedures for reconsideration and appeal. This includes details of the authority's internal review procedure and the applicant's rights to apply to the Information Commissioner and appeal to the Information Rights Tribunal (see **Chapter 10**).

Public authorities that employ information rights practitioners or staff who deal with both FOIA 2000 and EIR 2004 should be familiar with, at the very least, the Defra and ICO guidance. However, they should also be reviewing ICO and Tribunal decisions, if not routinely, then at least when they are trying to defend a particular position or decision. This will enable them to provide more detailed and reasoned refusal notices, supported by relevant authorities. Although applicants may be unhappy that their request has been refused, a more reasoned refusal notice may help them understand why it has been refused, and this could result in fewer complaints to the authority in the long run. It is certainly evident from many of the Information Commissioner's decision notices to date that he considers that many refusal notices are plainly inadequate.

CHAPTER 7

Exceptions to disclosure

7.1 INTRODUCTION

The right to access environmental information under EIR 2004 is not absolute. Although there is an unquestionably strong public interest in freedom of access to environmental information, it will not always be in the public interest to disclose certain information. One only has to think about the lengths that some people will go to in order to steal the eggs of birds of prey to realise that disclosing information about the location of nesting birds would not be in the public interest. There are clearly other imperative public requirements which the law seeks to protect; for example, there is a strong public interest in national security and public safety and it would not be in the overall public interest if the disclosure of information seriously compromised these. Similarly, there is a public interest in ensuring the right of a person to receive a fair trial, or in protecting commercially confidential information. Like all other access to information regimes, EIR 2004 seek to provide a balance between securing openness and prejudicing other public interest matters. They do this by the use of 'exceptions' to disclosure, which are to be found in EIR 2004, reg.12.

This is the first of three chapters which deal with the exceptions to disclosure. This chapter will begin with some background and general information; it will explain how public authorities should approach the exceptions and the public interest test. It will consider the impact of the presumption in favour of disclosure and the procedural and class-based exceptions. It will also examine the effect of EIR 2004, reg.5(6), which effectively disapplies other statutory prohibitions on disclosure.

Chapter 8 will examine the exceptions contained in EIR 2004, reg.12(5), namely where disclosure would adversely affect one of the matters specified in that regulation. The chapter will include a further examination of the public interest test as it relates to the specific exceptions.

Chapter 9 will examine the personal data exception and the relationship between EIR 2004 and DPA 1988.

7.1.1 Categorisation of EIR exceptions

The exceptions to disclosure under EIR 2004, reg.12 may be categorised into three groups:

1. refusals based upon procedural grounds – reg.12(4)(a)–(c);
2. refusals because the information falls into one of three class-based exceptions:

    (a) where the requested information includes personal data of which the applicant is not the data subject – reg.12(3);
    (b) where the request relates to incomplete material – reg.12(4)(d);
    (c) where the request involves the disclosure of internal communications – reg.12(4)(e);

3. refusals where disclosure of the information would adversely affect one of the matters specified in reg.12(5).

Apart from the personal data exception, all of the exceptions are subject to a public interest test which requires that in all the circumstances of the case the public interest in maintaining the exception outweighs the public interest in disclosing the information. (Although note the commentary at **7.5.1** below.) The exceptions must be interpreted restrictively and there is, in EIR 2004, reg.12(2), an expressly stated presumption in favour of disclosure.

In addition to the above public authorities need to bear in mind that explicit and important provision contained in EIR 2004, reg.5(6) which states that any enactment or rule of law that would prevent the disclosure of information in accordance with EIR 2004 shall not apply. This means public authorities cannot avoid disclosure under EIR 2004 by relying on other statutory bars; this will be discussed as relevant below.

7.1.2 EIR exceptions/FOIA exemptions

The aim of this book is to examine EIR 2004 in detail. However, EIR 2004 regime sits alongside FOIA 2000 and, in practice, information rights practitioners are likely to be more familiar with the provisions of FOIA 2000 than EIR 2004. On a number of occasions some public authorities have mistakenly dealt with requests for environmental information under FOIA 2000 rather than EIR 2004 and have refused to disclose citing one of FOIA 2000 exemptions. Given that several public authorities have 'got it wrong' (the Tribunal employs the analogy of a public authority backing the wrong horse) it is worth briefly identifying some of the key differences between the regimes:

*   EIR 2004 contains only 12 exceptions compared to 23 exemptions under FOIA 2000. (The reader should note the terminology here; EIR 2004 contains exceptions and FOIA 2000 has exemptions.)

- Apart from cases where the information includes personal data (EIR 2004, reg.12(2)), all of the exceptions in EIR are subject to the application of a public interest test. In contrast, under FOIA 2000, a number of exemptions are classed as 'absolute'. Providing information falls within the exemption description it is exempt from disclosure and there is no need for the public authority to consider the public interest in disclosure.
- In contrast with FOIA 2000, EIR 2004 contains an expressly stated instruction that 'A public authority shall apply a presumption in favour of disclosure'.
- Because EIR 2004 is based on a Directive, the list of exceptions in EIR 2004 is absolute and exhaustive and cannot be amended unilaterally by government.

7.1.3   EIR 2004, reg.5(6)

Before examining the exceptions it is necessary to consider the important provision in EIR 2004, reg.5(6) which states that 'any enactment or rule of law that would prevent the disclosure of information in accordance with these Regulations shall not apply'.

This means that any statutory bar on the release or disclosure of information cannot automatically be used to refuse a request for environmental information under EIR 2004. However, it is possible that the information could be withheld under one of the exceptions discussed below in this chapter and **Chapter 8**. The statutory bar may assist the public authority in determining whether an exception is engaged and also in assessing the public interest. For example, if an exception is engaged the existence of a statutory bar may indicate the pubic interest in withholding the information.

7.2   EXCEPTIONS

The exceptions to the duty to disclose environmental information under EIR 2004, reg.5(1) are contained within EIR 2004, reg.12. A public authority may refuse to disclose environmental information if:

(a)   an exception to disclosure applies under paragraphs (4) or (5); and
(b)   in all the circumstances of the case, the public interest in maintaining the exception outweighs the public interest in disclosing the information.

This is, however, subject to the provisions in paragraphs (2), (3) and (9) of EIR 2004, reg.12:

- reg.12(2) – a presumption in favour of disclosure;
- reg.12(3) – personal data;
- reg.12(9) – public authority not entitled to refuse to disclose information relating to emissions under an exception referred to in reg.12(5)(d)–(g).

These will be considered in detail later.

7.2.1   Discretionary nature of the exceptions

The fact that EIR 2004 contains exceptions does not mean that a public authority has to use them. Apart from requests for the disclosure of personal data (where release is only permitted if there is no breach of DPA 1998), all of the exceptions are discretionary. Even if a public authority is satisfied that it would be acting lawfully by refusing to disclose information it may still decide that it is going to make information publicly available.

7.2.2   Interpreting the exceptions restrictively

Faced with any statutory provision the skill of the practitioner is to understand what the provision means and how it should be applied. The traditional approach in English law is to interpret the words of an English statute literally, unless this produces an absurdity; in which case courts may have regard to the purpose of the provision. However, when tasked with interpreting national law which gives effect to a Directive, the domestic courts (and tribunals) are required to interpret the national law 'as far as possible, in the light of the wording and purpose of the Directive in order to achieve the result pursued by' the Directive. (*Marleasing SA* v. *La Commercial Internacional de Alimentacion SA* (Case C-106/89) [1990] ECR I-4135]).

The effect of this is that in interpreting EIR 2004 practitioners and lawyers should have regard to the wording and purpose of Directive 2003/4/EC. Indeed the High Court has observed that the Directive provides a 'powerful aid to the interpretation of [EIR 2004]' (see *Export Credits Guarantee Department* v. *Friends of the Earth* [2008] EWHC 638 (Admin); [2008] Env LR 40). As far as the wording is concerned, EIR 2004 is practically a verbatim re-enactment of the provisions of the Directive and therefore little can be gained from referring back to it. However, the Directive, unlike EIR 2004, contains a number of preambles (or recitals) which highlight the purpose of the Directive. Of most particular note in the context of the discussion in these chapters is Recital 16, which provides:

> The right to information means that the disclosure of information should be the general rule and that public authorities should be permitted to refuse a request for environmental information in specific and clearly defined cases. Grounds for refusal should be interpreted in a restrictive way, whereby the public interest served by disclosure should be weighed against the interest served by the refusal.

The Commissioner and Tribunal have made repeated references to this recital when considering whether the exceptions apply.

7.3   PRESUMPTION IN FAVOUR OF DISCLOSURE

Throughout the remainder of this chapter and **Chapters 8** and **9** we shall examine the nature and scope of each of the exceptions to see what is required before the exception is engaged. However, even if an exception is engaged or triggered this does not mean the information can automatically be withheld from the public. In addition, the public authority is required to consider whether 'in all the circumstances of the case the public interest in maintaining the exception outweighs the public interest in disclosure' (EIR 2004, reg.12(3)). This is known as the public interest test. The public interest test must be applied in the light of the presumption in favour of disclosure. The two concepts are therefore inextricably linked.

EIR 2004, reg.12(2) states that 'a public authority shall apply a presumption in favour of disclosure'. This contrasts with FOIA 2000 which fails to include an equivalent express provision. However, it is argued, in relation to FOIA 2000, that there is nevertheless an implied assumption that disclosure is the default position and openness is, in itself, to be regarded as something which is in the public interest. (See *Guardian News and Brooke* v. *Information Commissioner* (EA/2006/0011 & 0013).)

What is the effect of the expressly stated presumption in favour of disclosure? The Tribunal appears to have interpreted it in two ways:

- First, if there is in any given case 'doubt about the applicability of the exception that doubt must be resolved in favour of the disclosure' (*Burgess* v. *Information Commissioner and Stafford Borough Council* (EA/2006/0091)).
- Secondly, the presumption must also be applied in assessing the competing public interests. Since the presumption is in favour of disclosure, this must be rebutted by factors against disclosure. If the public interest in favour of maintaining the exception is equally balanced against the public interest in disclosure, then the information must be disclosed.

This view is echoed in the Defra's detailed guidance (para.7.3.4) which interprets EIR 2004, reg.12(2) to mean that 'if arguments are evenly balanced for withholding and disclosing information, the information must be disclosed' or, as the High Court put it 'to provide the default position in the event that the interests are equally balanced' (*Export Credits Guarantee Department* v. *Friends of the Earth* [2008] EWHC 638 (Admin); [2008] Env LR 40). For an excellent example of this see the Commissioner's decision notice in *Department of Energy and Climate Change* FER0184885; following an extensive evaluation of the competing public interests the Commissioner concluded that although there was not an overwhelming case for disclosing the information, the case for withholding was even weaker. Having regard to the presumption in favour of disclosure, the Commissioner ruled the information had to be disclosed. The Defra guidance does not appear to suggest that the presumption is a factor which could tip an unbalanced public interest from non-disclosure to disclosure.

7.3.1 Does the presumption in favour of disclosure apply to all of the exceptions?

As far as the wording of EIR 2004 is concerned, the answer to this question is yes. However, in November 2010 the Tribunal held, in the light of the Court of Appeal's decision in *Veolia ES Nottinghamshire Ltd* v. *Nottinghamshire County Council* [2010] EWCA Civ 1214, that the presumption in favour of disclosure of all environmental information held by public bodies 'must now be read subject to an exception in the case of any such information which is held by the public body subject to a legal duty of confidentiality' (*Staffordshire County Council and Sibelco UK Ltd* v. *Information Commissioner* (EA/2010/0015) [2010] UKFTT 573 (GRC)). Since the Directive does not actually require a presumption in favour of disclosure (this being a wholly domestic innovation), this interpretation (if correct) does not appear to breach the provisions of the Directive. (For further discussion see **8.8** and **8.9** in relation to EIR 2004, reg.12(5)(e) and (f).)

7.3.2 A note of caution

Although the Commissioner frequently refers in his decision notices to the presumption in favour of disclosure, he was criticised by the Tribunal when he failed to refer to it in his examination of the public interest test (see *Burgess* v. *ICO* (EA/2006/0091)). Public authorities should take note of this. When drafting refusal notices, public authorities are well advised to explain how they have factored EIR 2004, reg.12(2) into any decisions they take to withhold information.

7.4 PUBLIC INTEREST TEST

As noted at **7.3**, even if an EIR exception is engaged, the public authority is still required to consider whether 'in all the circumstances of the case, the public interest in maintaining the exception outweighs the public interest in disclosing the information'. This is phrased in a way that requires the public interest in maintaining the exception to be 'greater' than the public interest in disclosure. This inevitably therefore requires a public authority to balance the 'competing' public interests. This might be simply illustrated as:

Public interest in disclosure v. Public interest in maintaining the exception.

A public authority is only permitted to refuse to disclose if the public interest in maintaining the exception outweighs the public interest in disclosure, and as noted above this should be done in the light of the presumption in favour of disclosure.

For ease the public interest test is occasionally referred to as 'the PIT'. When applying the PIT, the authority is essentially making a judgement about whether, in the particular case, it serves the interest of the public better to withhold or disclose the information. The approach which public authorities (and the Commissioner and

Tribunal) must take was set out in two decisions of the Tribunal: *Department for Education and Skills* v. *Information Commissioner and the Evening Standard* (EA/2006/0006) and *Secretary of State for Work and Pensions* v. *Information Commissioner* (EA/2006/0040). Although both cases concerned FOIA 2000, the principles established apply equally to decisions under EIR 2004, reg.12 (see *Export Credit Guarantee Department* v. *Friends of the Earth* [2008] EWHC 638 (Admin)). Essentially, in applying the public interest test:

- every decision is specific to the particular facts and circumstances under consideration;
- the public authority's assessment of the public interest in maintaining the exception should focus on the public interest factors specifically associated with that particular exception, rather than on a more general consideration of the public interest in withholding the information (*Bellamy* v. *Information Commissioner and the DTI* (EA/2005/0023);
- it is relevant to consider what specific harm would follow from the disclosure of the particular information in question;
- the public authority is required to stand back and disregard its own interests except and in so far as those interests are properly viewed as part of the public interest.

The public interest test raises numerous questions, for example: What is the particular public interest that each exception seeks to protect? What is the public interest in disclosure?; What evidence is required when assessing the public interest? What happens when more than one exception is cited as grounds for refusal?

7.4.1 What is the public interest in the disclosure of environmental information?

The term 'public interest' is not defined within EIR 2004, however, it has been held that the public interest is that which serves the interest of the public. This is to be distinguished from something that merely interests the public (see *Lion Laboratories* v. *Evans* [1985] QB 526 (CA) at 537). For example, the private affairs of a public figure may well interest the public but it is not necessarily in the public interest for this information to be disclosed given that there is also a public interest in the protection of personal privacy. The public interest inherent in each exception will be examined throughout the chapters, but what is the public interest in disclosure of environmental information?

Access to environmental information is an end in itself but is also a means to an end. The disclosure of environmental information to the public is aimed at:

- facilitating a greater awareness of environmental matters;
- enabling a free exchange of views and more effective participation by the public in environmental decision making;

- improving accountability and transparency of environmental decision making;
- securing a better environment.

A review of the Commissioner's guidance note on the public interest and the many ICO and Tribunal decisions demonstrates that the arguments in favour of disclosure may be generic (i.e. increased accountability) and case specific (i.e. ensuring public monies are spent well in relation to a particular project). Arguments that have been used in favour of disclosure include:

- general arguments in favour of promoting transparency, accountability and participation;
- that disclosure might enhance the quality of discussions and decision making generally;
- if the subject matter of the request involves a large amount of public money, the public clearly has an interest in knowing how this money is being spent;
- the specific circumstances of the case and the content of the information requested in relation to those circumstances;
- the age of the information – the passage of time may impact upon the strength of the public interest arguments;
- the timing of a request, in respect of information relating to an investigation, may be relevant. This would depend on the stage the investigation had reached and how much information was in the public domain;
- the impact (beneficial) of disclosure upon individuals and/or the wider public.

The ICO guidance is careful to identify a number of factors which are irrelevant when applying the public interest test. These include:

- the identity of the person making the request. For example, it is irrelevant if the person making the request is a journalist who will use the information to embarrass a public authority;
- the possibility that the information could be misunderstood because it is too technical or complex. Such a paternalistic approach to the release of information is clearly unacceptable. If a public authority is genuinely worried about this then it could always take the step of releasing an explanatory note;
- the status of the information, for example, if it is classified or relates to senior individuals;
- the argument that disclosure will lead to poorer record keeping;
- the fact that the information is not accurate.

7.4.2 Public interest in maintaining the exception: aggregating the public interests

Where a public authority cites only one exception as grounds for refusing to disclose information then it needs only to consider the specific public interest that that particular exception seeks to protect and weigh it against the public interest in disclosure. It cannot rely on any public interest arguments in other exceptions; the examination must focus exclusively on the public interest which that particular exception seeks to protect.

However, difficulties have arisen where a public authority relies on more than one exception and in particular whether the EIR 2004 require or permit a further exercise involving the cumulation of the separate interests served by the two exceptions and their weighing together against the public interest in disclosure.. The issue was first raised before the Information Tribunal in *The Office of Communications* v. *Information Commissioner* (EA/2006/0078), Counsel for Ofcom and the additional party, T Mobile argued that in addition to conducting the PIT in relation to each exception engaged (in this case public safety and intellectual property rights) a public authority should also effectively 'aggregate' the separate interests served by the exceptions and weigh them together against the public interest in disclosure. The Tribunal rejected the argument and considered that each exception had to be considered separately for the purposes of the public interest balancing exercise and that it was not permissible to weigh the aggregate public interest in maintaining the exceptions against the public interest in disclosure. In the Tribunal's view such a process would result in a nonsensical outcome. However, on appeal the Court of Appeal favoured the arguments put forward by Ofcom and held that where more than one exception is found to apply, they must be considered together for the purpose of the public interest balancing exercise. In other words, the aggregate (or cumulative) public interest in maintaining the exceptions must be weighed against the public interest in disclosure. On further appeal, the Supreme Court was unable to agree the right approach to the public interest test, with a majority of three to two favouring the Court of Appeal's interpretation. In view of the uncertainty, the Supreme Court referred the question to the ECJ and asked whether a public authority is required to weigh the interests served by refusal to disclose, one at a time, against the public interests served by disclosure, or whether it is permitted, when carrying out the public interest balancing exercise, to take into account cumulatively a number of exceptions listed in the directive. The Court Of Justice delivered its ruling on 28th July 2011 and answered in the affirmative:

[t]he answer to the question referred is that Article 4(2) of Directive 2003/4 must be interpreted as meaning that, where a public authority holds environmental information or such information is held on its behalf, it may, when weighing the public interests served by disclosure against the interests served by refusal to disclose, in order to assess a request for that information to be made available to a natural or legal person, take into account cumulatively a number of the grounds for refusal set out in that provision.

Although the exceptions are listed separately in the directive this does not preclude cumulation given that the interests served by refusal to disclose may sometimes overlap in the same situation or the same circumstances. More significantly the ECJ held that the adoption of a cumulative approach is "not likely to introduce another exception in addition to those listed in that provision. It is worthy of note that the ECJ does not say that public authorities are 'required' to approach the PIT in this way; the exceptions are discretionary and the directive does not specify any particular procedure for examining the grounds for refusal in cases where a Member State has provided for such exceptions. This appears to suggest that Member States may adopt different approaches to the operation of the public interest test. In the light of this 'permissive' ruling the final arbiter will be the Supreme Court which is likely to uphold the Court of Appeal's decision. The cumulative approach is reflected in the Information Commissioner's guidance on 'The Public Interest Test' (Awareness Guidance No. 3, 1 July 2009).

7.4.3   The timing of the public interest test

The public authority needs to consider the public interest test at the time the request is made. If the request ultimately results in a complaint to the Commissioner or an appeal to the Tribunal then they too will assess the public interest at the time the request was made and not at the time of their investigation/hearing. The Tribunal has frequently been invited by applicants to reassess the public interest test in the light of new factors that have arisen since the original decision. This is hardly surprising given the lapse of time that may have occurred. However, the Tribunal is not prepared to do this. (See *Norman Baker* v. *Information Commissioner, Cabinet Office & National Council for Civil Liberties* (EA/2006/0045), which is a FOIA case, and also *The Department for Business, Enterprise and Regulatory Reform* v. *Information Commissioner & Friends of the Earth* (EA/2007/0072).) The only possibility is that the Commissioner may be willing to consider new facts that have come to light since the original decision but which might cast light on the balance of the public interest at the time when the question fell to be decided by the public authority.

7.4.4   Evidential issues

The public interest test is not an exact science; each case has to be decided on its own merits. EIR 2004 requires that in conducting the balancing act public authorities consider 'all the circumstances of the case'. This means that the content and the context of the requested information will be important factors, as will the timing of the request. Neither the Commissioner nor the Tribunal will be swayed by generic arguments or generalised contentions about inherent risk or possible harm. A public authority must be able to cite substantive reasons why it has concluded that the balance lies in favour of withholding information. Public authorities need to produce some clear, credible evidence about the harm that would flow from disclosure.

A public authority should always record the factors it has taken into account in conducting the public interest test as this will be particularly useful if its decision is investigated, on complaint, by the Information Commissioner.

7.5 REFUSALS BASED ON PROCEDURAL GROUNDS

EIR 2004, reg.12(4) permits a public authority to refuse to disclose information to the extent that:

(a) it does not hold that information when an applicant's request is received;
(b) the request for information is manifestly unreasonable;
(c) the request for information is formulated in too general a manner and the public authority has complied with EIR 2004, reg.9, which places a duty on the authority to provide advice and assistance to the applicant.

7.5.1 EIR 2004, reg.12(4)(a): Public authority does not hold information when applicant's request received

A public authority is only obliged to disclose the information it holds at the time the request is made. (For a discussion of the holding requirement see **6.2.4**) If the authority does not hold the information then it has no obligation to disclose. EIR 2004 do not require public authorities to create new records in order to deal with requests (see *Fowler* v. *Information Commissioner and Brighton and Hove City Council* (EA/2006/0071)).

Difficulties may arise where the applicant asks for information that is in the possession of an authority but is not immediately available in the form that the applicant requests. Public authorities should exercise caution before saying they do not hold information simply because it is not collated into a single document. The Commissioner will expect a more robust approach to dealing with requests.

Practical example

In *Defra* (FS50078600) Defra received an initial request for all copies of communications (including letters, emails, memoranda or minutes of meetings) between itself and the Department of Environment in Northern Ireland relating to the Urban Waste Water Treatment Directive in Northern Ireland (91/271/EEC). This first request was refused on a number of grounds. The applicant followed this up with a second request, this time for a list of all such information and communications, and in respect of each item the applicant wanted to know the date of the document, the name (if it had one), the type (i.e. email, letter), and the name of the sender and recipient. Defra refused to disclose this, stating that it did not hold a table or list of this kind and that it did not think it was reasonably incumbent on it to produce such a list. The Commissioner concurred with the complainant who argued that the fact that such a list did not exist was not relevant; Defra did not need to create new information but merely had to extract from its documents information it possessed and provide it in the requested format. The information was held by Defra at the time the request was made because the information requested was actually contained in documents which were in Defra's possession. Even though the request was for relatively little information from each document, it was still information that Defra held and it would not be too resource intensive to extract this information into a list.

This exception poses a further difficulty for applicants; if the public authority says it does not hold the information it will be very difficult for an applicant to know whether this is true or whether the public authority has not searched hard enough. As the Tribunal noted in *Bromley* v. *Information Commissioner and the Environment Agency* (EA/2006/0072): 'There can seldom be absolute certainty that information relevant to a request does not remain undiscovered somewhere within a public authority's records.' Mindful of this, the Commissioner, when called to investigate cases where this exception is raised, will consider whether the information is held on the balance of probabilities. This approach has been approved by the Tribunal in *Innes* v. *Information Commissioner* (EA/2009/0046) (a FOIA case).

The factors that the Commissioner will take into account in such cases include:

- the quality of the public authority's initial analysis of the request;
- the scope of the search based on that initial analysis;
- the rigour and efficiency with which the search was concluded; and
- the discovery of materials elsewhere whose existence or content point to the existence of further information within the public authority.

Public authorities are well advised to routinely record the steps that they have taken in order to produce evidence that will satisfy the Commissioner that the search has been considered, rigorous and efficient.

Practical example

The following example demonstrates that a public authority must know what information is held on its behalf. It also demonstrates that some applicants can be very determined in their quest for information. The applicant requested information from Wolverhampton City Council relating to the way in which garden boundaries for council house properties had been determined. The council advised the applicant that, despite making appropriate enquiries, it no longer held some of the information requested. The Commissioner decided that, in the absence of direct evidence undermining the council's denial, he was entitled to accept that documentation had not been retained due to the passage of time (see *Wolverhampton City Council* FER0120142). By the time the matter came before the Tribunal, the applicant had himself located the relevant information in the archives maintained by the Wolverhampton Archives and Local Studies Group (which was owned by the council). The Commissioner, at the appeal, conceded that the Council did in fact 'hold' the information at the time of the request (see also *Perrins* v. *Information Commissioner and Wolverhampton City Council* (EA/2006/0038)).

Good records management lies at the heart of both FOIA 2000 and EIR 2004. As the case above illustrates, it is imperative that a public authority knows what information it holds both within the authority and also within the authority's archives. Given the timescales for responding to requests for information, information rights practitioners need to be able to access information without unnecessary delay. Public authorities should have in place a records management policy which must also include an information retention strategy and a policy for dealing with emails and deleted emails. For an example of a request relating to deleted emails, see *Coventry City Council* (FS50086211).

Where a public authority does not hold the information it should serve a refusal notice but it should also consider whether it may need to transfer the request to another public authority that holds the information.

The public interest test

This exception is subject to the public interest test which is a little curious since it is difficult to see how the test operates if the public authority does not hold the information; even if the public interest squarely fell in favour of disclosure the public authority would still not hold the information. This 'oddity' was recognised by the Information Commissioner in *Chesterfield Borough Council* FS50260693. In March 2011, the Advocate General to the ECJ issued his Opinion in *Office of Communications* v. *Information Commissioner* (Case C-71/10) (Opinion of Advocate General Kokott, delivered on 10 March 2011). The case centres on the application of the public interest test (see **7.4**) but AG Kokott is clearly of the opinion that the 'not held' exception is not amenable to the public interest test. At the time of writing, the Court had not ruled on this issue however, it seems fairly conclusive that the public interest test does not, and cannot, apply to this exception.

7.5.2   EIR 2004, reg.12(4)(b): Request for information is manifestly unreasonable

If a public authority considers the request to be 'manifestly unreasonable' then it may refuse to disclose some or all of the information. This clearly begs the question, when will a request be manifestly unreasonable? What factors make it unreasonable? What about vexatious requests?

The first thing to note is that it requires more than that the request is too general. Where a request is formulated in too general a manner, a public authority is under a duty to help the applicant clarify the request (see duty to advise and assist at **6.3.2**). Volume and complexity alone do not make the request manifestly unreasonable.

The Commissioner's view is that a request is manifestly unreasonable if it is clearly and obviously unreasonable; there should be no doubt. When deciding whether a request is manifestly unreasonable, the principal question is whether the request could place a 'substantial and unreasonable burden on the resources of the public authority' (DEFRA Detailed Guidance, the Exceptions), particularly where, for example:

- it involves extensive scans of historic files;
- it involves searching large databases/files;
- extensive redaction is necessary;

- the retrieval would result in an unreasonable diversion of resources from the provision of essential public services (for example, diverting costs and staff from a public authority's core functions).

What then about vexatious requests? The word 'vexatious' does not appear in EIR 2004 but information rights practitioners will be familiar with its use in FOIA 2000, s.14 where a public authority can refuse a request for information where the request is vexatious. The Information Commissioner takes the view that, despite linguistic differences, both provisions were aimed broadly at achieving the same purpose, namely to ensure that applicants for information did not – as a result of their unreasonable requests – either jeopardise sound and effective administration within public institutions or otherwise unjustly harass public officials. This view is endorsed by the Tribunal (see *Carpenter* v. *Information Commissioner* (EA/2008/0046)).

In short, a request is likely to be manifestly unreasonable under EIR 2004 if would be vexatious under FOIA 2000, s.14. Therefore, the principles that have emerged in relation to what is 'vexatious' for the purposes of s.14 are of relevance, namely:

- Does the request have the effect of harassing the authority or distressing its staff?
- Could the request otherwise fairly be seen to be obsessive?
- Is the request designed to cause disruption or annoyance?
- Does the request lack any serious purpose or value?
- Does the request pose a substantial burden for the authority?

In the Commissioner's view at least two of the above must apply for a request to be manifestly unreasonable (see *Environment Agency* FER0347432). As a request may be manifestly unreasonable if it is vexatious, public authorities should consider the Commissioner's guidance on vexatious requests ('Vexatious and Repeated Requests', Awareness Guidance No.22, 1 March 2007), although this should not be adhered to in an overly structured way. In addition, Tribunal decisions on FOIA 2000, s.14 provide further understanding of what factors will be relevant. However, each case should be considered on its own facts. When considering the facts the public authority is not required to look at the request in isolation, it can consider both the history of the matter and what lay behind the request. Also it may be permissible to take into account the identity of the requestor. Although both FOIA 2000 and EIR 2004 are said to be both applicant and purpose blind, the Tribunal accepts that in the context of vexatious requests, identity and purpose can be very relevant in deciding whether a request is vexatious (see *Welsh* v. *Information Commissioner* (EA/2007/0088) (an FOIA case)). It is possible for an isolated single request to be unreasonable if it has the quality of being vexatious when it is construed in context.

If a public authority seeks to defend the use of this exception it should probably consider preparing a schedule of communications between itself and the applicant, background contextual information, and an indication of how much time it spent on the request before citing the exception.

Practical example

In *Robert Latimer* v. *Information Commissioner and the Environment Agency* (EA/2009/0018) the appellant made a request to the Environment Agency for information relating to a sewage treatment works near his home. This was refused on the basis that the request was manifestly unreasonable. Although the appeal related to this single request the Tribunal noted that the appellant had been communicating with the Environment Agency about this issue since 1992 and this had caused considerable stress to some Agency staff. The Agency had supplied the appellant with a great deal of information in the past, including explanatory notes. In total the Agency recorded some 699 communications regarding the appellant, the majority of which were between him and the Agency. The Tribunal also took into account the behaviour of the appellant (who had at times demanded that certain Agency staff resign and had levelled charges of incompetence, collusion and lying). Putting all of this into context, the Tribunal concurred that the request was manifestly unreasonable. See also *Easter* v. *Information Commissioner* (EA/2009/0092).

If the applicant requests the information in a particular format, this may also be manifestly unreasonable if the same considerations apply. Similarly, if extensive redaction is required then this may also make the request manifestly unreasonable.

Before a public authority decides that the request is manifestly unreasonable, it should first consider whether it has properly exercised its duty to advise and assist the applicant so as to clarify the nature of the request. This may make the request more manageable and negate the need to engage the exception.

The public interest test

The public interest in maintaining this exception is self-evident. Public authorities cannot be expected to deal with manifestly unreasonable requests which cause significant disruption and/or distress to the public authority or its staff. However, even if a public authority concludes that the request is manifestly unreasonable, it must still consider whether the public interest in disclosure outweighs any resource considerations. It is possible that the issues raised by the requestor are so important that the public interest in disclosure to the world at large prevails over the public interest inherent in this exception. There could be a fine balance between protecting an authority against manifestly unreasonable applications and the desire to ensure transparency.

7.5.3 EIR 2004, reg.12(4)(c): Request too general and public authority has complied with duty to provide advice and assistance

A request that is formulated in too general a manner may be difficult to respond to and could potentially impose a significant burden on the public authority. This exception allows the public authority to refuse to respond to such a request, but this is qualified; the public authority must be satisfied that it has fulfilled its obligation to advise and assist the applicant. A public authority cannot engage this exception if it has failed to comply with the duty.

Reflection point

Access to environmental information is intended to facilitate public participation in certain environmental decisions such as the grant of planning permission for projects that are likely to have significant effects on the environment. Often decisions concerning the location of a landfill or factory will impact on some of the poorest communities who may lack the expertise to formulate precise questions/requests for information. Environmental issues can be very complex and technical and applicants should not be deterred from making requests because they are unable to specify exactly what they need. Public authorities should ensure that the staff charged with dealing with EIR requests have the skills to assist applicants who need help in articulating their requests.

The public interest

The public interest in maintaining this exception is to all intents and purposes the same as that for the previous exception in EIR 2004, reg.12(4)(b) (see **7.5.2**). Although EIR 2004 require public authorities to help requestors formulate their requests '[t]here has to be a limit on how much time and effort it is appropriate for the [authority] to spend on answering queries from individuals' (see *Fowler* v. *Information Commissioner and Brighton and Hove City Council* (EA/2006/0071).

7.5.4 Handling difficult requests

The case of *Fowler* v. *Information Commissioner and Brighton and Hove City Council* (EA/2006/0071) demonstrates some of the real difficulties that public authorities face when dealing with people who make persistent and repeated requests. The case touches on all three of the procedural exceptions discussed above. The applicant, dissatisfied with the way in which Brighton and Hove City Council had dealt with a claim for compensation, appeared to have embarked on a campaign to challenge the council's new scheme to collect and recycle waste. During 2004 he engaged the council in very lengthy correspondence and with the advent of FOIA 2000 and EIR 2004 in 2005 he submitted numerous requests for information. It is clear that the applicant was persistent and had consumed a great deal of council time. The Tribunal set out some general observations about how a public authority may approach requests against a background when it has already replied to numerous similarly phrased requests and has provided substantial advice and assistance.

The Tribunal distinguished between:

- straightforward requests which can be answered relatively simply; and

- those which may require an individual reply. For example, in the *Fowler* case the council was asked why it thought its new system of waste collection was more efficient when it appeared to be less efficient.

  - A question like this, particularly based on a disputed premise, is difficult to deal with. Unless the public authority has a report or document which addresses such a question, it is not obliged by EIR 2004 to draft an individual reply. A public authority can legitimately claim that it does not hold this information.
  - It is open to a public authority to treat questions such as this as formulated in too general a manner. In *Fowler* the council had already offered substantial advice and assistance to the applicant and it could therefore rely on this exception.
  - The other option in more extreme cases is to invoke the manifestly unreasonable exception. As noted earlier, the Commissioner and Tribunal will consider this in context. In this case the Tribunal noted the 'obsessive' nature of the request and the remarkable forbearance of the council, suggesting that had this exception been raised they would have accepted it.

7.6 CLASS-BASED EXCEPTIONS

There are three class-based exceptions. In order for these exceptions to be engaged it is not necessary to identify any specific prejudice or harm flowing from the disclosure of the information in question. A public authority may refuse to disclose information if it falls into one of the following classes:

(a) the information includes personal data of which the applicant is not the data subject (EIR 2004, reg.12(3));

(b) the request relates to material which is still in the course of completion, to unfinished documents or to incomplete data (EIR 2004, reg.12(4)(d)); or

(c) the request involves the disclosure of internal communications (EIR 2004, reg.12(4)(e)).

7.6.1 EIR 2004, reg.12(3): Information includes personal data of which the applicant is not data subject

Disclosure of personal data is subject to the requirements of DPA 1998. Where a request for information includes a request for personal data then that element of the request must accord with the requirements of DPA 1998. If the person who makes the request is the data subject (the person about whom the personal data relates) then this element of the request will be treated as a data subject request under DPA 1998, s.7. If the person who makes the request is not the data subject then the public authority is prohibited from disclosing this information unless disclosure is in accordance with the requirements of EIR 2004, reg.13 which essentially requires that the disclosure of any personal data to another person does not infringe the requirements of DPA 1998. This exception and the relationship between EIR 2004 and DPA 1998 is considered more fully in **Chapter 9**.

This exception is not subject to the public interest test.

7.6.2 EIR 2004, reg.12(4)(d): Request relates to material still in the course of completion/unfinished documents/incomplete data

The purpose of the exception where the request relates to material which is still in the course of completion, to unfinished documents or to incomplete is to protect the 'thinking space' for government and other public authorities. The exception is (in the Commissioner's view) akin to the exemption contained at FOIA 2000, s.22 in that it is designed to exempt information that is intended for future publication. At first glance it would appear to offer public authorities an enormous opportunity to exclude information from EIR 2004 by simply labelling it 'draft' or incomplete. However, the Defra guidance (and the Arhus Implementation Guide) both caution that the mere status of material designated as 'draft' does not automatically bring it within this exception. The question can only be determined on a case-by-case basis having regard to the facts. For example, information contained in a survey where each individual stage of the survey could be regarded as if it were a separate survey.

Practical example

Plymouth City Council refused to disclose a Stage 2 Safety Audit Report for a pedestrian crossing scheme, on the basis that the report was only one in a series of three reports prepared during the implementation of the crossing scheme. The Commissioner required disclosure; the Stage 2 Report related to a distinct stage in the implementation of the crossing scheme and was a separate document. The exception was not engaged (see *Plymouth City Council* FER 0069925).

Does the public have a right to see initial drafts of documents/reports once completed?

The answer to this question appears to be no, given the Tribunal's decision in *Secretary of State for Transport* v. *Information Commissioner* (EA/2008/0052). The Secretary of State withheld a draft report prepared in advance of a final report which was published in 2006. Although the final report was in the public domain, the Secretary of State refused to disclose the draft. The Commissioner's view was that where a final version of the report existed then the draft was 'complete' and the exception could not be engaged since the rationale for the exception no longer operated.

The Tribunal considered this approach was unsustainable; no draft of any document could ever fall within this exception once there was a final version and this 'unfortunate conclusion' would mean that disclosure of such drafts could not be subjected to the public interest balancing exercise. The fact that a draft report itself related to another document (such as the final version) does not change its status as a draft; and a draft report is by its very name an unfinished document. Disclosure would be required only if the public interest in disclosure outweighed the public interest vested in this exception (see below). See also *Mersey Tunnel Users Association* v. *Information Commissioner & Halton Borough Council* (EA/2009/001); *Environment Agency* FER0210838; and *Department of Energy and Climate Change* FER0184885.

Duty to inform applicant where or when material will be completed

If this exception is being used then the public authority is required to advise the applicant of the name (if it knows it) of any other public authority that is preparing the information and also the estimated time by which the information will be finished and completed (EIR 2004, reg.14(4)).

The public interest test

As noted earlier it is not necessary to identify any specific prejudice or harm flowing from disclosure when a class-based exception is engaged. However, when considering whether the public interest in maintaining the exception outweighs the public interest in disclosure, it is relevant to consider what specific harm would follow from disclosure of the particular information in question. In order to do this, it is necessary to understand what interest this exception seeks to protect. Public authority staff need a safe space in which to work candidly and freely without being concerned that early drafts of reports will be disclosed. It is an important feature of policy making that public authorities (and any bodies that they work with, such as consultants or contractors) can freely analyse and discuss drafts. Disclosure might result in a loss of candour and frankness (known as the chilling effect – see **7.6.3** for further discussion of this argument). As far as the disclosure of incomplete data is concerned, it might be argued that releasing data at an 'early preparatory or contingency stage' might be misleading to the public. (See *Maile* v. *Wigan Metropolitan Borough Council* [2001] Env LR 11 which concerned the similar exception in EIR 1992.)

On the other hand, disclosure of draft material could cast light on how a final report had been arrived at and this could assist the public's knowledge of decision-making processes. Disclosure could also increase public confidence in the final version of reports if such disclosure revealed a process of peer review, reflection, adequate scrutiny and careful drafting. The factors that will be taken into account in balancing the competing public interests include:

- the timing of the request – whilst policy is in formulation it is highly unlikely that the public interest would favour disclosure of incomplete material or draft reports (unless, for example, it would expose wrongdoing by a public authority);
- the content of the information itself – every decision is specific to the facts and circumstances under consideration.

See *Department for Energy and Climate Change* FER0184885 which provides a valuable insight into the approach adopted by the Commissioner in relation to the public interest test for this exception.

7.6.3 EIR 2004, reg.12(4)(e): Request involves disclosure of internal communications

At first sight, this exception is capable of covering a vast amount of information held by public authorities and sits oddly with the stated purpose of the Regulations, the Directive or the Convention. The very wide formulation of this exception contrasts with the other more narrowly defined EIR exceptions and because it is class based there is no need to demonstrate that a particular interest will be adversely affected. Perhaps, of all the exceptions, this one most demands to be interpreted restrictively.

What are internal communications?

There does not appear to be a consensus between the Information Commissioner and the Tribunal on the interpretation of this exception. The Information Commissioner's 'Introduction to EIR 2004 Exceptions' published in September 2009 states that this exception 'should be interpreted broadly', but the Tribunal has stated that it finds this guidance 'unhelpful' (*South Gloucestershire Council* v. *Information Commissioner and Bovis Homes Ltd* (EA/2009/0032)). In the same case the Tribunal declined to devise a standard test as to what amounts to internal or external communication, for example, by reference to the nature of the communication or its audience. The question whether information constitutes an internal communication will therefore depend on the context and facts in each situation.

Communications between government departments

EIR 2004 state that internal communications includes communications between government departments. In *Friends of the Earth* v. *Information Commissioner and Export Credits Guarantee Department* (EA/2006/0073) the Tribunal rejected arguments put forward by Friends of the Earth that this was contrary to the Directive and internal communications should be limited to communications within a single government department. The Tribunal held that the exception applied to communications between separate governments departments.

Communications between different public authorities

Communications between public authorities that are not government departments, for example, between a central government department and a local authority, or between the Environment Agency and Defra are not covered by this exception (although, of course, they may be protected by one of the other exceptions listed in **Chapter 8**).

Communications with external bodies such as consultants

Public authorities frequently engage consultants to provide external expertise and services and to prepare reports. This is generally done on a commercial basis with some expectation, at least on the part of the consultant, of confidentiality. Information provided on this basis may be covered by exceptions in EIR 2004, reg.12(5) (see **Chapter 8**). However, in a number of instances public authorities have sought to withhold information prepared or supplied by consultants by citing the internal communications exception. Can communications between a public authority and a third party consultant be regarded as internal communications? There is no definitive answer; each case will be examined on its own particular set of facts (see above regarding the Tribunal's reluctance to devise a standard test). The factual and legal nature of the relationship between the public authority and third party provides the context of the communications but in the final analysis it is not the relationship but the communications themselves which are the determining factor.

The leading Tribunal decision on this issue concerned the draft report prepared by Sir Rod Eddington (the Chief Executive of British Airways plc), for the Secretary of State for Transport (*Secretary of State for Transport* v. *Information Commissioner* (EA/2008/0052)– see above at **7.6.2.**). The Tribunal concluded that, because Sir Eddington was firmly embedded within the civil service and acted as head of a team of civil servants (he also had an office within the Department for Transport and had a business card with the departmental logo) then his draft report constituted an internal communication. However, this decision was based on the particular facts of the case and was, in the Tribunal's word, exceptional. In *South Gloucestershire Council* v. *Information Commissioner and Bovis Homes Ltd* (EA/2009/0032) the Tribunal rejected the council's arguments that a firm of external consultants was integrated into the council. The factors that the Tribunal considered relevant in reaching this conclusion were:

- the council did not have the in-house expertise it required to carry out a detailed development appraisal of a site (which it required to conduct a delicate negotiation with a developer);
- the council engaged the consultants in the ordinary way by means of a contract for the provision of expert services;
- the consultants worked closely with the council but they were not seconded to the council nor were they 'embedded' into the organisation;

- the consultants did not take any decisions or otherwise act on the council's behalf;
- the consultant's role was important to the council because they brought an independent view from outside.

If a public authority relies on this exception, the refusal notice will need to explain why the public authority considers the information constitutes an internal communication, particularly where the communication is between the public authority and another body or consultant.

Internal communications and the public interest test

When considering whether the public interest in maintaining this exception outweighs the public interest in disclosure, it is relevant to consider what specific harm would follow from disclosure of the particular information in question. The public interest in this exception is similar to that in EIR 2004, reg.12(4)(d); public authorities need the space to think in private so that the 'formulation and development of government policy and government decision making can proceed in the self-contained space needed to ensure that it is done well' (Defra detailed guidance, para.7.4.5.8). The Commissioner and the Tribunal have dealt with a number of cases where this exception (and the largely corresponding exemptions in FOIA 2000, ss.35 and 36) have been cited. For example, *Lord Baker* v. *Information Commissioner and DCLG* (EA/2006/0042) and *Friends of the Earth* v. *Information Commissioner and the Export Credits Guarantee Department* (EA/2006/0073). Looking at these and other cases, the types of arguments in favour of maintaining the exception have revolved around the following:

- the so-called 'chilling effect' on free and frank discussions between civil servants and ministers;
- that disclosure will undermine the process of collective policy formulation;
- the damaging effects of disclosure on difficult or sensitive policy areas;
- that fear of disclosure will result in fewer notes and records being kept;
- damage to the relationship between decision makers and advisors and the fear that advisors will be less willing to give advice.

The arguments in favour of disclosure will include:

- the public needs to understand how and why decisions have been taken and the factors taken into account by decision makers;
- the need to ensure that decision makers have been properly advised;
- the information concerns an issue which is of significant importance and/or involves significant public expenditure;
- disclosure of information about the deliberative processes of government can improve those processes.

The public interest test reveals the tension between open government and good government; but each case will be decided on the facts. The Tribunal has demonstrated a fairly healthy scepticism about some of the arguments advanced in support of non-disclosure. General arguments about the chilling effect or possible wider risks have received little support from the Tribunal.

Practical example

Kent County Council refused to disclose internal council documents regarding a proposal to develop a lorry park in Kent. As well as providing secure overnight the proposed park would provide parking for lorries unable to use the M20 motorway due to traffic disruptions. Specifically the information concerned alternative sites for the park and the valuations of the associated sites. Although the information was contained in an internal communication the Commissioner decided the public interest favoured disclosure. There was a strong public interest in disclosing information which would inform public participation and debate around an issue of considerable public concern (*Kent County Council* FER219834).

CHAPTER 8

The 'adversely affects' exceptions: EIR 2004, reg.12(5)

8.1 INTRODUCTION

In addition to the procedural and 'class-based' exceptions discussed in **Chapter 7**, EIR 2004 provide, at reg.12(5), an additional seven exceptions where information may be withheld if its disclosure would adversely affect one of the following 'protected' interests:

(a) international relations, defence, national security or public safety;
(b) the course of justice, ability of a person to receive a fair trial or the ability of a public authority to conduct an inquiry of a criminal or disciplinary nature;
(c) intellectual property rights;
(d) the confidentiality of the proceedings of that or any other public authority where such confidentiality is provided by law;
(e) the confidentiality of commercial or industrial information where such confidentiality is provided by law to protect a legitimate economic interest;
(f) the interests of the person providing the information where that person:

(i) was not under, and could not have been put under, any legal obligation to supply it to that or any other public authority;
(ii) did not supply it in circumstances such that that or any other public authority was entitled apart from these Regulations to disclose it; and
(iii) has not consented to its disclosure;

(g) the protection of the environment to which the information relates.

Although public authorities exercise discretion as to whether they 'may' refuse to disclose information, in the case of these exceptions they can only do so if disclosure would adversely affect the interest protected by the exception. For a public authority to be able to withhold information under EIR 2004, reg.12(5) they need to consider two issues:

- First, whether the interest protected by the exception would be adversely affected by the disclosure. In other words, there needs to be an assessment of the consequences of disclosure. If disclosure would not have an adverse effect then there is no need to consider the public interest test the information should be disclosed because the exception has not been triggered.

- Second, if it is deemed that disclosure would have an adverse effect then the public authority must go on to consider the public interest test.

Considering adverse effects and the public interest is therefore a two-stage process.

However, these exceptions are subject to an important caveat. To the extent that the information is information on emissions then a public authority is prohibited from using the exceptions in EIR 2004, reg.12(5)(d)–(g). The impact of this will be considered later.

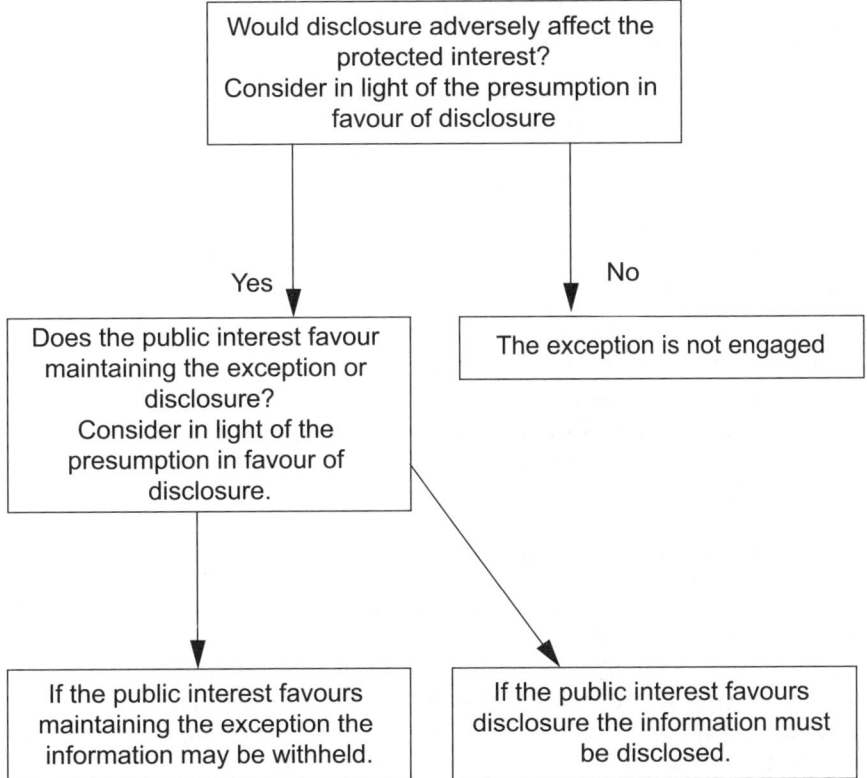

Figure 8.1 The 'adversely affects' exceptions

8.1.1 The general approach to these exceptions

There is an emerging body of decisions which can be referred to in determining how public authorities should approach these exceptions, both in general terms and also specifically for each particular exception. The Tribunal's decision in *Archer* v. *Information Commissioner* (EA/2006/0037) sets out the general approach that needs to be adopted:

1.   It is not enough that disclosure should simply affect the matters set out in EIR 2004, reg.12(5) as the effect must be 'adverse'.
2.   Refusal to disclose is only permitted to the extent of that adverse effect.
3.   It is necessary to show that disclosure 'would' have an adverse effect – not that it could or might have such effect.
4.   Even if there would be an adverse effect, the information must still be disclosed unless in all the circumstances of the case, the public interest in maintaining the exception outweighs the public interest in disclosing the information.
5.   All of these issues must be assessed having regard to the overriding presumption in favour of disclosure.

The result is that 'the threshold to justify non disclosure is a high one'. This does not mean that it is impossible, but the burden of proving adverse effect is difficult and requires more than generic assertions. Public authorities must be able to demonstrate how, and on what basis, they have reached the conclusion that the exception has been properly engaged.

Before examining each of the exceptions in turn it is important to consider some general questions, most particularly:

• What does 'would' mean? Is it sufficient to demonstrate that disclosure may adversely affect the protected interest?
• How 'adverse' does the affect need to be in order to trigger the exception?
• Does the public authority need to 'prove' the adverse affect and how can it do this if the adverse affect it is trying to avoid is in the future?

8.2   WOULD ADVERSELY AFFECT: THE DEGREE OF CERTAINTY REQUIRED

The requirement that disclosure would have an adverse effect is more stringent than the 'similar' prejudice-based exemptions under FOIA 2000. Under the Act it is sufficient that disclosure 'would or would be likely to' cause a particular harm or prejudice. It is therefore arguable that the threshold for engaging an adversely affects exception under EIR 2004 is higher than under the prejudice-based FOIA exemptions (see *Foreign and Commonwealth Office* v. *Information Commissioner and Friends of the Earth* (EA/2006/0065)). This raises certain questions. Does the word 'would' require a degree of certainty? What level of adverse effects is required? How can a public authority prove a future negative effect, or what evidence is required?

The Defra guidance offers little on the 'general' approach to be adopted; rather, it focuses on the individual exceptions. However, the guidance is not hugely consistent. For example, in relation to the intellectual property exception it notes that 'Any intellectual property rights … or other trade secret may be protected by this exception where *a potentially adverse effect can be reasonably anticipated*' (author's emphasis). In relation to the exception in EIR 2004, reg.12(5)(g), it states that the exception is 'applicable where disclosure of the information *could* adversely affect the interests of the individual or organisation who provided the information'. Public authorities should take care not to rely on the use of the word 'could' since EIR 2004, reg.12(5) clearly requires that the disclosure 'would' have an adverse effect.

The Information Commissioner maintains that the adversely affects exceptions in EIR 2004, reg.12(5) are broadly similar (but not identical) to the prejudice-based exemptions in FOIA 2000 (see FOIA Guidance, 'An Introduction to the Exceptions', September 2009 and 'Freedom of Information', Awareness Guidance No. 20.) This may be true but there are differences between the regimes and care should be taken not to interpret EIR 2004 by reference to the Act. Notwithstanding that note of caution, the Commissioner correctly recognises that the exceptions require a 'harm test' and that 'some harm must be at least probable, rather than merely likely'. In support of this, the Commissioner cites the Tribunal's decision in *Burgess* v. *Information Commissioner* (EA/2006/0091) in which the Tribunal laid down the principals that:

- 'would' means 'more likely than not'; and
- the adverse effect has to be 'real, actual or of substance'.

The 'more likely than not' approach is a pragmatic response; it recognises the difficulties inherent in proving a future negative. Whilst it is plainly not sufficient for a public authority to claim that releasing the information might result in an adverse effect, it can be difficult to prove that an adverse effect would occur beyond any doubt whatsoever. However, it must be at least more probable than not and there must be more than a theoretical risk.

8.2.1   What level of adverse effects is required?

The regulations are silent about the level of adverse effects required to trigger an exception. Clearly there needs to be a negative impact on the relative interest; the question is how much? Although the adverse effect has to be 'real, actual or of substance', the Tribunal also believes that the threshold for establishing an adverse effect is not particularly high. Citing the intellectual property exception in EIR 2004, reg.12(5)(c), the Tribunal notes that the purpose of the threshold was to filter out cases where infringement of intellectual property rights were 'either purely technical or so minimal that the exception may be disregarded at the outset without the public authority having to give consideration of the balance of public interest' (*The Office of Communications* v. *Information Commissioner* (EA/2006/0078)).

It should be noted that even though the extent of the adverse effect is not relevant at this stage, it is relevant when the public authority considers the public interest test (see *Archer* v. *Information Commissioner* (EA/2006/0037)).

8.2.2 What evidence is required or how can a public authority prove a future adverse effect?

The Tribunal accepts that it will not be possible for a public authority to prove the adverse effect beyond reasonable doubt, however, a civil standard of proof is required. The public authority will need to satisfy itself (and the Commissioner/ Tribunal in the event of an appeal) that on the balance of probabilities the relevant harm will be suffered.

8.3 EIR 2004, REG.12(5)(A): INTERNATIONAL RELATIONS, DEFENCE, NATIONAL SECURITY OR PUBLIC SAFETY

Where this particular exception applies, the public authority may refuse to either confirm or deny whether the information is held if to do so would be against the public interest. This is the only exception to which this option exists.

None of the phrases in this exception are defined within EIR 2004 and would therefore appear to afford considerable discretion to public authorities; however, they must be interpreted restrictively. The first limb (international relations) encompasses both international relations with other states and with international organisations, for example the United Nations or the International Court of Justice (see *Export Credit Guarantees Department* v. *Information Commissioner and Hildyard* (EA/2008/0071)). Curiously, the term 'national security' does not appear to have been defined in any domestic legislation. In the context of EIR 2004 it was held to mean the national security of the UK and its people and includes the protection of democracy and the legal and constitutional systems of the state, as well as military defence (see *Baker* v. *Information Commissioner and the Cabinet Office* (EA/2006/ 0045), a FOIA case). The public safety limb has been raised in cases which have a less obvious connection with public/national security. For example, the exception was raised successfully in relation to an environmental risk strategy report in respect of a local derelict mill (*Oldham Metropolitan Borough Council* FER0176570) and unsuccessfully by Plymouth City Council in relation to a request for information about a safety audit report for a pedestrian crossing scheme (*Plymouth City Council* FER0069925).

8.3.1 Adversely affects

It is likely that when a public authority considers the impact of disclosure on international relations it will have regard to any advice offered by the Foreign and Commonwealth Office. However, the Tribunal does not regard this as sufficient evidence of adverse effect; the adverse effect claimed must be objectively reasonable whether it is based on Foreign and Commonwealth Office guidance or a public authority's own risk assessment.

The national security exception was successfully used by the UK Atomic Energy Authority when it refused to disclose files containing information about the storage and safety of fissile and special nuclear material. The Commissioner accepted that the release of the information could enable terrorists or other attackers to gain access to nuclear materials. Not only would this pose a security threat, it would provide terrorists with the opportunity to undermine foreign policy and affect the economic well being of the country (see *UK Atomic Energy Authority* FS50117924).

The public safety limb was considered at some length by the Tribunal in the *Ofcom* case (*The Office of Communications* v. *Information Commissioner* (EA/2006/0078)). Ofcom argued that the disclosure of the information about the exact location of mobile telephone masts could result in the masts being targeted by criminals or terrorists and this would compromise the ability of the police and emergency services to respond to emergency calls. The difficulty in this case was that the information that was requested was available in the public domain but not easily searchable. Ofcom were required to demonstrate that the disclosure of those aspects of the database that were not already available to the public would contribute to the alleged risks. On the facts the Tribunal was prepared to accept that the release of the whole database would provide some assistance to criminals and this would increase, to some degree, the risks of attacks on the network and put public safety at risk.

8.3.2 Public interest test

The public interest that is protected by this exception is clear but it does not necessarily follow that the public interest will always fall in favour of maintaining the exception. For example, the sensitivity of information will normally diminish over time (although this may not always be the case). For example, the disclosure of information relating to the dumping of munitions during the Second World War may not adversely affect defence now. In the *Ofcom* case the Tribunal considered that notwithstanding any adverse effect to public safety, the public interest in disclosure outweighed the public interest in maintaining the exception. Although the adverse effect was sufficient to trigger the exception, it was not large in view of the information already available within the public domain.

8.3.3 No duty to confirm or deny

This is the only exception to which a public authority may refuse to confirm or deny that it holds the requested information, if conformation or denial would adversely affect the interests protected and it would not be in the public interest. In other words, a public authority may (where the above conditions are satisfied) simply refuse to say whether the information exists or whether it holds it (EIR 2004, reg.12(6) and (7)).

8.3.4 Ministerial Certificates: national security

Under EIR 2004, reg.15, a Minister of the Crown may issue a Ministerial Certificate which provides conclusive evidence that a refusal to disclose information is because the disclosure would adversely affect national security and it would not be in the public interest to disclose such information. Any appeal against a Ministerial Certificate is heard by the Upper Tribunal, but must be lodged with the First-tier (Information Rights) Tribunal before being transferred to the Upper Tribunal (see **Chapter 10**).

8.4 EIR 2004, REG.12(5)(B): THE COURSE OF JUSTICE/FAIR TRIAL/CRIMINAL OR DISCIPLINARY PROCEDURE

The course of justice, the ability of a person to receive a fair trial or ability of a public authority to conduct an inquiry of a criminal or disciplinary nature – although this exception refers to information relating to judicial matters, it must be recalled that EIR 2004 do not apply to a public authority to the extent that it is acting in a judicial or legislative capacity.

The exception contains three different limbs:

1. the course of justice;
2. the ability of a person to receive a fair trial; or
3. the ability of a public authority to conduct an inquiry of a criminal or disciplinary nature.

The exception exists in part to ensure that there should be no disruption to the administration of justice, including the operation of the courts, and no prejudice to the right of individuals or organisations to a fair trial (see *Kirkaldie* v. *Information Commissioner & Thanet District Council* (EA/2006/001)). Although this is a widely stated exception, it does not explicitly name legal professional privilege (LPP) and it has been argued on a number of occasions (for example, *Creekside Forum* v. *Information Commissioner and the Department for Culture, Media and Sport* (EA/2008/0065)) that it should not include information covered by LPP.

8.4.1 Does the exception include information subject to LPP?

Despite the absence of the phrase 'legal professional privilege' (and in contrast to the analogous FOIA 2000, s.42 exemption) it appears to be beyond dispute that legal advice is capable of falling within this exception (see *Kirkaldie* v. *Information Commissioner & Thanet District Council* (EA/2006/001) and *Maiden* v. *Information Commissioner and Borough Council of King's Lynn and West Norfolk* (EA/2008/0013)). Although there is no direct reference to legally privileged information within this exception, there is no express prohibition on privileged information being included (*Rudd* v. *Information Commissioner and the Verderers of the New Forest* (EA/2008/0020)). Legal advice provided by an in-house lawyer could also be protected under the internal communications exception in EIR 2004, reg.12(4)(e) but that would clearly not extend to legal advice provided by an external legal advisor.

What information is covered by LPP?

LPP is a set of rules or principles which are designed to protect the confidentiality of legal or legally related communications and exchanges between a client and his legal advisor. The fundamental principle of LPP is that a client must be certain what he discusses with his lawyer in confidence will not be disclosed. Information is not 'privileged' simply because it was sent by, or to, a lawyer; the information must relate to a legal context. LPP does not attach to information of a purely factual nature. There are two categories of LPP and both are covered by this exception:

- confidential communications between lawyers and their clients for the purpose of obtaining legal advice (legal advice privilege); and
- confidential communications where the sole or dominant purpose is litigation (litigation privilege) (see *Bellamy* v. *Information Commissioner* (EA/2005/0023)). Litigation privilege applies only if there is a reasonable prospect of litigation and it also includes communications with third parties outside the lawyer–client relationship providing they were made to assist the lawyer to prepare the case.

FOIA 2000, s.42 applies to all information in respect of which a claim for LPP can be maintained. Indeed, such privilege can be maintained regardless of whether litigation is in prospect or not and regardless of the effect of disclosure of the specific material in question. In contrast, EIR 2004, reg.12(5)(b) only applies if the disclosure of the information would adversely affect one of the identified interests. In *West* v. *Information Commissioner* (EA/2010/0120) the Tribunal thought it arguable that EIR 2004, reg.12(5)(b) might not apply in a case where there is no prospect of litigation and pure 'legal advice privilege' is relied on; presumably as disclosure might not affect the course of justice or ability of a person to receive a fair trial.

Given that the Tribunal is emphatic that EIR 2004, reg.12(5)(b) includes information subject to LPP, requestors have inevitably raised arguments that the specific disputed information is not subject to LPP. The following arguments have been advanced to and rejected by the Tribunal:

Argument	Reason rejected
The information relates to judicial review which is not a litigious process sufficient to assert LPP.	LPP applies as much to judicial review proceedings as to any other type of litigation.
LPP only attaches to criminal litigation.	LPP attaches to all litigation.

Argument	Reason rejected
There is no need for LPP when proceedings are at an end.	The Tribunal rejected this on the basis that the advice may have a generalised importance that goes beyond the four corners of a particular dispute. However, the currency of the advice and whether it relates to a live issue will be relevant in assessing the adverse effect of disclosure and the public interest balance (see *Woodford* v. *Information Commissioner* (EA/2009/0098)).
LPP does not extend to in-house lawyers.	The same requirements of confidentiality and candour apply whether advice is provided by an employed lawyer or independent legal professional.
The time limit for judicial review has expired and so LPP no longer attaches to the advice.	LPP applies without time limit (subject to the public interest test).

The disclosure of information subject to LPP constitutes one of the major themes of the Tribunal's decided case law since the introduction of FOIA 2000 and EIR 2004. That is hardly surprising given the courts' traditional adherence to the view that that information subject to LPP is always protected from disclosure (see **8.4.4**).

Waiving LPP

Once a document/information is privileged it remains privileged unless there has been waiver. If privilege has been waived then the exception is not engaged. Waiver of LPP for one document/advice in a series of documents may also waive privilege in the other related documents; however, this will depend entirely on the facts of the case. The Commissioner and Tribunal will not allow a public authority to 'hide' behind this exception in circumstances where they have either expressly or impliedly waived privilege. In considering whether privilege has been waived the Commissioner/Tribunal will look at all the circumstances of the case:

- Whether the legal advice has been put into the public domain in some other form. In *Kirkaldie* v. *Information Commissioner* (EA/2006/001) the Tribunal found that privilege had been waived because Thanet District Council had provided a summary of the disputed legal advice at a full council meeting.
- Whether the public authority has 'promised' that it will disclose the information.
- Whether the public authority has disclosed previous advices (see *Maiden* v. *Information Commissioner and Borough Council of King's Lynn and West Norfolk* (EA/2008/0013)).

It may be possible to redact the privileged information from a document and, in such circumstances, disclosure of the unprivileged part will not waive privilege in the remaining part.

8.4.2 Fair trial and criminal or disciplinary inquiries

Although the majority of the cases where this exception has been raised relate to LPP it should be recalled that the exception refers to disclosure that would adversely affect the right to fair trial or the ability of a public authority to conduct an inquiry of a criminal or disciplinary nature.

The ability to receive a fair trial is not limited to court proceedings and can include administrative proceedings. Given the introduction of the administrative sanctions in environmental enforcement (as a result of the Regulatory Enforcement and Sanctions Act 2008), this could have greater application in the future. In *Watts* v. *Information Commissioner* (EA/2007/0022) the Tribunal made some useful observations about this aspect of the exception. First, the test under EIR 2004, reg. 12(5)(b) is harder for a public authority to overcome than under the broadly equivalent FOIA 2000, s.30, which provides that information is exempt if it has at any time been held by it 'for the purposes' of criminal proceedings. Second, the Tribunal exhorts a cautious approach in making the assessment because of the importance of not prejudicing a fair trial in criminal proceedings. If, on a sensible reading of the documentation in question, its disclosure would not adversely affect the prospects of a fair trial, then the fact that the information has some connection with the subject matter of a prosecution will not be sufficient justification for non-disclosure.

The final limb is where disclosure would adversely affect the ability of a public authority to conduct an inquiry of a criminal or disciplinary nature. This raises the question whether the exception applies to information that relates to enquiries which are not strictly 'criminal' in nature but may nevertheless result in the imposition of some sort of penalty, for example an administrative fine. The ruling of the ECJ in relation to the 1990 Directive suggests that the answer is yes. The exception also applies to information held by a public authority when it is conducting preliminary investigations with a view to embarking on criminal or disciplinary proceedings, but does not reach as far as information where there is the hypothetical possibility of future legal proceedings (*Mecklenburg* v. *Kreis Pinneberg der Landrat* (Case C-321/96) [1998] ECR I-3809).

8.4.3 Adversely affects

The fact that information is subject to LPP is not the critical factor; the only relevant consideration is whether disclosure would adversely affect either the course of justice, the ability of a person to receive a fair trial or the ability of a public authority to conduct an inquiry of a criminal or disciplinary nature. If a public authority intends to withhold information under this exception, particularly information subject to LPP, they need to consider how disclosure would seriously affect the protected interests; it is not sufficient to make generic claims that the disclosure of privileged information will always automatically have an adverse effect. A public authority seeking to rely on this exception will need to explain how disclosure of the specific information in question will have an adverse effect and what that adverse effect would be. The factors that are relevant in considering adverse effect include:

- Whether the litigation to which the information relates is in prospect; the disclosure of legal advice obtained by one side to prospective litigation without corresponding disclosure the other way would clearly be unfair and tend to undermine the course of justice in the particular case.
- Whether disclosure will damage a public authority's ability to deal with future similar cases/issues.
- The 'value' of the information to the parties. In *Department of the Environment for Northern Ireland* FER0082261 the information was sufficiently innocuous so as not to adversely affect any purported legal action; disclosure would not benefit to any degree the complainant in terms of defending any prospective enforcement action and neither would the Department be disadvantaged to any degree.

The level of adverse effect is not relevant here; it only needs to be sufficient to trigger the exception. However, in *West* v. *Information Commissioner* (EA/2010/0120) the Tribunal pointed out that where no specific adverse effect had been identified as likely to flow from disclosure of the particular advice in question, the weight of the public interest in maintaining the exception is reduced or not increased.

8.4.4 Public interest test

In *R* v. *Derby Magistrates' Court* ex parte *B* [1996] AC 487 Lord Taylor of Gosforth described LPP as:

> a fundamental condition on which the administration of justice as a whole rests ... I am of the opinion that no exception should be allowed to the absolute nature of legal professional privilege once established.

The absolute nature of LPP was confirmed by the House of Lords in 2004 in *Three Rivers District Council* v. *Governor and Company of the Bank of England (No.6)* [2004] UKHL 48. On the face of such pronouncements it would appear that information subject to LPP could never be disclosed. However, it is clear that this is no longer the case; the advent of legislation including EIR 2004 and FOIA 2000 mean that information subject to LPP must be disclosed if the public interest in disclosure outweighs the public interest in maintaining legal professional privilege.

An examination of the Tribunal's decisions in relation to this exception reveals that there is a strong built-in public interest in upholding LPP generally. The public interest vested in this exception has been well rehearsed before the Tribunal in both

FOIA and EIR cases. The decision in *Bellamy* v. *Information Commissioner* (EA/2005/0023) (an FOIA case) provides a useful review of the relevant principles established by the higher courts and the public interest factors in favour of maintaining this exception. The public interest must be assessed in all the circumstances and this means that a public authority cannot maintain a blanket refusal to disclose information simply because it is protected by LPP. There are a number of key factors, which as a matter of principle, will favour maintaining this exception:

- A client must be able to consult his lawyer in confidence; legal advice cannot be effectively obtained unless the client is able to put all the facts before his advisor without fear that this information will be disclosed and used against him. This principle is a fundamental condition on which the administration of justice as a whole rests.
- A person may be deterred from seeking legal advice if he or she cannot be certain of complete candour in communications with his or her legal advisor. In the case of a public authority there is a very strong public interest in a public authority being able to obtain frank legal advice based on a consideration of all the relevant facts, before deciding whether to use public funds to embark on enforcement actions or legal proceedings.
- Full and frank legal advice aids public authorities to comply with their legal obligations. Without such advice public authorities may not be able to carry out their duties effectively or lawfully.
- Disclosure of legal advice may prejudice a public authority's ability to litigate in the future or to defend its legal interests.
- LPP has been held to be part of the right to privacy guaranteed by art.8 of the ECHR (*Campbell* v. *United Kingdom* (1992) 15 EHRR 137).

Given the strong public interest inherent in this exception, at least equally strong, compelling and specific countervailing arguments need to be advanced to override the public interest inherent in it (*Mersey Tunnel Users Association* v. *Information Commissioner and Merseytravel* (EA/2007/0052)). Of course, there is a general public interest in a public authority being held to account for decisions it makes but, as the Tribunal notes in *Archer* v. *Information Commissioner* (EA/2006/0037) disclosure of legal advice is not the only means to achieve that. The following arguments have been advanced in favour of disclosure:

- If legally privileged material were evidence of malfeasance or fraud or corruption then there would be a very strong public interest argument in favour of disclosure (*Creekside Forum* v. *Information Commissioner and the Department for Culture, Media and Sport* (EA/2008/0065)). However, there must be cogent evidence of wrongdoing.
- Public authorities should be accountable for decisions; if a public authority uses public funds to start proceedings/enforcement actions but does not pursue them then the public should know why.

- Knowing that public authorities act appropriately in relation to the advice given.
- Despite the importance of LPP, Parliament did not make this an absolute exception and in any event there is a presumption in favour of disclosure.
- The scope of the dispute; for example, in *West* v. *Information Commissioner* (EA/2010/0120) the legal advice related to a dispute between a leaseholders' group and the public authority and had a bearing on the financial position of a large number of leaseholders and, indirectly, on a larger number of council tax payers.
- The age of the advice contained in the information is relevant. The passage of time would, as a general principle, favour disclosure. However, if the legal advice is still 'live' then this would suggest the information should not be disclosed.

8.5   EIR 2004, REG.12(5)(C): INTELLECTUAL PROPERTY RIGHTS

Public authorities hold a wide range of information which may be subject to some form of intellectual property protection. For example, the authority may have commissioned a report which is prepared by an outside organisation and is subject to copyright, or a company bidding for a contract may have disclosed information subject to a patent protection. The intellectual property right may be held by the public authority itself or some other public sector organisation or may be held by a private sector body such as a company. The fact that the information is subject to some form of intellectual property right does not take it outside the scope of EIR 2004. Providing the protected information is held by the public authority and concerns environmental information it is potentially discloseable. Copyright Designs and Patents Act (CDPA) 1988, s.50(1) states that an act 'specifically authorised by an Act of Parliament' does not infringe copyright. Hence disclosure under FOIA 2000 and EIR 2004, even if it involves providing a copy of a document which is a copyright work (either of the public authority or a third party)does not infringe copyright. It should be noted however, that any further copying by the requestor will infringe copyright. Disclosure does not mean that the rights become wholly valueless; once disclosed the information is free in the public's hands, subject to the private law rights which the owners of the intellectual property rights might enforce.

This exception is not triggered unless disclosure would adversely affect an intellectual property right and the public interest in maintaining this exception is greater than the public interest in disclosure. The net result of this is that there will be circumstances where information is subject to some form of intellectual property right, such as copyright, but nonetheless must be disclosed. The fact that disclosure would involve infringements of intellectual property is, at most a balancing factor against disclosure, not an absolute bar. The public interest in disclosure might override the rights in question.

8.5.1   What information is covered?

Since intellectual property rights are not defined by EIR 2004, reference has been made to the Convention establishing the World Intellectual Property Convention (WIPO Convention) (1967) which defines intellectual property rights as:

> the rights relating to – literary, artistic and scientific works ... protection against unfair competition and all other rights resulting from intellectual activity in the industrial, scientific, literary or artistic fields.

Intellectual property rights include copyrights, patents, trademarks and protected designs. They may be in the form of, for example, an invention, a manuscript, a suite of software or a business name. In order to engage this exception it will be necessary to identify a specific intellectual property right; it is not enough to assert that the type of information is commonly protected by an intellectual property right or is commercially confidential (see *Veterinary Medicines Directorate* FER0137609). Similarly, the fact that use of the data could be protected by an intellectual property right is equally not sufficient to trigger the exception (*Queen's University Belfast* FS50163282).

Many public authorities maintain a significant amount of information in an electronic database and as such this may be protected under CDPA 1998, s.3A. However, in order to establish a database right the maker must demonstrate that a substantial investment has been made in obtaining, verifying or presenting the contents of the database. If the Commissioner is not satisfied that a database meets this requirement he will not regard the database as benefitting from a database right. Similarly, a database is only protected under CDPA 1998, s.1 if it has originality in the selection or arrangement of its content. Public authorities that seek to engage the intellectual property exception in respect of database information need to check first whether the database meets the legislative requirements. If not then the exception cannot be engaged.

8.5.2   Adversely affects

Since the exception under EIR 2004, reg.12(5)(c) is intended to protect the interests of the holder of an intellectual property right (rather than intellectual property rights in principle), it is necessary to demonstrate the intellectual property rights holder would suffer an adverse effect as a result of disclosure of protected information. Disclosure of copyrighted or protected information does not of itself infringe the intellectual property right; it is only if the information, once in the public domain, is used that there may be a breach of the right and thus a possible adverse effect.

In order to trigger this exception:

- The infringement of the intellectual property right must be more than just a technical infringement (which in other circumstances might have led to a court awarding nominal damages or even exercising its discretion to refuse to grant the injunction that would normally follow a finding of an infringement).

- The infringement must be one that would result in some degree of loss or harm to the right holder. The test for establishing an adverse effect is not particularly high. The purpose of the adverse effect test is to:

  > filter out those cases where the infringement has been either purely technical or so minimal that the exception may be disregarded at the outset, without the public authority having to give consideration to the balance of public interest. (*The Office of Communications (Ofcom)* v. *Information Commissioner* (EA/2006/0078) para.48)).

  However, the degree of harm is also relevant when conducting the public interest test.

The factors that the Tribunal considers relevant in deciding whether intellectual property rights would be adversely affected include:

- Whether disclosure of commercially valuable information would result in the loss of ability to exploit the intellectual property right, through licensing, and cause a loss of potential revenue.
- The difficulty of policing any breaches of the property right. Although disclosure via EIR 2004 or FOIA 2000 does not involve an implied license to exploit information commercially or to use it in a way that would infringe an intellectual property right, the reality is that policing such rights becomes very difficult. That is particularly the case where the information is stored in a form in which it may be instantaneously transmitted to many third parties with limited scope to trace either the source or the destination and in a format that may easily be reconfigured.
- Release of the information to competitors or suppliers may give them a competitive edge. For example, in *Ofcom* it was argued that release of the data would enable landowners to anticipate where the mobile network operators wanted to locate further base stations and this would enable them to increase the rental or price of land.

The question is whether the specific intellectual property rights of the owner will be adversely affected; in other words, this is an assessment of the impact on the private rights of the property owner. This is not the same thing as the general public interest in maintaining intellectual property rights, which are assessed at the public interest stage.

8.5.3 Public interest test

Even if disclosure would involve an intellectual property right being adversely affected this is only a balancing factor against disclosure; it is not an absolute bar. The public interest may override the rights in question, depending on the facts of the case. The public interest factors in favour of maintaining this exception have rarely been rehearsed since the majority of the cases where this exception has been cited have failed at the adverse effect hurdle. The only Tribunal decision to date is *The Office of Communications (Ofcom)* v. *Information Commissioner* (EA/2006/0078) where the Tribunal did not spend much time looking at the public interest arguments in favour of the exception. However, there is self-evidently a public interest vested in favour of protecting intellectual property rights in general, and it may not be in the public interest for a public authority to use public monies to defend an action for breach of a protected right. In *Ofcom* the Tribunal considered the potential public interest detriment arising from the mobile network operators (as owners of the intellectual property rights) refusing to continue licensing the information to make a limited version available to the public. For such detriment to be relied upon the intellectual property right owner would need to carry out any such threats.

The public interests in disclosure will, of course, relate to the content of the information and the extent to which that information facilitates greater openness and transparency and accountability. (See again *Ofcom* where there was strong public interest in disclosing the disputed information.)

Given that disclosure may result in an infringement of an intellectual property right, to what extent can any 'benefit' arising from the use of that information be taken into account when assessing the public interest? The Court of Appeal (*The Office of Communications* v. *Information Commissioner* [2009] EWCA Civ 90) held that even where the use of information breaches an intellectual property right(s), its use may have both beneficial and adverse consequences and both can be taken into account in assessing where the public interest lies. A public authority is entitled, when assessing the public interest, to take into account the benefit arising from the use of information even if that use would be in breach of intellectual property rights. Of course, the extent to which this might tip the balance will depend on the use to which the information may be put; in the *Ofcom* case it was going to be used to assist with epidemiological research.

8.5.4 Releasing copyright material

Disclosure of information protected by an intellectual property right does not mean that the rights become wholly valueless. If a public authority discloses information which is subject to an intellectual property right then it must make the applicant aware of this fact. Responsibility then falls upon the applicant to secure the necessary licence from the copyright holder should they wish to make multiple copies or issue copies to the public. If the copyright is vested with the public authority, the Re-Use of Public Sector Regulations 2005, SI 2005/1515 will apply (see **11.10**).

8.6 EIR 2004, REG.12(9): INFORMATION RELATING TO EMISSIONS

Before looking at the remaining exceptions in EIR 2004, reg.2(5)(d)–(f) it is important to recall EIR 2004, reg.12(9) which provides that if:

the environmental information to be disclosed relates to information on emissions, a public authority shall not be entitled to refuse to disclose that information under an exception referred to in paragraphs 5(d) to (g).

When the Commissioner is forced to adjudicate on the use of the exceptions under reg.12(5)(d)–(f) he will normally start his analysis by considering whether the information in question relates to information on emissions. If he concludes that it does then he will not go on to consider the exceptions. For example, see *Department for Business, Enterprise and Regulatory Reform* FER0085500. Public authorities would be well advised to adopt the same approach; there is no point in trying to justify the use of one of the following exceptions if the information relates to information on emissions.

The term 'emissions' is used twice in EIR 2004. First, emissions are included (at EIR 2004, reg.2(1)(b)) in the list of 'factors' which make up the definition of environmental information in so far as the factors are likely to affect one of the elements of the environment (see **3.3**). The term is also used in EIR 2004, reg.12(9). As far as reg.12(9) is concerned, the following points should be noted:

- The term 'emissions' should be given its plain and natural meaning.
- Inclusion of the phrase 'relates to information' means that reg.12(9) is not restricted to cases where information falls within the definition of 'environmental information' only by virtue of EIR 2004, reg.2(1)(b).
- Any environmental information that relates to emissions is capable of falling within EIR 2004, reg.12(9) (i.e. information on activities that affect or are likely to affect emissions). For example:

  – environmental risk assessment information as part of an approval process relating to sheep dip. In view of the manner in which sheepdip may enter the wider environment through drips, sheep walking through water courses, etc. the Commissioner concluded that the information about the impact of such a product constituted information relating to emissions (*Veterinary Medicines Department* FER013760).
  – a report submitted to a government department as part of an application for a grant towards the costs of a power plant. The key aim of the grant scheme was to reduce carbon emissions. The decision to offer a grant or not was likely to affect the reduction of carbon emissions and the grant was a measure designed to protect the elements of the environment by reducing emissions (*Department for Business, Enterprise and Regulatory Reform* FER0085500).

- Emissions are not limited to emissions that have already taken place and could include past, present and future emissions.
- A useful extrinsic aide to the term is provided in Directive 2008/1/EC on integrated pollution prevention and control; 'emissions' are defined as 'the direct or indirect release of substances, vibrations, heat or noise'.

8.7   EIR 2004, REG.12(5)(D): CONFIDENTIALITY OF THE PROCEEDINGS PROVIDED BY LAW

Confidentiality of the proceedings of that or any other public authority where such confidentiality is provided by law – this exception relates to the confidentiality of proceedings of the public authority that receives the request and also the confidentiality of the proceedings of any other public authority. However, the exception is qualified; the confidentiality of the proceedings must be provided for by law. This raises two questions:

1.   Which proceedings are covered?
2.   When are the confidentiality of proceedings provided for by law?

8.7.1   Which proceedings are covered?

EIR 2004 provides no definition of the term 'proceedings'. However, it is clear that the term is not likely to encompass every meeting held or procedure carried out by a public authority, particularly bearing in mind the need to interpret the exceptions restrictively. In order to fall within this exception it appears that proceedings must have a certain level of formality, for example, formal meetings at which deliberations take place on matters within a public authority's jurisdiction.

The following appear to be proceedings under this exception:

- proceedings where a public authority exercises its statutory decision-making powers (for example, a local authority planning committee);
- a range of investigative, regulatory or other activities carried out according to a statutory scheme, for example, consideration of a planning application or a disciplinary hearing;
- legal proceedings (*Archer* v. *Information Commissioner and Salisbury District Council* (EA/2006/0037)) and mediation proceedings;
- the statutory process of investigating and determining objections under the Audit Commission Act 1998 where confidentiality is provided by law (*Mark Heap (District Auditor)* FER0265816);
- the Commissioner's investigation of a complaint under EIR 2004, reg.18 (see **10.10**) (*Information Commissioner* FER029464).

Where the proceedings involve a meeting (for example, a local authority council meeting), the issue of whether information discussed at the meeting falls within this exception depends, according to the Tribunal, on whether the information was prepared exclusively for discussion at the meeting in question. In order to 'qualify' under this exception it would appear that the information must be prepared exclusively for that meeting (see *Archer* v. *Information Commissioner and Salisbury District Council* (EA/2006/0037)).

The Commissioner has rejected the argument that the term is so expansive as to cover 'any' business conducted by a public authority or its officials. For example, correspondence between the Department for Media, Culture and Sport with the Royal Household did not constitute proceedings (FS50154684).

Practical example

Defra held a series of meetings with Tesco and various other supermarkets; the meetings covered, *inter alia*, energy and waste targets. Defra refused to disclose the minutes and details of the meetings citing this exception but the Commissioner rejected the idea that 'discussions' could properly be considered as proceedings, even if the meetings were held on a confidential basis (*Defra* FER0098306/7).

Confidentiality of proceedings provided for by law

A public authority cannot just unilaterally decide that proceedings are 'confidential'; the confidentiality must be provided for by law. The exception does not protect proceedings that a public authority considers should remain confidential; the confidentiality must be provided for by national law, be that the common law or a specific enactment. The Commissioner's stance is that the focus of the exception is on cases where there is a specific statutory provision, although he accepts that, in some cases, the phrase 'where such confidentiality is protected by law' may include the protection given by the courts in the event of action taken for breach of confidence. If disclosure of information obtained during proceedings (such as the Commissioner's investigative proceedings) constitutes a criminal offence then this would indicate that the confidentiality has been provided for by law. To the extent that the proceedings are legal, confidentiality is provided for by the common law in relation to LPP.

Example – Local authorities

The Local Government Act 1972 and the Local Government (Access to Information) Act 1985 aim to provide for greater public access to local authority meetings, reports and documents subject to specified confidentiality provisions. The Local Government Act 1972, s.100A states that:

'The public shall be excluded from a meeting of a principal council during an item of business whenever it is likely, in view of the nature of the business to be transacted or the nature of the proceedings, that, if members of the public were present during that item, confidential information would be disclosed to them in breach of the obligation of confidence; and nothing in this Part shall be taken to authorise or require the disclosure of confidential information in breach of the obligation of confidence.'

Emissions

A public authority cannot use this exception if the information in question relates to information on emissions. In *Department for Business, Enterprise and Regulatory Reform* FER0085500 the Commissioner required the disclosure of a due diligence report prepared by consulting engineers in support of a capital grant scheme application; the report was prepared within the framework of a measure likely to affect emissions of carbon dioxide (CO_2). Consequently, the Commissioner, taking a very broad approach to EIR 2004, reg.12(9), took the view that the information in the report related to emissions and could not be withheld under this exception.

8.7.2 Adversely affects

If disclosure would breach a statutory prohibition on disclosure then it is probable that this would have an adverse effect on the confidentiality of proceedings. If the proceedings are of an investigative and adjudicatory nature, disclosure might hamper the capacity of the public authority to exercise its regulatory or investigative functions, particularly where the information has been supplied by third parties on a voluntary basis (such as witnesses). See, for example, the Information Commissioner's Notice addressed to himself (FER0269464). In *Mark Heap (District Auditor)* FER0265816, the Commissioner accepted the exception was engaged without explaining why there would be any adverse effect. However, the District Auditor was under a statutory duty not to disclose the disputed information unless certain specified circumstances existed; otherwise disclosure was prohibited and constituted a criminal offence. Presumably, the Commissioner considered that this would constitute an adverse effect, although this is a matter of conjecture in this case. In other cases the Commissioner has explained why, in his view, disclosure would not cause adverse effect, but his explanations have remained confidential to the public authority concerned in the event of an appeal by the public authority. (For example, *Colchester Borough Council* FS50196456.)

Note

Although a statutory prohibition on disclosure may be enough to satisfy the adverse affect test, public authorities need to be aware of the provisions of EIR 2004, reg.5(6) which state that any enactment or rule of law that would prevent disclosure in accordance with EIR 2004 will not apply (see **7.1.1**).

8.7.3 Public interest test

Disclosure of information about the proceedings of a public authority will contribute a greater openness and may increase understanding and trust of the public authority and its decision-making processes. Offset against this, releasing information may undermine the work of a public authority. In *Mark Heap (District*

Auditor) FER0265816 there was a public interest in maintaining the confidentiality of the District Auditor's investigations because disclosure could undermine the relationship between him and local authorities and witnesses regarding acquiring information necessary to conduct his investigations.

8.8 EIR 2004, REG.12(5)(E): CONFIDENTIALITY OF COMMERCIAL OR INDUSTRIAL INFORMATION, ETC.

This exception is concerned with the protection of confidential commercial and industrial information, but the potentially wide scope of the exception is limited by two important caveats: the confidentiality must be protected by law and must be provided to protect a legitimate economic interest. The aim of the exception is to avoid disclosure which would adversely affect such legitimate economic interest. The reason for including this exception is clear; public authorities are provided with a substantial amount of information from third parties in the context of, *inter alia*, tenders, contracts, viability reports for planning applications, lease agreements and surveys. Some information will be supplied as part of a legal obligation; other information will be supplied on a cooperative or voluntary basis. Either way, disclosure of commercially sensitive information could expose the public authority or third parties to adverse consequences, for example, by allowing competitors to find out about pricing structures. Moreover, disclosure of confidential information by a public body may result in a breach of the third parties' rights under art.1, Protocol 1 of the ECHR.

In order for the exception to be triggered it is necessary to go through a series of tests/questions:

1. Is the information commercial or industrial in nature?
2. Is the information subject to a duty of confidence which is provided by law?
3. Is confidentiality required to protect a legitimate economic interest?
4. Would the confidentiality required to protect a legitimate economic interest be adversely affected by disclosure?

8.8.1 Is the information commercial or industrial in nature?

The information covered by this exception will be commercially sensitive, such as trade secrets, information supplied by contractors as part of a tendering exercise or information held by regulators. Neither the Tribunal nor the Commission have paid a great deal of attention to this because in the main it is reasonably self-evident that the information in question is either commercial or industrial.

8.8.2 Is the information subject to a duty of confidence which is provided by law?

The party seeking to rely on this exception must establish that it has a right to protect the information by law; this includes domestic statute law, EU legislation and also the common law of confidentiality. It may be the case that the information provided by a third party is done so as part of a regulatory regime (for example, the Environmental Permitting regime) which prescribes that information is provided in confidence; however, even that is not conclusive because it will still be necessary to consider whether disclosure would have an adverse effect and whether the public interest favours disclosure. Alternatively, the confidentiality may arise because of the common law duty of confidence.

Common law duty of confidence

Essentially a duty of confidence arises when confidential information comes to the knowledge of a person (public authority) in circumstances where he has notice, or is held to have agreed, that the information is confidential, with the effect that it would be just in all the circumstances that he should be precluded from disclosing the information to others (*Attorney General* v. *Guardian Newspapers Ltd (No.2)* [1990] 1 AC 109). The common law rules relating to confidentiality and breach of confidence are continually evolving, particularly since the implementation of the Human Rights Act 1998; a detailed examination is outside the scope of this handbook. Readers are commended to read the ICO decision in *Cabinet Office* FS50114757, which refers to the test for breach of confidence laid down in *Coco* v. *AN Clark (Engineers) Ltd* [1969] RPC 41 and the High Court decision in *Secretary of State for the Home Department* v. *British Union for the Abolition of Vivisection and the Information Commissioner* [2008] EWHC 892 (QB) in relation to FOIA 2000, s.41.

The test that the Tribunal uses in relation to this exception was laid down in the *Ofcom* decision (EA/2006/0078). A party relying on this exception must establish:

1. the information has the necessary quality of confidence about it (trivial information will not be confidential);
2. the information has been given in circumstances which give rise to a reasonable expectation that confidentiality would be maintained; and
3. the unauthorised use of that information is to the detriment of the person who provided the information.

The Tribunal will examine any claims about confidentiality by reference to these three requirements, all of which must be satisfied. It will be necessary to examine all the circumstances, including the circumstances in which the information was provided to the public authority, the nature of the information and how such information has previously been handled. In *Ofcom*, for example, the Tribunal decided that the exception was not engaged; although the second and third tests were satisfied, the information did not have the necessary quality of confidence.

Information has the necessary quality of confidence

Information that is trivial, or already in the public domain, does not have the necessary quality of confidence. Information will not have the quality of confidence if it transpires that it has been disclosed to some other person without any obligation of confidence being imposed on them. If the information forms part of a publicly available body of information but in encrypted form it may lose its quality of confidence if it is accessible to anyone with the skill to decrypt (see *Mars* v. *Teknowledge* [2000] FSR 138) or if it takes a great deal of time and effort to extract the information.

Information does not have the quality of confidence merely because the parties have agreed that it should be confidential or because the information has been marked as 'confidential' or 'secret'. The existence of an agreement between the parties that the information is to be treated as confidential is a factor to be taken into account but cannot of itself be conclusive. Even if a document or contract is marked as 'confidential' this does not mean that all of the information contained within it is confidential; certain parts may be commercially confidential whereas as other parts may not. For example, in *R* v. *Secretary of State for the Environment, Transport and the Regions*, ex parte *Alliance Against the Birmingham Northern Relief Road (No.1)* [1999] JPL 231 (a case concerning the corresponding exception under the EIR 1992) the High Court recognised that a compensation provision within a contract was precisely the type of information to which commercial confidentiality attaches.

Information has been given in circumstances which give rise to a reasonable expectation that confidentiality would be maintained

The test laid down in *Coco* v. *AN Clark (Engineers) Ltd* [1969] RPC 41 is invariably the starting point for consideration; it requires an examination of the circumstances to assess whether any reasonable person, standing in the shoes of the recipient of the information (the public authority), would have realised that upon reasonable grounds the information was being provided to him in confidence. The Tribunal will look at all the circumstances of the case and the behaviour and usual practices of the parties. For example, not withstanding that information was supplied during the planning process, which is meant to be open and public, the usual practice of Bristol City Council, at the relevant time, was that viability reports and cost estimates were accepted in confidence (*Bristol City Council* v. *Information Commissioner* (EA/2010/0012)). The supplier of the information therefore had a reasonable expectation that confidentiality would be maintained.

Difficulties arise when information is provided where there is no express statement that the information is confidential but there is a belief that the information will be maintained as confidential. For example, in *North Western and North Wales Sea Fisheries Committee* v. *Information Commissioner* (EA/2007/0133) information was provided by leaseholders under a duty arising from a lease which did not contain an express confidentiality clause; although not determinative, this was a relevant consideration when determining whether the information had the necessary quality of confidence. In the *Fisheries* case the Tribunal considered that since the information was provided to a public authority that had obligations over a fishery that was within a Site of Special Scientific Interest (SSSI) and a Special Protection Area (SPA), which are not privately owned, this was a strong indicator that the information provided would be open to wider public scrutiny.

Confidential information is protected by the ECHR

The party seeking to rely on this exception must establish that it has a right to protect the information by law and this includes ECHR, art.1, Protocol 1. In *Veolia* v. *Nottinghamshire County Council* [2010] EWCA 1214, Rix LJ concluded that valuable commercial confidential information could amount to a possession for the purposes of ECHR, art.1, Protocol 1. Unrestricted disclosure of such information would amount to an interference with the art.1, Protocol 1 right to possession. The Tribunal considered the effect of *Veolia* in *Staffordshire County Council* v. *Information Commissioner & Sibelco* [2010] UKFTT 573 (GRC) and elaborated the following points in relation to this exception:

- disclosure of confidential information by a public authority engages the ECHR rights of the holder of the confidence;
- EIR 2004 must have an exception read into it to exempt the disclosure of confidential information in order to give effect to those ECHR rights;
- the rights conferred by art.1, Protocol 1 are qualified and subject to the application of the public interest test and there is a strong public interest in the maintenance of valuable commercially confidential information.

In *Nottinghamshire County Council* v. *Information Commissioner* (EA/2010/0142) the Tribunal held that if information amounted to a possession under art.1, Protocol 1 then there was also a right to privacy in respect of that information under ECHR, art.8(1). Article 8(1) is a qualified right and breaches of art.8 rights may be justified. In the Tribunal's view the balancing exercise required in art.8 cases could be done by the public interest test under EIR 2004.

8.8.3 Is confidentiality required to protect a legitimate economic interest?

If the commercially confidential information does not protect a legitimate economic interest then the exception cannot apply. Economic interests in activities that are unlawful cannot be protected under this provision. The economic interest will depend on the nature of the information.

Practical example

South Gloucester Council successfully engaged this exception in relation to a development appraisal report prepared by consultants. The report was prepared to assist the Council in negotiating a s.106 planning agreement (under the Town and Country Planning Act 1990) with a development company. The Tribunal held that the purpose of the s.106 agreement was to secure an economic advantage and therefore protected the council's legitimate economic interest (*South Gloucestershire Council* FER0127659)

8.8.4 Would disclosure adversely affect the confidentiality required to protect a legitimate economic interest?

The question is whether the disclosure of the confidential information would adversely affect the legitimate economic interests that such confidentially was designed to protect. The obvious adverse effect of disclosure is that a public authority exposes itself to an action for breach of confidence and the consequent costs to the authority, but strictly speaking this is not relevant at this stage; it does however, become a very significant consideration at the public interest stage. Factors to consider in assessing the adverse effect include:

- whether disclosure will prejudice the commercial interests of the person who provided the information (for example, disclosure to competitors, suppliers or potential contractors – see *Yorkshire Water* FS50172335);
- the nature of the market in which the supplier of information operates; for example, in a market with few suppliers and customers, disclosure of price-sensitive information could lead to price parallelism and the diminution of competition;
- whether the adverse effect is such that the third party would be able to obtain redress through the courts;
- whether the information has been made available to the public in some other way and whether this has caused any adverse effect. For example, a company may refuse to allow the disclosure of information which it has already made available in some other form via a planning application.

The decision notice issued against *East Sussex County Council* FER0099394 provides a detailed examination of the adverse effect test in relation to information supplied during a tendering exercise.

8.8.5 Public interest test

It has already been noted that disclosure of confidential information engages the ECHR right of the holder of the confidence. In *Staffordshire County Council (and Sibelco)* v. *Information Commissioner* (EA/2010/0015) the Tribunal considered (in the light of the Court of Appeal's decision in the *Veolia* case (see **8.8.2**)), that the

144

presumption in favour of disclosure of all environmental information must now be read subject to an exception in the case of any environmental information which is held by a public authority subject to a legal duty of confidentiality. This represents a quite radical departure from the wording of EIR 2004. In short, the presumption in favour of disclosure is effectively displaced for this exception (if the Tribunal's interpretation of the *Veolia* case is correct). The consequence of this is that it may be more difficult for the public to access environmental information that is subject to a duty of confidence.

The types of arguments that have been rehearsed in favour of maintaining the exception include:

- There is a public interest in public bodies abiding by agreements, made in good faith, in respect of information provided to them on a voluntary basis.
- Disclosure will damage a public authority's reputation for maintaining confidential information and this could deter third parties from dealing with the public authority or supplying information to them.
- Disclosure may result in third parties being unwilling to continue to supply information on a voluntary basis, thus hampering the ability of a public authority to fulfil its statutory functions (see *Staffordshire County Council* v. *Information Commissioner* (EA/2010/0015); [2010] UKFTT 573 (GRC)).
- Disclosure will result in the public authority being exposed to an action for breach of confidence. It is not necessary for the public authority to be actually sued but it will be necessary to look at all the circumstances to consider whether, in the event of disclosure, there would be a reasonable expectation that an action, if brought, would succeed.
- The information is already available in an aggregated form sufficient to provide information to the public and there is little or no public interest in it being available in a disaggregated form so as to reveal the position of individual companies.

Arguments that favour disclosure include:

- The information concerns the use of public land or an area protected by environmental protection legislation (see, in particular, *North Western and North Wales Sea Fisheries Committee* v. *Information Commissioner* (EA/2007/0133) where the information related to mussel farming in an SSSI.
- The information relates to an activity that has an adverse effect on the environment, for example, mining, and there is a strong public interest in the public knowing the human and environmental consequences associated with such activities.
- The information relates to an environmental decision (such as planning permission) which is likely to have significant effects on the environment and therefore falls within the public participation limb of the Aarhus Convention.
- Disclosure will enable the public/local communities to participate fully in the above mentioned decision-making processes.

145

- The need to ensure that public authorities act scrupulously in decisions in which they have a vested interest.

For a particularly useful examination of the public interest balancing exercise in relation to this exception, see *Staffordshire County Council* v. *Information Commissioner* [2010] UKFTT 573 (GRC) (EA/2010/0015).

8.8.6 Difference between EIR 2004, reg.12(5)(e) and FOIA 2000, s.41

EIR 2004, reg.12(5)(e) exception is broader than the corresponding FOIA. s.41 exemption, which is expressly limited to information received in confidence by a public authority where disclosure by the authority would amount to an actionable breach of confidence. EIR 2004 exception (unlike FOIA 2000, s.41) applies to commercially confidential information that belongs to the authority or that has been disclosed to the authority by a third party.

It has been argued that the words 'provided by law' should be limited to meaning 'imposed on the public authority by law' and the exception should only apply where the public authority owes a duty of confidentiality to a person from whom it had obtained information, and not where a confidentiality obligation is owed to the public authority. However, the Tribunal has rejected such an interpretation. Wherever the law recognises the confidentiality of the information as deserving of legal protection, the confidentiality is provided by law (see *South Gloucester County Council* v. *Information Commissioner* (EA/2009/0032)).

8.8.7 Implications for the private sector

A third party supplier of information (such as a contractor) may seek to prevent the information from being disclosed by marking it as confidential but, as was noted at **8.8.2**, this is not determinative. Where a third party is concerned that there may be requests for disclosure under EIR 2004 or FOIA 2000 they would be well advised to supply the public authority with cogent evidence why the information should be protected as commercially or industrially confidential and also justify a period for the information to remain confidential. The latter point is suggested in recognition of the fact that information may cease to be sensitive over time and the exception should be limited to the minimum time necessary to protect the commercial or industrial interest.

Emissions

Information on emissions can never be deemed commercially confidential. The result is that, even if EIR 2004, reg.12(5)(e) is engaged, the effect of reg.12(9) is that the exception may not be relied on.

8.9   EIR 2004, REG.12(5)(F): INTERESTS OF THE PERSON PROVIDING THE INFORMATION

A public authority may not disclose information where disclosure would adversely affect the interests of a person who has voluntarily provided that information. EIR 2004 do not actually define who is a person for these purposes but it must be taken to mean any natural or legal person.

This exception may only apply if the person who supplied the information:

1.   was not under (and could not have been put under) a legal obligation to supply it to that or any other public authority;
2.   did not supply it in circumstances such that that or any other public authority was entitled apart from EIR 2004 to disclose it; and
3.   has not consented to its disclosure.

All three conditions must be satisfied, which means that this will be a difficult exception to engage.

8.9.1   The person voluntarily supplied the information

The person must have supplied the information to the public authority on a voluntary basis; they will not be deemed to have voluntarily supplied it if they were required to supply it by law or could have been required to supply it by law. Examples of where information is supplied voluntarily include:

- the submission of views to a public authority during a consultation process – there is no requirement that the public does this (*Dainton* v. *Information Commissioner* (EA/2007/0020));
- reporting a pollution incident – this could also be used to protect whistleblowers;
- informal pre-planning application correspondence between a developer and a local planning authority (*Redcar and Cleveland Borough Council* FER0066999);
- informal discussions with a regulatory body prior to submission of an application for some form of environmental permit.

8.9.2   The person did not supply it in circumstances such that that or any other public authority was entitled apart from EIR 2004 to disclose it

The exception will not apply if the person voluntarily supplied the information in circumstances where the public authority is entitled to disclose it under a provision other than EIR 2004. For example, a person may supply information to a public authority for inclusion on a public register (see **Chapter 11**). However, in the main, such information is usually provided as a result of some other statutory provision, in which case the first condition of this exception would not apply. However, it may be the case that a person supplies additional information on a voluntary basis but the circumstances are such that the public authority would be entitled to disclose it. For example, the operator of an environmental permit is required to provide certain information for inclusion on the public register but he may choose to supply additional information which is not strictly required; where this happens this exception will not apply.

8.9.3   The person has not consented to its disclosure

If the person supplying the information has consented to disclosure, the exception cannot apply. The person supplying the information may at the time of supply expressly or impliedly make it clear that they do not consent to disclosure. If the public authority is not certain then it should consult the party providing the information to ascertain whether they are willing to consent to disclosure. The Defra guidance suggests that suppliers of volunteered information should be encouraged to consent to release where appropriate and such consent can be sought in advance, when the information is collected, but can be sought later in response to a particular request or in order to proactively disseminate the information.

8.9.4   Adversely affects

It is the interests of the provider of the information that would be adversely affected, as opposed to the interests of the public authority. Whether the person providing the information will be adversely affected will depend on the circumstances of the case. For example, where information supplied is by way of a complaint, revealing the identity of the person who supplied the information could have an undesirable effect on the relationship between the complainant and the person complained of, and this would be sufficient to cause an adverse effect. However, it may be possible to redact any information which reveals the identity of person who supplied the information to avoid causing any adverse effect to him or her.

8.9.5   Public interest test

The public interest vested in this exception includes the following arguments:

- Disclosure of information supplied on a voluntary basis may result in an unwillingness to disclose further information and such loss of cooperation would not be in the public interest. For example, tipping off regulatory bodies about pollution incidents and environmental crimes must be in the public interest.
- There is public interest in safeguarding the free flow of information to public authorities to enable them to fulfil a variety of functions more effectively.

- Public authorities with regulatory responsibilities for the environment (such as local authorities and the Environment Agency) often seek to develop constructive dialogue with those bodies that they regulate and this could be undermined if information voluntarily supplied as part of this process was disclosed to the world at large.
- There is a public interest in developers being able to approach planning authorities for frank and confidential advice before submitting planning applications.

On the other hand, there are some strong public interests in favour of disclosure which include:

- Disclosure would lead to more transparency and could improve public confidence in regulatory regimes and promote understanding of why decisions were taken.
- Disclosure would enable the public to understand the nature of the relationship between, for example, a local planning authority and a developer and ensure that the developer did not exert any undue influence.
- Also in the context of planning issues, which are often emotive and provoke considerable response from the public, local planning authorities should be as open as possible about the planning process so as to ensure important debates are not clouded by accusations of malpractice or maladministration.
- Protecting individuals from malicious complaints and avoiding the waste of public resources investigating such complaints.

In assessing the relative balance of public interests it will be necessary to have regard to the sensitivity of the information (see *Foreign and Commonwealth Office* FER0081530).

Emissions

If the information requested is information on emissions into the environment then this exception is not available and the information should be released (EIR 2004, reg.12(9)).

8.9.6 Contrast with FOIA 2000, s.41 exemption

The broadly corresponding FOIA 2000 exemption is s.41. Under FOIA 2000 this is an absolute exemption; however, it is also a more limited exemption. Under FOIA 2000, s.41 information is only protected by the exemption if the information was obtained by the public authority from any other person (including a public authority) and the disclosure of the information to the public (other than under FOIA 2000) would constitute an actionable breach of confidence by that other person. EIR 2004, reg.12(5)(f), albeit subject to the adverse effect test and the public interest balancing exercise, is not so narrowly defined.

8.10 EIR 2004, REG.12(5)(G): PROTECTION OF THE ENVIRONMENT

A public authority may refuse to supply environmental information in order to protect the environment to which it relates. This is perhaps the most logical and important of all the exceptions, at least in the context of the overarching aims of EIR 2004. There is no corresponding exemption under FOIA 2000. At the time of writing there was only one ICO decision (*Department for Business, Enterprise and Regulatory Reform* FER0085500) and no Tribunal decisions relating to this exception. Therefore, there is a lack of guidance about the way in which this exception has been interpreted. However, when assessing the adverse effect and the public interest test, public authorities are recommended to consult with relevant nature conservation public authorities. Information is also available from the National Biodiversity Network website (**www.nbn.org.uk**) and public authorities are recommended to consult this when considering whether to engage this exception.

The Defra guidance cites disclosure of information about the location of nesting sites, rare habitats and vulnerable archaeological sites as examples of information that may be protected by this exception. It also suggests that information about possible SSSIs should not normally be made available until a formal notice is served, especially if there is any risk that making information available prematurely could result in pre-emptive damage being caused to a site before it was protected.

8.10.1 Adversely affects and the public interest test

For the exception to be engaged the public authority must be able to establish that disclosure would adversely affect the environment and must apply the considerations laid down in the *Archer* case discussed at **8.1.1**. In the absence of any decisions relating to this, one can only surmise about the degree of evidence that would be required to establish that there 'would' be an adverse effect. However, it must be recalled that disclosure is to the world at large. So, for example, even if the applicant is a sympathetic body such as the RSPB, it is more likely than not that the information could be used by a person to damage the environment.

It will rarely be in the public interest to release information that would result in damage to the environment or prejudice the ability of a public authority to promote or engage in policies that protect the environment.

This exception was considered in *Department for Business, Enterprise and Regulatory Reform* FER0085500 where the Department withheld information relating to an application to the Bio Energy Capital Grants Scheme for grant aid towards a power plant. Amongst the purposes of the grants scheme was the reduction of carbon dioxide emissions as a means to combat climate change. The Department believed that any disclosure of information that may dissuade potential future applicants from applying to the Bio-Energy Capital Grants Scheme would adversely affect the protection of the environment. Unfortunately, there is no discussion of this exception because the Commissioner concluded that the information requested had to be disclosed by virtue of EIR 2004, reg.12(9), which applied to the whole of the disputed report.

Emissions

As noted at **8.6** this exception does not apply to information which relates to emissions.

CHAPTER 9

Environmental information and personal data

Andrew Watson

9.1 INTRODUCTION

The Data Protection Act (DPA) 1998 was introduced in order to comply with the Data Protection Directive (Council Directive 95/46/EC on the protection of individuals with regard to the processing of personal data and on the free movement of such data). DPA 1998 provides legal standards on how organisations use the personal data of individuals ('the data protection principles') as well as giving a range of rights to individuals to access and control how their data is used.

DPA 1998 overlaps with EIR 2004 where the information requested is both environmental information and also about individuals.

EIR 2004 contains two data protection related exceptions. These cover two situations:

- first, where the information is about the person making the request; and
- second, where it is about third parties.

EIR 2004, reg.5(3) covers the situation where the person makes a request for information which includes personal data about themselves. In those circumstances there is no obligation to disclose the personal data under EIR 2004. Instead the person may access that information directly via DPA 1998.

Where third party information is sought then EIR 2004, reg.12(3) only permits disclosure where EIR 2004, reg.13 can be complied with. Unlike the other EIR exceptions this is mostly an absolute exception. While the public interest test applies to all of the other EIR exceptions it only applies to part of the personal data exception.

However, before a public authority can begin to apply these exceptions it must understand when DPA 1998 applies. Not all information held by an organisation about individuals is caught by DPA 1998.

9.2 DATA PROTECTION DEFINITIONS

The obligations under DPA 1998 are imposed on 'data controllers'. The data controller is the organisation which decides how and why the data should be used. In the majority of cases this will be the public authority which is dealing with the EIR 2004 request. The 'data subject' is the individual who is the subject of the information.

DPA 1998 only applies if the information being dealt with is 'personal data'. Before information about an individual is caught by the Act two questions must be answered:

1. Is the information data?
2. If it is data then is it personal?

If you cannot answer yes to both of these questions then DPA 1998 does not apply and you cannot rely on EIR 2004, regs.5 or 13 to refuse to disclose the information.

9.2.1 What is data?

Data does not just mean written documents. It can include electronic, visual, audio or other forms of recorded information. DPA 1998, s.1 provides five categories of information which count as data.

'Data' is defined as information which:

(a) is being processed by equipment operating automatically in response to instructions given for that purpose;
(b) is recorded with the intention that it should be processed by means of such equipment;

The above two categories essentially include all information which is held electronically or intended to be held electronically. It includes information held on the whole range of electronic gadgets which have become so prevalent in modern life. It will include information held on PCs, in emails, and on laptops, mobile phones, iPads or digital cameras.

(c) is recorded as part of a relevant filing system or with the intention that it should form part of a relevant filing system;

A relevant filing system is defined as:

> any set of information relating to individuals to the extent that, although the information is not processed by means of equipment operating automatically in response to instructions given for that purpose, the set is structured, either by reference to individuals or by reference to criteria relating to individuals, in such a way that specific information relating to a particular individual is readily accessible.

In his technical guidance on 'Determining what information is data for the purposes of the DPA' the Information Commissioner advises that the key issue is:

the existence of a structure to the record keeping which facilitates ready access to information and an understanding that the structure will be used whenever a new record is added to the information set.

The Court of Appeal put the level of sophistication required by a filing system rather more highly. In *Durant* v. *Financial Services Authority* [2003] EWCA Civ 1746 the court held that a relevant filing system was one which had 'a level of sophistication equivalent to that of a computerised file'.

It is worth bearing in mind that a relevant filing system does not have to consist of a row of cabinets, drawers and files. The key issue is the ease with which you can access information about individuals from the system rather than the physical format of the data.

(d)   does not fall within (a), (b) or (c) but forms part of an accessible record as defined by section 68;

Accessible records are defined in DPA 1998, s.68 and include health, education, housing and social services records. This category is only used if the data does not otherwise fall into categories (a)–(c).

(e)   is recorded information held by a public authority and does not fall within any of paragraphs (a) to (d).

Category (e) is a catch-all provision introduced by FOIA 2000. Essentially, it makes all records held by public authorities count as data, regardless of the form or format in which they are held.

9.2.2   Is the data personal?

Even if information is 'data' within the meaning of DPA 1998, it is also necessary to decide whether the data is personal. If data is not personal data then the provisions of DPA 1998 do not apply and nor can either of the exceptions in EIR 2004 be relied on. It is therefore vital to always establish whether information is data within the general definition discussed above and then whether it is personal data.

'Personal data' is defined in DPA 1998, s.1 as data which relates to a living individual who can be identified from that data, or be identified from that data and other information which is in the possession of, or is likely to come into the possession of, the data controller. The definition includes 'any expression of opinion about the individual and any indication of the intentions of the data controller or any other person in respect of the individual'.

9.2.3   Does the data relate to an identifiable living individual?

The provisions of DPA 1998 only apply to individuals. If the information is about a company, society or other non-individual then the exception does not apply. However, it is worth bearing in mind that information about sole traders or partnerships may well identify individuals and therefore be caught by DPA 1998. In addition, the Act only applies to living individuals. Information about the deceased is not covered by DPA 1998 even if it would otherwise be private, personal or embarrassing.

Even if the information is about individuals it must still not be possible to identify them from the data or other data held or likely to be held. This does not just include information where individuals are named. The use of identifiers, markers or other systems for separating out records of different people will suffice. If it is possible to distinguish data about one individual from that data about others then the individual will be identifiable.

However, even if the data is about an identifiable living individual it will still not necessarily be 'personal data'. The data must relate to the individual which has been an issue of some controversy.

In the leading case of *Durant* v. *Financial Services Authority* [2003] EWCA Civ 1746 Lord Justice Auld identified two concepts which he felt were of assistance in deciding whether data was personal data within DPA 1998. The first of these was that the information should be 'biographical' in that it should go beyond simply a record of a data subject's participation in an event which has no personal significance and 'in respect of which his privacy could not be said to be compromised'. The second notion was that the information must have the data subject as its focus as opposed to some other event in which he had an interest. Essentially, the data must affect the individual's privacy, whether in their personal or family life, professional or business capacity.

Practical example

In *Department for Business, Enterprise and Regulatory Reform v. Information Commissioner* (EA/2007/0072), Friends of the Earth sought disclosure of details of meetings and correspondence between Minsters and senior civil servants with members of the Confederation of British Industry in relation to energy policy. The information sought included letters, minutes and other documents which included the names of a range of different civil servants. The Tribunal held that the names of people in those documents were personal data as they would have biographical significance for the individuals. The information recorded the individuals' employers, where they were at a particular time and that they took part in a meeting which might be of career or business significance.

The Information Commissioner has provided guidance on when personal data will relate to an individual ('Data Protection Technical Guidance: Determining What is Personal Data' (2007)). The Commissioner identifies a series of points to consider when determining whether data is personal:

(a)   the data is obviously about an individual;

(b)   the data is linked to an individual such that you can obtain information about them;

(c)   the data can be used to inform or influence actions or decisions about the individual;
(d)   the data has biographical significance to the individual;
(e)   the data focuses on the individual;
(f)   the data might impact on an individual whether in their family, personal, business or professional life.

If it is determined that the information requested is personal data then the exceptions in EIR 2004, regs.5 and 13 may apply. However, there is an additional category of personal data which is important to identify – 'sensitive personal data'.

Sensitive personal data is subject to more restrictions as to how and when it can be used. This will be relevant when trying to apply the exceptions and one must therefore be able to distinguish between normal and sensitive personal data.

Sensitive personal data is personal data which consists of information as to the data subject's:

(a)   racial or ethnic origin;
(b)   political opinions;
(c)   religious beliefs or beliefs of a similar nature;
(d)   membership of a trade union;
(e)   physical or mental health or condition;
(f)   sexual life;
(g)   involvement in the commission or alleged commission of a criminal offence;
(h)   involvement in criminal proceedings, their disposal or sentence.

9.3   HOW DO THE EXCEPTIONS WORK?

Once it has been determined whether or not the information requested is personal data then decide whether or not one of the exceptions applies.

EIR 2004, reg.5(3) provides that:

> To the extent that the information requested includes personal data of which the applicant is the data subject, paragraph (1) shall not apply to those personal data.

Essentially, if the applicant asks for their own personal information then there is no obligation for a public authority to provide it under EIR 2004. This does not mean that they are unable to access that information; it simply means that the authority should not provide it under EIR 2004.

DPA 1998 includes a provision allowing individuals to gain access to their own personal data. DPA 1998, s.7 allows an individual to request copies of any or all of his or her personal data which is held by the data controller. Such requests must be made in writing and satisfy that he or she is the data subject, and a fee may be charged. Fees can vary depending on the sector and there is a maximum of 40 calendar days allowed to provide the information.

If an applicant makes a request for his or her own personal data, which is also environmental information, then the request can be refused under EIR 2004. It should then be treated as a subject access request under DPA 1998, s.7. If the EIR 2004 request has been made orally then the requestor can be asked to remake it in writing and to pay the fee. The time to reply will not begin to run until these conditions are met.

EIR 2004, reg.12(3) provides that:

> To the extent that the [environmental] information requested includes personal data of which the applicant is not the data subject, the personal data shall not be disclosed otherwise than in accordance with regulation 13.

EIR 2004, reg.13 provides that third party personal data may only be withheld where one of two conditions is met. The first condition is that the disclosure of the personal data to a member of the public:

(a)   would contravene any of the data protection principles; or
(b)   would contravene section 10 of DPA 1998 and in all the circumstances of the case, the public interest in not disclosing the information outweighs the public interest in disclosing it; or
(c)   otherwise than under the regulations would contravene any of the data protection principles if the exemptions in DPA 1998, s.33A(1) were disregarded.

Paragraph (c) applies to category (e) personal data (see **9.2** above). Category (e) data is generally exempt from the operation of many sections of the Act, including many of the principles. This paragraph effectively means that all forms of personal data are treated equally when deciding whether or not the data protection principles apply.

The second condition is that the information is exempt from DPA 1998, s.7(1) (the subject access provisions).

9.3.1   What are the data protection principles?

There are eight data protection principles which set out the minimum expected standards which data controllers should meet when dealing with personal data. They are as follows:

1.   Personal data must be processed fairly and lawfully and in accordance with a condition in Schedule 2 or Schedules 2 and 3 in the case of sensitive personal data.
2.   Personal data should only be obtained for one or more specified and lawful purposes and must not be used for any other incompatible purpose.
3.   Personal data must be adequate, relevant and not excessive in relation to the purpose it is being processed for.
4.   Personal data must be accurate and where necessary kept up to date.

5.   Personal data must not be kept for longer than is necessary.
6.   Personal data must be processed in accordance with the rights of the data subject.
7.   Appropriate technical and organisational measures must be taken to prevent the unauthorised or unlawful use of the data or its accidental loss or damage.
8.   Personal data must not be transferred outside of the European Economic Area unless the destination country provides an adequate level of protection in relation to the data.

When considering whether or not the exception applies, the first principle is usually the most relevant as it contains the most general and wide ranging obligation on data controllers.

Practical example

In *De Mello* v. *Information Commission and the Environment Agency* (EA/2008/0054) the applicant was the subject of an investigation by the Environment Agency (EA) following a complaint about a septic tank on his property. He sought disclosure of the details of the complaint and the person who made it. The EA provided some basic details of the nature of the complaint but no more. The Tribunal found that a person making a complaint to a public authority had an implicit expectation of confidentiality and that their personal data would not be disclosed. As such, release of their personal data would be a clear breach of the first principle in that disclosure would be unfair to the data subject and the appeal was therefore rejected. It is, however, worth bearing in mind that the Tribunal specifically commented that if the EA had checked with the complainant about whether or not he objected to disclosure then significant expense might have been avoided.

There are three elements to consider when applying the first data protection principle:

1.   Is the disclosure lawful?
2.   Is the disclosure fair?
3.   Can the disclosure meet one of the qualifying conditions in Schedules 2 and/or 3?

The issue of lawfulness is unlikely to arise as disclosure under EIR 2004 will provide a lawful basis to disclose. That is not to say that lawfulness should be ignored. While 'lawfulness' is not defined in DPA 1998, it has been defined as 'something which is contrary to some law or enactment or is done without lawful justification or excuse' (*R* v. *R* [1991] 4 All ER 481). Therefore the existence of, for example, a statutory bar on disclosure would prevent disclosure being lawful and the exception would apply.

Whether or not disclosure will be fair is a fact-specific issue which will vary in every case. However, the Information Commissioner has identified a number of factors which are likely to be relevant when deciding on the issue of fairness such as:

1.   What is the nature of the information and how serious are the consequences of disclosure on the individual?
2.   How was the information obtained and is it in the public domain?
3.   What are the reasonable expectations of the individual about what might be done with their data?
4.   Where does the balance lie between the impact on the individual and the principle of transparency and openness in EIR 2004?
5.   What are the legitimate interests of the public in having access to the information?

Defra suggests in its guidance that it is permissible to ask the applicant why they want to see another person's personal data when assessing the issue of fairness. This is at odds with the Information Commissioner's approach which requires a balance to be struck between the effect on the individual and the legitimate interests of the public at large, rather than necessarily the particular interests of the applicant.

Practical example

In *Surrey Heath Borough Council and Keith McCullen* v. *Information Commissioner* (EA/ 2010/0034) the applicant sought disclosure of information relating to a grant of planning permission. The applicant was concerned that a planning officer had received more favourable treatment than a member of the public would have. The council's monitoring officer had completed an investigation into the allegations and provided a report. The council withheld the report but provided a précis. The applicant sought the remainder of the material. On appeal it was decided that much of the material was both environmental information as well as being the personal data of a range of people including members of the local authority's staff, a planning agent and the person seeking planning permission. The Tribunal found that it would not be unfair to disclose a number of items of personal data for a variety of reasons. These included, for example, that the report contained no criticism of the person it related to; the professional role of a number of the individuals; that the data was an assessment of the way some planning officers had done their job; and, even where the report was critical, the fact that it was about the authority's CEO meant disclosure would not be unfair. The Tribunal also found that disclosure of some of the material would be unfair but that it should still have been disclosed but redacted.

The DPA 1998 Schedule conditions provide a justification for processing personal data and data controllers must be able to identify a relevant condition whenever they process personal data. As such, when considering the exception in EIR 2004 the public authority must consider whether or not the proposed disclosure would meet one of the conditions in Sched.2. If the data is sensitive personal data then the authority must also identify a condition in Sched.3.

9.3.2   Schedule 2 conditions

The Sched.2 conditions are:

1.   the data subject has given consent;
2.   the processing is necessary for the performance of a contract to which the data subject is a party;
3.   the processing is necessary for the data controller to comply with a legal obligation to which they are subject except where it is imposed by a contract;
4.   the processing is necessary to protect the vital interests of the data subject;
5.   the processing is necessary for the exercise of various public functions;
6.   the processing is necessary for the purpose of legitimate interests.

Additional conditions have been added in statutory instruments but they are not likely to be applicable when dealing with a request for information. Of these conditions it is condition 6 which is most often referred to when considering whether or not disclosure under EIR 2004 could be justified.

9.3.3   How does the 'legitimate interests' condition work?

Schedule 2(6) provides that processing personal data will be justified where:

> the processing is necessary for the purpose of legitimate interests pursued by the data controller or a third party to whom the data are disclosed, except where the processing is unwarranted in any particular case by reason of prejudice to the rights and freedoms or legitimate interests of the data subject.

Essentially, this condition means that an applicant may be able to seek disclosure of personal data where they have a legitimate interest in receiving it unless that disclosure would create an unwarranted interference with the data subject's rights. The condition effectively imports a form of public interest test into what is otherwise an absolute exception.

The issue of disclosure of personal data is one which has arisen in numerous cases. The most well known of these is *Corporate Officer of House of Commons* v. *Information Commissioner* (EA/2007/0060) which dealt with the issue of MPs' expenses. While this case related to an application under FOIA 2000, the issues under that Act when looking at the disclosure of personal data are the same as under EIR 2004.

Here the Tribunal stressed that when applying Sched.2(6) regard had to be had to the Data Protection Directive and to art.8 of the ECHR. The provisions were aimed at protecting the privacy of the individual and disclosure should only occur where it was necessary, that is, there was a pressing social need, and where the interference with the individual's private life was justified and proportionate to the aim which was being pursued.

In making its decision the Tribunal drew upon two questions asked in *Samaroo* v. *Secretary of State for the Home Department* [2001] EWCA Civ 1139):

1.   Can the legitimate aims of the applicant be achieved in ways which interfere less with the privacy of the data subject (which might include their families or others around them)?

2.   If the aims of the requestor cannot be met by less intrusive means then would the disclosure have an excessive or disproportionate adverse effect on the legitimate interests of the data subject?

Practical example

In *Imogen Bickford-Smith* v. *Information Commissioner* (EA/2010/0032) the applicant sought release from the Rural Payments Agency of details of claims for subsidies made in relation to 'Adjacent Commons' under the single payment scheme. This information was both environmental, as it related to the administration of land in the New Forest, and personal, as it included names, addresses and other details of individuals. The Tribunal held that the applicant did have a legitimate interest in disclosure of the personal data which related to successful applications by sole traders or partnerships. There was a general public interest in transparency and scrutiny of a public authority's actions and the scheme involved significant amounts of public money and had been subject to some controversy. However, this only applied to successful applicants who had received funds and therefore it would be unfair to disclose details of unsuccessful applicants. Information about applicants who were not sole traders or partnerships would be released as in those cases the information would not be personal data and therefore the exception could not apply. It is, however, worth bearing in mind that in this case the Tribunal also considered that the impact on the privacy of the individuals affected would be limited.

When deciding whether or not the disclosure would be an unwarranted interference with the rights of the data subject, the Tribunal will take into account a range of factors.

The knowledge of the data subject will be an issue. The Tribunal will look at what information was given to the individual when their information was collected, what they were told would happen to it and what their reasonable expectations might be. However, overarching claims that information will not be disclosed are unlikely to be effective, especially where the personal data relates to someone within the public sector. Organisations cannot rely on blanket claims that they will never disclose information as these fail to give any consideration to the impact of EIR 2004 or FOIA 2000.

However, that is not to say that a claim to confidentiality or non-disclosure is irrelevant. For example, where a specific confidentiality agreement has been entered into, this will create a strong argument that disclosure of that information would be an unwarranted interference as the agreement creates a reasonable expectation that the information will not be disclosed.

The extent to which an individual might have a reasonable expectation that their information will not be disclosed will vary depending on the circumstances of the case. The nature of the information is important; it will determine the extent to which there is interference in private life. However, the status of the individual is also a key consideration. The Information Commissioner and the Tribunal have both accepted that those who hold public office and who are responsible for public expenditure or those who hold senior positions have a lower expectation of privacy where it relates to their public role. In such circumstances they can, and should, expect greater scrutiny, even where it reveals information about their private lives.

Practical example

In *Creekside Forum* v. *Information Commissioner and the Department for Culture, Media and Sport* (EA/2008/0065) members of a local pressure group sought details of the information considered by the Department when making a decision about whether or not Borthwick Wharf should be subject to a certificate of immunity from listing. These papers included representations made by a number of individuals, some in a private capacity and others on behalf of various organisations. The Department had a policy in place that those who made submissions on a personal basis would not be identified and those who wrote on behalf of organisations would not be identified if they expressed a concern at being identified. The Tribunal found that those who made submissions on a personal basis had a legitimate expectation of privacy which outweighed the legitimate interests of the pressure group. Disclosure of their details would expose them to further lobbying or disputes given the local nature of the issues. The individuals were acting in a private capacity and were not publically accountable. However, the Tribunal also found that those acting on behalf of an organisation had a much lower expectation of privacy. Their personal data would be disclosed unless they had previously expressed a concern about release or they were a junior member of the organisation with limited responsibility or accountability.

9.3.4   Schedule 3 conditions

Where the information which is requested is sensitive personal data then disclosure of it will breach the first principle if there is no qualifying Sched.3 condition. These conditions mirror, to an extent, those under Sched.2 but are generally narrower. However, there is no equivalent in Sched.3 to the legitimate interest condition in Sched.2. As such it is much more difficult to identify any relevant conditions which might apply where the information is sensitive personal data.

In such circumstances it is unlikely that the disclosure of sensitive personal data can be justified under EIR 2004. However, it may be possible to disclose the data if it can be rendered anonymous. In such circumstances it would cease to be personal data and therefore the exception would not apply.

9.4   SECTION 10 OF DPA 1998

EIR 2004, reg.12(3) exception will also apply if the disclosure would breach DPA 1998, s.10. Section 10 provides that a data subject may give notice to a data controller to require them to stop, or not to start, processing their personal data where the processing is likely to cause substantial damage or substantial distress and that the damage or distress is unwarranted. Such a notice is not effective where any of the first four conditions in Sched.2 apply (see **9.3.2**).

When such a notice is served the data controller must decide whether or not to accept it and, if it is accepted, the extent to which it is accepted. If the data controller rejects the notice then the individual can seek to enforce it through an application to the county court.

Where a data subject has provided a s.10 notice which has been accepted by the data controller or enforced by the court then the exception in EIR 2004, reg.12(3) arises and disclosure may not be permitted. However, this part of the exception is qualified and therefore the public interest test will apply (see **Chapter 7**).

9.5 SUBJECT ACCESS

The second condition which applies when deciding whether or not the exception applies is where the information is exempt from DPA 1998, s.7. Section 7(1) gives every individual a right to know what information is held about them by a data controller and to be provided with a copy of the data. This right is, however, subject to a number of exemptions. Where those apply then the exception in EIR 2004 may also apply. This effectively means that an applicant cannot gain access to personal data about an individual which the individual himself or herself could not gain access to.

However, this part of the exception is qualified and therefore the public interest test will apply (see **Chapter 7**).

There are numerous exemptions which apply in DPA 1998 and its associated statutory instruments. This chapter cannot hope to cover them all, however, we will attempt to identify the most relevant ones. A number of these exemptions make reference to prejudice which is likely to occur. In this context 'likely' does not mean more probable than not but instead that there must be a significant and real risk, more than just a mere possibility (see *R (on the application of Lord)* v. *Secretary of State for the Home Department* [2003] EWHC 2073).

9.5.1   DPA 1998, s.28: National security

An exemption from DPA 1998, s.7(1) applies where it is necessary to safeguard national security. However, before this provision can be relied upon a Minister of the Crown must sign a certificate certifying that the exemption applies.

9.5.2   DPA 1998, s.29: Crime and taxation

Personal data which is processed in order to prevent or detect a crime or assess any tax or duty is exempt from DPA 1998, s.7(1) where release of the data would be likely to prejudice any of those aims.

In addition, the exemption applies where the information is processed for the purpose of discharging a statutory function and it has been received from someone who held it for the purpose of detecting or preventing crime or assessing taxation.

This would cover, for example, the situation where the personal data was shared between a law enforcement organisation and a partner public authority.

9.5.3   DPA 1998, s.31: Regulatory activity

This exemption covers a wide range of regulatory activities carried out by public authorities. It covers investigations into improper conduct in the financial services, the regulation of charities and securing health and safety amongst others. The exemption will only apply if the disclosure would be likely to prejudice the regulatory activity.

9.5.4   DPA 1998, s.33: Research history and statistics

If the personal data is being used only for research purposes (which includes statistical and historical purposes) then it is exempt from DPA 1998, s.7(1) if three conditions apply:

1. the data must not be used to make decisions in relation to specific individuals;
2. the data must not be used in such a way that substantial damage or substantial distress is likely to be caused to an individual; and
3. the results of the research must not be made available in such a form that identifies any individual.

9.5.5   DPA 1998, s.30: Health, social work and education

Information about an individual's physical or mental health may be exempt from DPA 1998, s.7(1). This will only apply where the disclosure would be likely to cause serious harm to the person's mental or physical health. If the data controller is not a health professional then he or she must consult with an appropriate health professional on whether or not the risk is likely to arise.

It is unlikely that it would be necessary to rely on this provision as information about a person's health is sensitive personal data and disclosure is unlikely to be fair in any case.

9.5.6   DPA 1998, Sched.7: Legal professional privilege

If the personal data contains information to which a claim for legal professional privilege could be maintained then it is automatically exempt from DPA 1998, s.7(1).

9.6   NEITHER CONFIRM NOR DENY

When a request for environmental information is received which includes personal data it is possible that even disclosing whether or not the information exists could disclose the personal data. For example, if an application requests details of any successful criminal proceedings for fly tipping then simple confirmation that the data is held but refusing to disclose it potentially discloses some personal data, i.e. that there is a criminal conviction if an individual can be identified. As such, EIR 2004, reg.13(5) allows a public authority to respond to a request by neither confirming nor denying that the information exists. However, this can only be relied on where confirming or denying would breach one of the principles; or would breach a s.10 notice, or where the information would be exempt from the subject access rights.

9.7 SUMMARY

The following flowchart provides a basic structure for dealing with a request for environmental information which might also be personal data.

Question 1: Does the information requested fall within one of the five categories of data?	
Yes – go to Question 2.	No – the personal data exceptions do not apply.
Question 2: Does the data relate to a living identifiable individual?	
Yes – go to Question 3.	No – the personal data exceptions do not apply.
Question 3: Is the identified individual the person making the request?	
Yes – refuse the request under EIR 2004, reg.5(3) and treat it as a subject access request under DPA 1998, s.7(1). You may need to seek confirmation of their identity and can charge the appropriate fee.	No – go to Question 4.
Question 4: Have any of the people identified in the information requested previously issued a s.10 notice to prevent use of the material which you have accepted?	
Yes – the exception in EIR 2004, reg. 12(2)(a)(ii) applies and you must apply the public interest test. Then go to Question 5.	No – go to Question 5.

Question 5: Would the individuals who are identified in the information requested be able to obtain it if they made a subject access request under DPA 1998, s.7(1)?

Yes – go to Question 6.	No – the exception in EIR 2004, reg. 13(3) applies and you must apply the public interest test. Then go to Question 6.

Question 6: Would disclosure of the information to the general public be fair?

Yes – go to Question 7.	No – the exception in EIR 2004, reg. 13(2)(a)(i) or (b) applies and you must not disclose the information.

Question 7: Would disclosure of the information to the general public be lawful?

Yes – go to Question 8.	No – the exception in EIR 2004, reg. 13(2)(a)(i) or (b) applies and you must not disclose the information.

Question 8: Does disclosure of the information to the general public meet a condition in DPA 1998, Sched.2?

Yes – the information may be disclosed provided that it is not sensitive personal data.	No – the exception in EIR 2004, reg. 13(2)(a)(i) or (b) applies and you must not disclose the information.

Question 9: Is the information requested sensitive personal data?

Yes – go to Question 10.	No – the personal data exception does not apply and you may disclose the data.

Question 10: Does the disclosure of the sensitive personal data meet a condition in DPA 1998, Sched.3?

Yes – the personal data exception does not apply and you may disclose the data.	No – the exception in EIR 2004, reg. 13(2)(a)(i) or (b) applies and you must not disclose the information.

CHAPTER 10

Enforcement and appeals

10.1 INTRODUCTION

One of the fundamental failings of EIR 1992 was that the only way in which a dissatisfied applicant could challenge a public authority's decision not to disclose information was by way of judicial review. Even the most tenacious of applicants would have had to think twice about embarking on such risky and expensive litigation to secure information. Directive 2003/4/EC addressed this problem head on by imposing a requirement on Member States to adopt procedures that meet the 'access to justice' requirements of art.9 of the Aarhus Convention. In particular, the Convention (art.9) and the Directive (art.6) require independent and impartial procedures to be put in place that are both expeditious and either free or inexpensive. EIR 2004 have fulfilled this requirement by establishing a procedure which enables an applicant to complain about the way in which a public authority has handled his or her request without the need to go to court or to incur great expense. To date only two cases have reached the domestic courts having exhausted the review procedures built into EIR 2004.

Under EIR 2004 an applicant who is not satisfied with the way in which a public authority has handled a request for environmental information or (more usually) thinks that their request has been wrongfully refused may take the following action:

1. Complain to the public authority about the way it has handled the request or ask the authority to reconsider its decision (the internal review procedure).
2. If the internal review procedure does not satisfy the applicant they can complain to the Information Commissioner.
3. The Information Commissioner will (subject to some exceptions) investigate the complaint and issue a decision notice which is legally binding on the public authority (subject to a right of appeal). This may require the public authority to disclose the requested information.
4. Both the applicant (complainant) and the public authority have the right to lodge an appeal to the First-tier Tribunal (Information Rights) against the Information Commissioner's decision notice.
5. Any party to the proceedings before the Information Rights Tribunal may seek leave to appeal, on a point of law, to the Administrative Appeal Chamber (AAC) of the Upper Tribunal.

6.   Any further appeals are to the Court of Appeal subject to permission to appeal.

In addition, EIR 2004 have put public authorities under the supervisory control of the Information Commissioner by conferring on him various powers of enforcement. Before looking at the review and appeals procedures, this chapter will commence with an examination of the powers and functions of the Information Commissioner in ensuring that the legal rights and obligations conferred and imposed by EIR 2004 are respected and observed.

10.2 FUNCTIONS OF THE INFORMATION COMMISSIONER IN RELATION TO EIR 2004

The Information Commissioner is responsible for ensuring that public authorities comply with the obligations imposed by EIR 2004 and ensuring that the rights of access to environmental information are observed.

- EIR 2004, reg.18 provides that, subject to some modification, the following provisions of FOIA 2000 apply to EIR 2004: Part IV (Enforcement); Part V (Appeals); and Sched.3 (Powers of Inspection). The principal modification concerns Ministerial Certificates; where a Minister issues a Ministerial Certificate, FOIA 2000, Part IV (Enforcement) does not apply.
- EIR 2004, reg.16(5) applies the general functions of the Information Commissioner under FOIA 2000, s.47 and the power of the Commissioner to give practice recommendations under FOIA 2000, s.48.

The unfortunate consequence of this 'import' is that it requires some cross referencing between EIR 2004 and FOIA 2000. To aid understanding, references to EIR 2004 and the corresponding FOIA 2000 sections are given as appropriate.

10.2.1 Ministerial Certificates

There is one significant caveat to the application of FOIA 2000 enforcement provisions to EIR 2004 and that arises in consequence of EIR 2004, reg.18(3). This which states that Part IV (Enforcement) of FOIA 2000 shall not apply in any case where a Ministerial Certificate has been issued in accordance with EIR 2004, reg.15(1). (see **8.3.4**). Under EIR 2004, reg.15 a Minister may issue a certificate certifying that a refusal to disclose information is because disclosure would adversely affect national security and it would not be in the public interest to disclose this. The Ministerial Certificate is conclusive evidence of the matter. Where this happens the Information Commissioner has no enforcement powers and cannot issue any notices.

10.2.2   The Commissioner's general functions in respect of EIR 2004

The Information Commissioner's general functions in respect of EIR 2004 are as follows:

- to promote good practice by public authorities generally and, in particular, to perform his functions so as to promote observance by public authorities of the requirements of EIR 2004 and the EIR Code of Practice (EIR 2004, reg.16(5); FOIA 2000, s.47(1));
- to inform and advise the public, as he considers appropriate, about the operation of EIR 2004, about good practice and about any other matters that come within the scope of his functions (EIR 2004, reg.16(5); FOIA 2000, s.47(2));
- the Commissioner may assess whether a public authority is following good practice but only if the public authority consents (EIR 2004, reg.16(5); FOIA 2000, s.47(3));
- to determine (except in certain circumstances) whether or not a public authority has, when responding to a request, complied with its obligations under Parts 2 and 3 of EIR 2004 (EIR 2004, reg.18; FOIA 2000, s.50(2)).

10.2.3   The Commissioner's powers in respect of EIR 2004

In fulfilment of these functions, the Information Commissioner has the power to:

- issue a Code of Practice on EIR 2004; the Code is to provide guidance to public authorities as to the practice that the Commissioner considers is desirable;
- issue decision notices, enforcement notices and information notices (EIR 2004, reg.18, FOIA 2000, as.50–52);
- issue written practice recommendations to a public authority (EIR 2004, reg.16(5); FOIA 2000, s.47(1)). A practice recommendation is issued where the Commissioner considers that a public authority's practice does not conform to the Code of Practice;
- obtain a warrant to enter and search premises in order to obtain evidence where the Commissioner suspects that a public authority is failing to comply with its obligations under EIR 2004 or with any notices issued or where he suspects an offence under EIR 2004, reg.19 (obstructing the disclosure of information);
- certify to a court that a public authority has failed to comply with a decision, information or enforcement notice in order that the court can investigate and sanction as a contempt of court if appropriate (EIR 2004, reg.18; FOIA 2000, s.54);
- prosecute any EIR public authority that commits an offence under EIR 2004, reg.19 (obstructing disclosure of information);
- charge for his services under EIR 2004, reg.16 (FOIA 2000, s.47(4)) but only with the consent of the Secretary of State.

The Commissioner does not have the power to:

- impose any fines on any public authority in breach of its EIR 2004 obligations. Although the Commissioner has now been given the power to impose fines for breaches of DPA 1998, he does not have the power to impose a fine on any public authority that breaches either EIR 2004 or FOIA 2000;
- award any compensation, or demand that compensation be paid by a public authority, to a complainant who has suffered some loss in consequence of a breach of the regulations;
- make a costs order against the parties involved in a complaint that he is required to determine.

10.2.4   The Commissioner's approach to monitoring and enforcement

The ICO has published a 'Freedom of Information Regulatory Action Policy' which seeks to provide more detail on the ICO's approach to regulatory action, including investigating complaints and serving appropriate notices. The document 'A Robust Approach to FOI Complaint Cases' also details the 'robust complaints handling criteria' which are applied to complaints.

In terms of monitoring, the Commissioner recognises that there are a number of reasons why public authorities may not achieve full compliance with EIR 2004 or its Code of Practice and he will therefore seek to focus on the more serious or repeated examples of poor performance. In particular, the Commissioner has identified timeliness as an area that is particularly problematic and which warrants attention. To this end he has developed some 'rules of thumb' which will be used to focus attention on those public authorities experiencing the most difficulty. These are identified as those authorities:

- where the Commissioner has received six or more complaints concerning delay within a six-month period;
- which appear to have exceeded the time for compliance by a significant margin on one or more occasions;
- where it appears that less than 85 per cent of requests are receiving a response within the appropriate timescales

10.3   THE INFORMATION COMMISSIONER'S NOTICES

In order to fulfil his role the Commissioner has the power under EIR 2004 to serve three different types of legally enforceable notices. These are:

- information notices (EIR 2004, reg.18; FOIA 2000, s.51);
- decision notices (EIR 2004, reg.18; FOIA 2000, s.50);
- enforcement notices (EIR 2004, reg.18; FOIA 2000, s.52).

10.3.1 Information notices

The Information Commissioner may serve an information notice (EIR 2004, reg.18; FOIA 2000, s.51) on a public authority in two circumstances:

(a)   if he has received a complaint about the public authority; or

(b)   he reasonably requires the information to help him determine whether a public authority has complied with its duties under Parts 2 and 3 of EIR 2004 or to help him determine whether the practice of a public authority conforms to the EIR Code of Practice.

The Information Commissioner will not normally serve an information notice unless the circumstances demand it and where he intends to serve the notice he will, where possible, warn the authority in advance. This may be enough to get the public authority to release the information without recourse to the notice. An information notice:

- requires the public authority to provide the information specified in the notice; it may also require the disclosure of unrecorded information (FOIA 2000, s.50(8)), for example, statements from officers dealing with the request.
- must specify the reasons why it is being served. If it is being served in consequence of a complaint, this must be stated, or if it is for the purposes of determining whether the public authority has complied with EIR 2004 and/or the Code of Practice, the notice must specify why the Commissioner thinks the information is relevant.
- must specify how and when the information is to be provided. The deadline for providing the information to the Commissioner cannot expire before the period within which the public authority can appeal the notice, which is 28 days from the service of the notice.

The right of appeal against an information notice is provided by EIR 2004, reg.18 (FOIA 2000, s.57). If the public authority does commence an appeal against the information notice then it does not have to provide the information required by the notice until the appeal has either been decided or withdrawn (FOIA 2000, s.51(4)).

The Information Commissioner can cancel an information notice by written notice to the authority on which it was served.

Under FOIA 2000, s.51(5) an information notice cannot require a public authority to disclose:

(a)   any communication between a professional legal advisor and his or her client made in connection with the giving of legal advice to the client with respect to his or her obligations, liabilities or rights under EIR 2004 (or FOIA 2000); or

(b)   any communications between a professional legal advisor and his client, or between the legal advisor or his or her client and any other person, made in connection or in contemplation of proceedings under or arising out of EIR 2004 (or FOIA 2000) (including proceedings before the Tribunal) and for the purposes of such proceedings.

This limitation only arises in the circumstances listed above. The Commissioner can require disclosure of other legally privileged information not concerning the operation of EIR 2004 or FOIA 2000. Even in circumstances where the public authority is withholding information under EIR 2004, reg.12(5)(b) (see **8.4**), the Commissioner can obtain legally privileged information to determine whether the exception has been correctly engaged. In addition, the public authority cannot refuse to provide information to the Commissioner (or later the Tribunal) on the grounds that it would be a breach of confidence and make them either civilly or criminally liable.

A public authority may appeal an information notice.

10.3.2 Decision notices

The Commissioner can only issue a decision notice (EIR 2004, reg.18; FOIA 2000, s.50) following a complaint about a public authority's handling of a request. Not all complaints will result in a decision notice; the Commissioner is not required to make a decision:

(a)   if the complainant has not exhausted the internal review procedure which is provided by the public authority in conformity with the EIR Code of Practice;

(b)   where there has been undue delay in lodging the complaint;

(c)   where the application is frivolous or vexatious;

(d)   where the application has been withdrawn or abandoned.

In addition, the Commissioner may conclude that he is not going to adjudicate the complaint; where this happens he will not issue a decision notice but he must notify the complainant that he has not made a decision and give his reasons (FOIA 2000, s.50(3)(a)).

If none of the above apply and the Commissioner has investigated a complaint and found that the public authority has failed to comply with EIR 2004, regs.5(1), 6, 11 or 14 he must serve a decision notice on both the complainant and the public authority concerned. The decision notice:

(a)   may conclude that the public authority has complied with its duties under EIR 2004 and/or uphold the public authority's decision;

(b)   if the Commissioner decides the public authority has not complied with its duty to make information available under EIR 2004, reg.5(1) or has failed to comply with EIR 2004, regs.6, 11 or 14, must set out what steps that the authority is required to take and the time frame for compliance. There is nothing to stop the decision notice dealing with other matters, for example, inappropriate charges under EIR 2004, reg.8. Typically a decision notice will require the public authority to:

- reconsider its response in the light of any specified factors or exceptions;
- disclose the information; or

- provide the information in the format requested.

(c)   may indicate that the public authority was in breach of EIR 2004 but need take no action. This might arise where the public authority has subsequently disclosed the information requested.

(d)   must include a statement of reasons and details of the right of appeal.

There is no statutory time limit for the time period for compliance and in any event this will largely depend on the circumstances of the case. However, the time limit cannot be earlier than 28 days from date of service as this is the period within which the recipient has a right to lodge an appeal to the Information Rights Tribunal. Unless the public authority appeals the decision, it must comply with it. Unlike enforcement and information notices, it does not appear that the Commissioner can cancel a decision notice once he has issued it. However, see below at **10.3.4** in relation to the ministerial veto under EIR 2004, reg.18(6)/ FOIA 2000, s.53.

Both the public authority concerned and the complainant may appeal the decision notice.

10.3.3   Enforcement notices

The Information Commissioner has the discretionary power to serve an enforcement notice (EIR 2004, reg.18; FOIA 2000, s.52) where he is satisfied that a public authority has failed to comply with any of the requirements of Parts 2 and 3 of EIR 2004.

The enforcement notice:

- must contain a statement of the requirements of EIR 2004 which the Commissioner considers the public authority has breached and his reasons for believing the public authority has breached this/these requirement/s;
- can require the public authority to take such steps as the Commissioner specifies and within the time period laid down by the Commissioner in the notice;
- must tell the public authority that it has a right of appeal against the notice;
- cannot require the steps to be complied with before the end of the period within which the public authority may appeal the notice and, if an appeal is brought, the public authority need not comply with the notice until the appeal has been determined.

The Commissioner has the right to cancel the enforcement notice by giving written notice to the public authority concerned. An enforcement notice may be overridden by ministerial veto. A public authority may appeal the enforcement notice.

10.3.4   Ministerial veto

EIR 2004, reg.18(6) imports the controversial provisions of FOIA 2000, s.53 into EIR 2004 which enable a Minister to 'override' a decision or an enforcement notice served on a government department, the Welsh Assembly or any other public authority designated by the Secretary of State for the purposes of this provision. This is referred to as a ministerial veto and arguably breaches the Directive, which does not allow for the conferral of such a power. The power may be exercised by an accountable person who is a Minister or the Attorney General. This power does not apply to information notices.

After an enforcement or a decision notice has been served (or after it has been upheld or modified on appeal by the Information Rights Tribunal) a Minister may issue a certificate on the Information Commissioner which effectively 'overrides' the enforcement/decision notice. The certificate must be issued within 20 working days of service of the notice and it must state that the Minister has, on reasonable grounds, formed the opinion that in respect of the request there was no failure to comply with EIR 2004, reg.5(1). The effect of the ministerial veto is that the enforcement or decision notice ceases to be of effect. In other words, the politician's view will prevail over the Commissioner's. The Minister is required to lay the certificate before Parliament and (where relevant) the Welsh or Northern Ireland Assembly but not before it is issued to the Commissioner. The Minister must also notify the complainant and give reasons why he has issued the certificate, although he is not obliged to disclose information covered by an EIR exception.

There is no possibility of appeal against a ministerial veto and therefore the only way it may be challenged is by way of judicial review. The Commissioner, public authority concerned and the applicant/complainant are likely to have sufficient interest (standing) to bring the matter before the High Court but they would need to demonstrate that the use of the veto was irrational or unlawful. Given that the Directive does not provide for such a course of action it could be argued that a ministerial veto is per se unlawful, however, this remains conjecture because, at the time of writing, the power to veto has not been exercised.

10.3.5   Non-compliance with notices

On receipt of one of the above notices, the public authority concerned must either appeal the notice within 28 working days of the notice being served or comply with its terms within the time period specified in the notice. Unless the notice has been 'overridden' by a ministerial veto, the failure to comply with it is regarded as contempt of court. The Information Commissioner has the power to certify (in writing) to the court that the public authority has failed to comply with the notice and the court will proceed with the matter as a civil contempt (FOIA 2000, s.54). Public authorities should be aware that if contempt is established then not only does the court have the power to fine an authority it may also sequestrate the authority's assets, issue an injunction or commit an individual to a prison sentence. Committal to prison and sequestration are only to be used in the most serious of cases and therefore are highly unlikely to be used in the context of EIR 2004. However, a court may choose to impose a fine on the defaulting public authority. The difficulty with establishing a civil contempt of court is that the criminal standard of proof applies (beyond reasonable doubt).

10.3.6 Appeals against notices

Under EIR 2004, reg.18(2)(b); FOIA 2000, Part V:

- decision notices may be appealed by the complainant or the public authority;
- enforcement and information notices may be appealed by the public authority;

Where the decision notice or enforcement notice relates to certain transferred public records (EIR 2004, reg.17(2)–5)), the appeal may be made by the public authority or the responsible authority. The appeals procedure is considered below at **10.11**.

10.4   EIR 2004, REG.16(5)/FOIA 2000, S.48: PRACTICE RECOMMENDATIONS

Although not strictly an enforcement power, the Commissioner has the power to issue practice recommendations to any public authority that he considers is not to be conforming with the EIR Code of Practice. As the name suggests, the purpose of a practice recommendation is to suggest steps that the public authority can take to ensure that it complies with the code and meets its obligations under EIR 2004. Practice recommendations will address matters of poor practice and will often be made by agreement and following a practice assessment (under FOIA 2000, s.47(3); EIR 2004; reg.16(5)). The Commissioner is not bound to issue a Practice Recommendation; he may decide it is more appropriate, in the circumstances, to deal with the matter informally by letter or to hold discussions with the authority concerned.

In contrast to the notices discussed above there is no sanction for failing to comply with a practice recommendation because a practice recommendation is not a tool of enforcement. In this respect practice recommendations are non-enforceable, but this does not mean a public authority should treat them lightly. A public authority that receives a practice recommendation must be falling short of the good practice required by the Code and in this respect the recommendation serves as a warning to the authority that it needs to address its practices. For example, the practice recommendation may deal with shortcomings in the advice and assistance offered to applicants, or poor quality refusal notices. The Commissioner is more likely to issue a practice recommendation in response to repeated poor practice but he can also issue one for a single incident of very poor practice.

A public authority that does not heed the recommendations may find itself not only facing adverse publicity but also continuing practices which could breach EIR 2004 and the Commissioner will take this failure into account when deciding whether to take formal action against the authority. The Commissioner's office will monitor compliance with the practice recommendations.

There are no rights of appeal against a practice recommendation.

10.5   EIR 2004, REG.19: OFFENCES

The only criminal offence created by EIR 2004 is provided by EIR 2004, reg.19 and this applies where a request for environmental information has been made to a public authority and the applicant would have been entitled to that information under EIR 2004 but for the commission of the offence. A person commits this offence if he alters, defaces, erases, destroys or conceals any record with the intention of preventing its disclosure to the applicant. This mirrors the offence created by FOIA 2000, s.77. The offence can be committed either by a public authority or by any person who is employed by, is an officer of, or is subject to the direction of, the public authority. A government department cannot be prosecuted but the offence can be committed by a civil servant and a person acting on behalf of either of the Houses of Parliament.

This is a summary offence triable only in the magistrates' court and conviction may lead to a fine of up to level 5 on the standard scale (currently £5,000). Prosecutions are brought by the Information Commissioner, although EIR 2004, reg.19(4) enables prosecution by some other person but only with the consent of the Director of Public Prosecutions.

It is also an offence to:

- intentionally obstruct a person in the execution of a warrant (see below); or
- fail, without reasonable excuse, to give any person executing a warrant such assistance as he may reasonably require for the execution of the warrant (EIR 2004, reg.18(1), FOIA 2000, Sched.3).

10.6   POWERS OF INVESTIGATION

The Commissioner's powers of entry/inspection are exercisable where the Commissioner has reasonable grounds to suspect a public authority:

- has failed to comply with Parts 2 and 3 of EIR 2004 or one of his notices
- of committing an offence under EIR 2004, reg.19.

If the Commissioner wishes to enter property with a view to securing evidence of the above, he must obtain a warrant from either a circuit or district judge. A warrant may authorise entry to any premises in order to search the premises and inspect/ seize any documents or other materials which may evidence the suspected breaches. A warrant can allow the Commissioner to operate and test any equipment where information may be recorded; the most obvious example being information stored on a computer. Except in an emergency or where compliance with the steps detailed below would defeat the object of entry (for example, where a public authority might destroy evidence), a judge cannot agree to issue a warrant unless he is satisfied that:

- the Commissioner has given the occupier of the premises in question seven days' notice in writing demanding access to the premises; and

  - the access demanded was reasonable but was unreasonably refused; or
  - the occupier granted access to the premises but unreasonably refused to comply with a request from the Commissioner or his staff to carry out the powers of inspection mentioned above; and

- the occupier has, after the refusal, been notified by the Commissioner of the application to obtain a warrant and the occupier has had the opportunity of being heard by the judge.

The warrant should be exercised at a reasonable time unless there are grounds for suspecting the evidence would not be found at that time. Once granted, the person executing the warrant (which is likely to be an officer of the ICO) is able to use such reasonable force as may be necessary. Schedule 3 contains further procedural details about the execution of the warrant.

The warrant does not allow the Commissioner or his staff to inspect the following:

- information whose disclosure would adversely affect national security (EIR 2004, reg.18(4)(h));
- information that is subject to legal professional privilege between a professional legal advisor and his client in connection with the giving of legal advice to the client with respect to EIR 2004 or made in contemplation of proceedings under or arising out of EIR 2004. However, this does not include any material held by a third party or to anything held with the intention of furthering a criminal purpose.

See **10.5** in relation to offences relating to the execution of a warrant.

10.7   COMPLAINTS ABOUT BREACHES OF EIR 2004

10.7.1   Grounds for complaint

Given the range of duties imposed on public authorities by EIR 2004, it is not difficult to see the scope for things going wrong and hence possible complaints. The Directive demands that the review procedures put in place cover situations where the applicant's request has been 'ignored, wrongfully refused (whether in full or in part), inadequately answered or otherwise dealt with in accordance' with the requirements of the Directive. In EIR 2004 this translates as allowing applicants to complain about:

- bodies that claim they are not subject to EIR 2004;
- public authorities claiming they do not hold the requested information;
- public authorities claiming the information is exempt under FOIA 2000 in circumstances where the requested information is environmental information;
- public authorities not providing the information requested within the time limits;
- public authorities not providing adequate advice and assistance;
- public authorities refusing to provide the information in the form or format requested;
- public authorities charging unreasonable fees for providing the information or charging fees where such charges are prohibited;
- public authorities not providing the information as soon as possible or within the deadline of 20 working days (or 40 working days if the time period has been extended);
- public authorities refusing to supply some or all of the information requested, or failing to give adequate reasons for the refusal.

10.7.2   How will the applicant know how to complain?

In practice what is most likely to trigger a complaint is where a public authority has issued a refusal notice under EIR 2004, reg.14 because it is claiming that the information is covered by an exception under EIR 2004, reg.12(1) or EIR 2004, reg.13(1). The refusal notice must inform the applicant of the public authority's internal review procedures under EIR 2004, reg.11 and of the enforcement and appeal provisions. Hence the refusal notice will direct the applicant to the internal review procedure, details of which should also be available on the public authority's website.

However, as noted above, a refusal to disclose is not the only circumstance where an 'aggrieved' person might complain. The applicant may have been provided with the information but not in the form or format requested, or may feel that he has not received sufficient advice and assistance in formulating his or her request or has been inappropriately charged; in which cases the applicant will not have been issued a refusal notice. In these circumstances the applicant may not be aware of the internal review procedure. However, if the applicant writes to the authority (either by letter or email) and it is clear that he is complaining, this is sufficient to trigger the internal review procedure under EIR 2004, reg.11(2). If the applicant phones with a complaint then they should be advised that any complaint must be put in writing (see **10.8.1**). Details of the public authority's internal review procedure must be made available to the public, probably via the authority's website/publication scheme. This may not necessarily appear under the heading of internal review but it should be easy for a person to establish how to make a complaint.

10.8   EIR 2004, REG.11: INTERNAL REVIEW PROCEDURE

A sceptic might be forgiven for thinking that the internal review procedure is going to be a waste of time because it is more likely than not that the public authority will uphold its original decision or consider it has complied with its obligations under EIR 2004. The Code of Practice, however, states that it should be possible for a public authority, having undertaken an internal review, to either reverse or amend its original decision. The value of an internal review is that it allows the applicant to ask the public authority to rethink its decision without having to embark on a more formal complaints procedure and without having to incur any cost. For instance, if the authority has stated that it does not hold the information, the review may throw up the fact that it does. If the complaint is about the way in which the public authority has discharged its responsibilities to advise and assist, the complaint may result in an improvement in service performance.

10.8.1   Written representation

Unlike the original request which could be verbal, EIR 2004, reg.11 requires that the request for reconsideration/complaint must be made in writing. The written request can be sent electronically (an email will suffice) but it must be made within 40 working days after the date on which the applicant believes that the public authority has failed to comply with the requirement. The complainant does not need to expressly refer to EIR 2004, reg.11 or even use the words 'internal review' to trigger this process, although it may be advisable to make it clear in some way that this is the purpose of the correspondence. As noted at **10.7.2** above, any written reply from an applicant expressing dissatisfaction with the authority's response to a valid request for environmental information should be treated as a complaint and should trigger the internal review process.

Substantiating the complaint; formulating the arguments

There is no requirement on the part of a complainant to give detailed explanations of why or how they consider the public authority has failed to comply with EIR 2004 or has wrongfully refused the request, although of course they should explain why they are complaining. However, complainants would be well advised to provide as much detail as possible, for example, detailing when they made the request, how they made it, what information they were trying to obtain and whether they asked for help and advice. Where the complainant is challenging a refusal to disclose information, he or she should consider the reasons cited by the public authority in the refusal notice and may consider whether he or she has any arguments that can be raised to counter these reasons. EIR 2004, reg.11(3) recognises that the applicant may submit supporting evidence and indeed the public authority must consider it where it has been submitted. If the public authority has stated that an exception is engaged and the public interest lies in favour of maintaining the exception, then the

179

complainant may want to put forward arguments in favour of the public interest in disclosure. It is evident from some of the Commissioner's decision notices that some complainants have presented quite carefully marshalled arguments about why the information should be released, why exceptions are not engaged, or why the public interest favours disclosure. Certainly a complaint that is clearly structured and well argued is likely to be more difficult to rebut or at least may generate a more carefully formulated and reasoned refusal.

If the complainant is not certain about his arguments then there are various sources of information he might consider using to gain some assistance. Apart from books such as this, the Defra and ICO guidance on EIR 2004 and, in particular, EIR 2004 exceptions are useful starting points. These explain how Defra and the ICO interpret the duties and exceptions under EIR 2004. In addition, both the ICO and Information Rights Tribunal websites contain all the Information Commissioner's decision notices and Tribunal decisions. These are now (largely) searchable by category or regulation and enable the public to see how the Commissioner and the Tribunal have responded to different cases which have raised similar issues. Although each case will always be considered on its own set of facts, and whilst the Tribunal's decisions do not set any precedent, previous decisions can be a very useful guide to the way in which the Information Commissioner/Tribunal would resolve the matter. Complainants should consider whether any decisions support their arguments and should try and cite these in their letters of complaint.

10.8.2 Handling the internal review procedure

Once the written representation, whatever form it takes, is received then it should be handled in accordance with the public authority's internal review procedure and the authority should also conform to the requirements of EIR 2004 Code of Practice. EIR 2004, reg.11 requires that:

- the internal review should be dealt with 'as soon as possible' but in any event within 40 working days from the time when the complaint was received and the applicant must be notified of the public authority's decision;
- the public authority must consider any supporting evidence produced by the applicant;
- the internal review procedure must be free of any charge.

Although EIR 2004 does not specify this, a public authority will need to log the complaint to ensure it meets with the deadline of 40 working days and, as a matter of good practice, it should acknowledge receipt of the complaint. The applicant should be advised of the authority's target day for responding to the complaint. If it becomes apparent that the process will take longer, perhaps because of the complexity of the issues involved, then the complainant should be updated and the delay explained.

10.8.3 Outcome of the review procedure

Once the public authority has reviewed its decision or its handling of the request, it must reach a decision as to whether it has complied with EIR 2004. Where the public authority decides that it has failed to comply with EIR 2004, the notification to the applicant must include a statement of:

- how the authority has failed to comply;
- what action the authority has decided to take to comply with EIR 2004; and
- the period within which that action is to be taken.

In addition, EIR 2004 Code of Practice recommends that:

- where the outcome of a complaint is that information should be disclosed which was previously withheld, the information in question should be disclosed with immediate effect;
- where the outcome of a complaint is that the procedures have not been properly followed by the authority's staff, the authority should apologise to the applicant. The authority should also take appropriate steps to prevent similar errors occurring in future;
- where the public authority affirms its decision to withhold information, the applicant must be informed of his right to apply to the Information Commissioner.

As far as the applicant is concerned, the outcome of the review procedure will either resolve the matter or not. If not then the applicant has the right to complain to the Information Commissioner in the same way that an aggrieved applicant would under FOIA 2000. A failure to deal with a complaint properly may constitute a breach of EIR 2004, reg.11 (see, for example, *Cabinet Office* FER0162453). An applicant may complain to the Information Commissioner about procedural breaches of EIR 2004, reg.11.

10.8.4 Monitoring complaints

The Code of Practice requires that public authorities monitor complaints in order to review and improve their procedures and in particular to avoid similar errors occurring again.

10.9 COMPLAINING TO THE INFORMATION COMMISSIONER

If a member of the public is dissatisfied with the outcome of the internal review procedure then he or she may lodge a complaint with the Information Commissioner's Office under EIR 2004, reg.19 (FOIA 2000, s.50(1)). The reader should note that FOIA 2000, s.50 does not actually use the word 'complaint', it states that any person may 'apply' to the Commissioner, but for the sake of ease this may be referred to as a complaint, and the dissatisfied applicant as the complainant. The dissatisfaction may arise because of the way in which the original request for information was handled or because the public authority refused to supply the information (or refused to supply it in a particular format) or because of the way in which the internal review procedure was conducted. The purpose of applying/complaining to the Commissioner is to ask the Commissioner to reach a decision on whether the public authority has dealt with the request in accordance with the requirements of EIR 2004. If the public authority has refused to disclose the information requested, the Commissioner has the power to order disclosure.

Before applying to the Commissioner a complainant would be well advised to read the ICO's 'Freedom of Information Act 2000 and the Environmental Information Regulations 2004: When and How to Complain' (2007) (hereafter referred to as 'the Complaints Guide'). This is available via the ICO website (**www.ico.gov. uk**).

10.9.1 Formalities

An application (complaint) to the Information Commissioner must be made in writing; it may be posted or submitted electronically via the ICO website, using the online complaints form. The complaints form requires the complainant to provide the following:

- A copy of the initial request. If the applicant no longer has this then he or she will need to produce some evidence that the request was submitted, for example, a recorded delivery receipt. If the public authority has acknowledged receipt of the request, this can be provided as useful evidence.
- A copy of the public authority's initial response (the refusal notice) unless the complaint is about a lack of response.
- A copy of the complaint made to the public authority as part of its internal review procedure.
- A copy of the public authority's response to the internal review procedure (unless the public authority did not respond).
- Any other information the complainant considers relevant. For example, any arguments that the complainant submitted to the public authority as part of the internal review process.
- Contact details.

There is no fee to pay.

The application should be made by the person who made the original request or a named person acting on his or her behalf. A name and contact details must be provided; the Information Commissioner will not deal with anonymous complainants. The completed form and supporting documents must be sent in the post to the Customer Services Team, Information Commissioner's Office, Wycliffe House, Water Lane, Wilmslow, Cheshire, SK9 5AF, or alternatively it can be emailed to casework@ico.gsi.gov.uk. The email should say 'Complaint to the ICO' in the subject line. The website does not offer fax as a means of communication.

The application and supporting documentation should be sufficiently detailed and clear; the Commissioner will not take any formal action if there is not enough information to support the complaint or if the information is unclear. In such cases the ICO will write to the applicant requesting additional information and the complaint will be closed until this is provided. As with the internal review procedure there is no statutory requirement for the complainant to advance any arguments about why the public authority has breached the regulations or why the information should be disclosed. If the complainant has done this for the internal review procedure then he or she should provide copies of his or her arguments to the Commissioner.

Timing

The application to the Commissioner must be made without 'undue delay' otherwise the Commissioner is not required to take formal action. The phrase 'undue delay' is not defined in EIR 2004 or FOIA 2000 but the Complaints Guide suggests that the complaint should be made as soon as possible and within two months of receiving the public authority's final response.

10.9.2 Handling the complaint: initial steps

Acknowledging receipt of the complaint

The ICO should acknowledge to the complainant that it has received the complaint. The Information Commissioner must also contact the public authority as soon as possible and within 10 working days of receiving the complaint. This may be done by phone or email to speed communications up. Wherever possible, communications between the ICO and public authorities should be by email. In practice, contact will usually be with the designated information rights officer where the authority has one; the Commission staff will be aiming to establish a single line of communication with one person. The Commissioner will provide the public authority with details of the complaint and will request that the public authority provides (to his office) all of the information relevant to the application. He will also invite the authority to make any comments on the complaint.

Initial evaluation and allocating the complaint

A case officer within the case reception unit (which acts in a sort of triage capacity) will consider whether the complaint is eligible for consideration. This initial evaluation stage enables the ICO staff to determine whether the Commissioner is going to investigate or whether the matter can be resolved quickly without further investigation, for example, by advising the complainant that he or she needs to exhaust the internal review procedure before complaining to the ICO. If the Commissioner decides that he is under a duty to investigate the complaint, or that he intends to investigate the complaint, then he will notify the complainant and advise him or her what the next steps are. If the Information Commissioner decides to take the case on it will be allocated a case reference number and passed to the complaints resolution team. Any communications with the public authority or complainant should refer to this case number. The actual investigation can, in some instances, take several months; however, the Commissioner will aim to provide the public authority and the complainant with a monthly progress report.

10.9.3 Information Commissioner not obliged to investigate all complaints

FOIA 2000, s.50 provides that the Commissioner is not required to (but he has discretion, so may) take a decision in the following four circumstances:

(a) If the complainant has not exhausted the internal review procedure which is provided by the public authority in conformity with EIR 2004 Code of Practice. However, the Commissioner may choose to investigate in circumstances where the public authority has ignored the request for an internal review or has refused to undertake one.
(b) Where there has been undue delay in making the application. It was noted above that the application should be made as quickly as possible but in any event within two months of the public authority's final response.
(c) Where the application is frivolous or vexatious.
(d). Where the application has been withdrawn or abandoned.

If the Commissioner decides that he is not going to take a decision then he must notify the complainant that he has not made any decision as a result of one of the grounds above (FOIA 2000, s.50(3)). There is no appeal against this decision; an applicant would need to seek judicial review of the Commissioner's decision.

10.10 INVESTIGATING THE COMPLAINT

10.10.1 Obtaining information from the public authority

In some circumstances it may be possible for the Commissioner to reach a decision with very little further investigation or without requiring any additional information from the public authority. If further information is needed then the relevant case worker will normally contact the public authority concerned and will ask them to provide relevant information. These initial requests for further information will be informal. The Commissioner is likely to want to find out how the public authority responded to the initial request and how it communicated with the applicant. He may want to see copies of the withheld or redacted information. The public authority may consider using this invitation as an opportunity to present their arguments in support of their actions or reasons for withholding the information. If the public authority has withheld information then it may be sensible to explain why it considers the exception is engaged and what factors it took into account when undertaking the public interest balancing exercise. A transparent and reasoned approach is likely to help the Commissioner reach a conclusion more quickly. The public authority may consider supplying third party expert evidence in some circumstances.

The public authority concerned is expected to provide all the information requested by the Commissioner within 20 working days or sooner if possible. Any request for further information must be met within 10 working days. If the public authority cannot meet these deadlines then it must explain its reasons to the Commissioner. However, if the public authority fails to provide the information or the Commissioner believes that it is being unreasonably withheld or delayed he has the power to serve an information notice or, if the circumstances demand it, prosecute the public authority under EIR 2004, reg.19.

10.10.2 Visiting the public authority to inspect documents and information

It may be necessary or expedient for a staff member of the ICO, or the Commissioner himself, to visit the public authority's offices and examine the information in situ, for example, if the information is particularly sensitive and the Commissioner agrees it should not be circulated beyond the public authority in question. A public authority may request that only the Commissioner or nominated staff have access to the information where stringent security considerations apply. The Commissioner should not refuse unless there are overriding reasons why provision of the information to or inspection by other staff would significantly obstruct the discharge of his statutory functions. It might also make sense for practical reasons for the Commissioner or his staff to see the information in situ, for example where there is a considerable volume of information or where it would help to have the information explained by appropriate staff in the public authority.

10.10.3 Can the Commissioner share information disclosed to him?

The Commissioner and his staff are potentially privy to information of a very sensitive or confidential nature. They will commit an offence if they disclose, without lawful authority, any information provided which relates to an identified or identifiable person or business and which is not available to the public from any other sources (DPA 1998, s.59). Information supplied to the Commissioner will be held securely and not disclosed to the complainant or a third party (unless the public authority consents or all appeal procedures have been exhausted). The Commissioner will also retain it only for as long as is necessary.

10.10.4 Powers of entry and search warrants

In order to investigate a complaint and/or to determine whether there has been a breach of EIR 2004, the Information Commissioner may need to inspect the premises of the public authority. The Information Commissioner's powers of inspection have been considered at **10.6**.

10.10.5   Burden of proof

When examining the evidence and considering the arguments presented, the Commissioner must bear in mind that there is an expressly stated presumption in favour of disclosure (EIR 2004, reg.12(2)). The public authority will need to justify why it has chosen to withhold information in the light of this presumption and therefore the burden of proof would seem to fall squarely on the public authority. The complainant may marshal arguments about why an exception is not triggered or why the public interest favours disclosure but it is ultimately for the public authority to justify its position. The Commissioner will expect to be given evidence about any assertions made by public authorities in respect to both adverse effect (where applicable) and the public interest test.

10.10.6   Time limits for investigation

There is no statutory time limit for the Information Commissioner to complete his investigation. The Information Commissioner should, however, respond in an efficient and timely manner.

10.10.7   Outcome of the investigation

Following his investigation and determination of the complaint, the Commissioner must either:

* notify the complainant that he has not made any decision because of one the grounds referred to at **10.9.3** above; or
* serve a decision notice. (FOIA 2000, s.50(3); EIR 2004, reg.18).

The decision notice may uphold the public authority's decision or conclude that it has complied with its obligations under EIR 2004. Alternatively, the decision notice may record that the public authority is in breach of its EIR 2004 obligations and/or may require disclosure of the disputed information. As noted at **10.3.5**, non-compliance with a decision notice is treated as contempt of court.

10.11   APPEALS TO THE INFORMATION RIGHTS TRIBUNAL

Appeals against notices issued by the Commissioner, including decision notices, are heard by the First-tier Tribunal (Information Rights). Prior to 17 January 2010 the Tribunal was simply called the Information Tribunal but was renamed following the overhaul of the tribunals service by the Tribunals, Courts and Enforcement Act (TCEA) 2007 and is referred to hereafter as the Information Rights Tribunal.

The Information Rights Tribunal is a First-tier Tribunal and it sits within the General Regulatory Chamber. The TCEA 2007 established the Upper Tribunal which has been sitting since January 2010; it hears appeals from the First-tier Tribunal on questions of law, exercises powers of judicial review in certain circumstances and enforces decisions made by the First-tier Tribunals. Prior to the establishment of the Upper Tribunal, appeals from the Information Rights Tribunal, on a point of law, were to the High Court. There were only two appeals relating to EIR 2004 (the *Ofcom* and *Export Credits Guarantee Department* cases discussed at **8.3**).

The Information Rights Tribunal has 16 judges including a principal judge (at the time of writing, Professor John Angel). In addition, there are currently 36 non-legal members of the Tribunal. Non-legal Tribunal members are appointed on the basis of their experience in information rights matters. The Information Rights Tribunal divides into panels to deal with appeals and each panel has a chairman (or deputy chairman) who is legally qualified and who nominates an equal number of members. A panel usually consist of three members in total.

Decisions of the First-tier Tribunal are binding on the parties but do not establish a legal precedent.

10.11.1 Jurisdiction of the Information Rights Tribunal

The Information Rights Tribunal hears appeals against notices issued by the Information Commissioner under, *inter alia*, FOIA 2000, EIR 2004, DPA 1998 and the Privacy and Electronic Communications (EC Directive) Regulations 2003, SI 2993/2426. Specifically, in the context of EIR 2004, the Information Rights Tribunal hears appeals against:

- information notices;
- decision notices; and
- enforcement notices.

It is important to note that in relation to decision notices the appeal is against the Information Commissioner's notice and not the public authority's original decision. The Commissioner is the respondent.

10.11.2 Grounds for appeal

The only two grounds for appeal are that:

(a) the notice is not in accordance with the law. This might apply, for example, where it is argued that the Commissioner has not interpreted the provisions correctly; or

(b) the notice involved the exercise of discretion by the Commissioner and the Commissioner ought to have exercised his discretion differently. Typically this will apply in cases where it is argued that the Commissioner has reached the wrong conclusion in relation to the public interest test.

If neither of these grounds for appeal exists then the Information Rights Tribunal must dismiss the appeal. If they are well founded then the Tribunal can uphold the appeal or substitute the notice. When the Tribunal is hearing the appeal it is entitled to review any finding of fact on which the notice in question was based.

10.11.3 Who can appeal?

- Both the applicant/complainant and the public authority have an automatic right of appeal against any decision notice issued by the Information Commissioner.
- Public authorities also have a right of appeal against information and enforcement notices.
- Where the appellant is an applicant lodging an appeal against a decision notice then the Tribunal has the power to order the public authority to be joined as a party to the appeal. The Tribunal can do this of its own motion or in response to an application by one of the parties.
- In addition, an interested third party who does not enjoy an automatic right of appeal may ask the Information Rights Tribunal to join them to the appeal. For example, in the *Ofcom* case (see **Chapter 8**) T Mobile applied to be joined as an additional party because the information that was subject to the dispute had been provided by them and they were resisting disclosure. Conversely, in *East Riding of Yorkshire Council* v. *Information Commissioner* (EA/2009/0069) the Stanley Davies Group, the applicant, was ordered to be joined as a third party to the appeal.

If a third party wishes to be joined to the appeal it must notify the Information Rights Tribunal by way of a written application, referred to as a joinder notice (three copies are required). The joinder notice must contain the usual contact details and explain, *inter alia*, why the third party has an interest in the appeal and whether he/she/it supports the appeal. This is then sent to the Commissioner and the public authority concerned. The joinder notice needs to be drafted with care because it is treated as the third party's reply to the notice of appeal in the event the Information Rights Tribunal agrees to join them to the appeal.

10.12 PROCEDURAL RULES

The procedural rules of the Information Rights Tribunal are laid down in the Tribunal Procedure (First-tier Tribunal) (General Regulatory Chamber) Rules 2009, SI 2009/1976 (L.20) as amended. (Any references to rules below are references to this statutory instrument.) It is not our intention to go through every aspect of these rules, rather to identify some key provisions. The relevant rule has been identified for ease of cross-referencing. The Information Rights Tribunal website provides guidance to appellants and respondents as well as the appropriate forms that need to be completed.

The overriding objective of the procedural rules is to enable the Information Rights Tribunal to deal with cases fairly and justly, which includes:

- dealing with cases in ways that are proportionate to the importance of the case, its complexity and the anticipated costs and resources of the parties;
- avoiding unnecessary formality;
- ensuring, so far as practicable, that the parties are able to participate fully in the proceedings;
- using any special expertise of the Tribunal effectively;
- avoiding delay as far as compatible with proper consideration of the issue.

Subject to the provisions of the TCEA 2007, the Information Rights Tribunal may regulate its own procedures and may, *inter alia*:

- give directions in relation to the conduct of proceedings at any time and amend, suspend or set aside an earlier direction;
- extend or shorten the time for complying with any rule or practice direction unless this would conflict with some other statutory time limit;
- consolidate or hear together two or more sets of proceedings (or parts of) which raise common issues, or treat a case as a lead case;
- permit or require a party to amend a document;
- permit or require a party or another person to provide documents, information or submissions to the Tribunal or a party;
- deal with an issue in the proceedings as a preliminary issue;
- hold a hearing to consider any matter including a case management issue;
- decide the form of hearing and adjourn or postpone a hearing;
- require a party to produce a bundle for a hearing;
- stay proceedings;
- in certain circumstances, transfer proceedings to another court or tribunal if that court or tribunal has jurisdiction relating to the proceedings;
- suspend the effect of its own decision pending determination by the Tribunal or the Upper Tribunal of an application for permission to appeal against that decision.

10.12.1 Notice of appeal (rule 22)

Appeals to the Tribunal must be lodged, by a notice of appeal (NoA), within 28 days of service of the Information Commissioner's decision notice. Appellants who need extra time before lodging a formal appeal (for example, to draft the grounds for appeal) may request an extension of this 28-day period unless the Information Rights Tribunal exercises a discretion to extend this because it considers it just and right to do so. Applicants will need to provide a full explanation of why they require extra time. This issue has been addressed at length by both the First-tier Information Rights and Upper Tribunals in *Prof Sikka* v. *Information Commissioner* (EA/2010/ 0054 and GIA/1488/2010).

The appellant must include the following in the NoA:

- a copy of the Information Commissioner's decision being appealed;
- name and address of appellant and representative (if any);
- the result the appellant is seeking and the grounds for appeal;
- whether the appellant wishes to have an oral hearing or hearing on the papers only;
- the name and address of the relevant public authority;
- if the application is lodged outside the 28 days, the reasons why the Information Rights Tribunal should hear the matter.

The NoA must be sent to The First-tier Tribunal (Information Rights), General Regulatory Chamber, Arnhem House Support Centre, PO Box 9300, Leicester, LE1 6ZX.

Upon receipt of a properly completed NoA the Tribunal will issue an acknowledgment and a copy of the NoA will be sent to the Information Commissioner and any other joined respondent. Both are required to respond within 28 days.

10.12.2 The response (rule 23)

The Information Commissioner has 28 days to respond to the NoA although this period may, in special circumstances, be extended. The response must include the usual contact details and any other information required by a practice direction or direction; and the respondent must indicate whether he would be content for the case to be dealt with without an oral hearing. The Information Commissioner must include a statement as to whether and why he opposes the appellant's case and details of the reason behind the contested notice. The Commissioner must also send a copy of his response to the appellant. The same applies to any other respondent.

The Information Commissioner may respond by asking the Tribunal for the matter to be struck out either because the Tribunal is not entitled to hear the matter and/or the NoA discloses no reasonable grounds to hear the appeal.

After considering the NoA and the Commissioner's reply the Tribunal may dismiss the appeal summarily if it considers it proper to do so, but the Tribunal must notify the appellant that it intends to do this and allow the appellant to make written representations and request a hearing.

The appellant will be given a copy of the Information Commissioner's response and has the opportunity of providing further written submissions to the Tribunal but these must be sent within 14 days after the date on which the Commissioner or Tribunal sent the response to the appellant (rule 24).

10.12.3 Directions (rule 6) and entry directions (rule 18A)

The Information Rights Tribunal may give directions either on its own motion or on the application of one or more of the parties. Where the party makes a request for directions they must do so in writing with supporting reasons. The Information Rights Tribunal must notify the parties (and any other person affected by the direction) in writing, of its direction, unless the Tribunal considers there is a good reason not to do so. A party may challenge a direction.

The purpose of directions is to determine the scope and format of the hearing. As noted above, the Tribunal may also give a direction adding, subtracting or removing a party as an appellant or a respondent, either of its own motion or on the application of a third party (rule 9).

The Information Rights Tribunal may also give an 'entry direction' which requires the occupier of any premises (including the offices of a party) to permit entry to specified persons in order to allow such persons to inspect, examine, operate or test relevant equipment and materials. An entry direction will allow the inspection of computer equipment and examination of documents and materials connected with the processing of personal data or the storage, recording or deletion of other information.

In some cases the Tribunal may hold a directions hearing which is usually conducted by the chairman or deputy chairman and may involve all the parties meeting or it may be conducted by telephone.

10.12.4 Representation (rule 11)

There is no requirement that the parties are represented by legal advisors; the process is meant to be relatively informal (compared to a court hearing) and inexpensive. In about 60 per cent of Tribunal cases (this includes FOIA cases) the appeal is brought by the person who requested the information and in the great majority of these cases that person represents themselves. To this end the Information Rights Tribunal publishes guidance for unrepresented appellants. There is no legal aid to support applicants before the Information Rights Tribunal but some lawyers may be willing to undertake pro bono work in this area. A party may appoint a representative, who need not be legally qualified, to represent them in the proceedings. In practice, most public authorities do instruct counsel.

10.12.5 Confidentiality of information (rule 14)

As a general rule, information that is relevant to court proceedings should, as far as possible, be available to all of the parties. However, given the nature of the appeals (disputes over whether information should be disclosed) it will inevitably be necessary for the Tribunal to determine (and see) which information is to remain confidential from the other party(ies). The Tribunal will need to see this information in order to be able to judge whether it is covered by the exception claimed, and during the hearing it may be necessary to exclude some of the parties where such information is considered. To this end the Information Rights Tribunal may:

(a) make an order prohibiting the disclosure or publication of specified documents relating to the proceedings;

(b) make an order prohibiting the disclosure or publication of any matter likely to enable members of the public to identify any person the Tribunal considers should not be identified;

(c) give a direction prohibiting the disclosure of a document or information to a person if the Tribunal is satisfied that disclosure would be likely to cause that person or some other person serious harm and having regard to the interests of justice it is proportionate to give such a direction. If a party wishes information to be protected on this basis, they must provide the excluded document or information to the Tribunal and explain why the information should not be disclosed to the second party. Even if the Tribunal gives such a direction they may choose to provide the information to the second party's representative providing that it is not disclosed to any person without the Tribunal's consent.

The Tribunal may also give a direction to the parties that they must disclose information to the Tribunal on the basis that the Tribunal will not disclose the information to other persons or other specified persons. Where the case involves matters of national security, the Tribunal must ensure that information is not disclosed contrary to national security. Finally, when the Tribunal conducts proceedings and records its decision it must not undermine the effect of any order or direction given for national security.

10.12.6   Witnesses (rule 16)

The Tribunal has the power to summon witnesses either of its own initiative or on the application of one of the parties. It may do this by way of a summons requiring the person to attend a hearing or by order requiring the person to answer questions or produce documents that are in the person's control. The person must be given 14 days' notice or such shorter period as the Tribunal directs. This is subject to an important caveat: no person can be compelled to give any evidence or produce any document that the person could not be compelled to give or produce in a trial court.

10.12.7   The hearing (rules 32–36)

Under rule 32 the Information Rights Tribunal must hold a hearing before making a decision unless each party has consented to the matter being determined without an oral hearing and the Tribunal is satisfied that the matter can be dealt with on paper. However, this is subject to the caveat that if the Tribunal has held a hearing to consider a preliminary issue and following that no other issue needs to be determined, the Tribunal may dispose of the proceedings without holding a hearing.

The NoA form allows the applicant to indicate which option they prefer and the respondent and other parties are also permitted to express a preference, but the final decision rests with the Tribunal. The Tribunal will take into account whether there is disagreement about the facts of the case or where there are complicated legal arguments to be addressed.

The case may be dealt with on the basis of the papers alone; the parties may wish to put written witness statements before the Tribunal and they will need to set out their arguments in writing. The Tribunal will meet and will discuss the papers without needing to hear any oral evidence. This meeting will take place in private.

Oral hearings, where they take place, are usually heard by the panel at the Tribunal offices and each party is entitled to attend. Where it is anticipated that there will be considerable public interest then the oral hearing (if there is one) may be relocated to larger premises. Witnesses may be called and each party is expected to make their submissions before the Tribunal. As a general rule, all hearings must be held in public. However, given the nature of some of the information subject to the appeal, the Tribunal may direct that a hearing, or part of it, be held in private. The usual order for proceedings is as follows:

- introductions;
- in some cases the parties may be invited to make an opening statement;
- the tribunal will hear witness evidence (first witnesses called by the appellate followed by the Commissioner's witnesses and then any witnesses called by any other party);
- witnesses may be questioned by the party who called them and then by the other parties;
- the Tribunal may ask the witnesses questions either during or after the examination of the witnesses;
- the party that called the witness may ask further questions to clarify any issues arising from the questions asked by the other parties or the Tribunal;
- the parties may make final oral submissions to the Tribunal. The legal arguments will be examined at this stage.

10.12.8 Timescales

The Tribunal will try to deal with the appeal as quickly as possible, however, this will depend upon the cooperation of the parties. The actual timescale between receipt of the NoA and the final decision will often depend on whether there is a paper or oral hearing. An appellant may seek an early determination of the appeal but they must do this within the NoA and provide reasons why the matter should be expedited.

10.12.9 Costs (rule 10)

As a general rule, each side pays its own costs. However, the Information Rights Tribunal can make an order for costs on the application of one of the parties or of its own motion at any time or up to 14 days after its final decision. It may make an order only if it considers:

- that a party has acted unreasonably in bringing, defending or conducting the proceedings; or
- the Commissioner's decision was unreasonable.

Before making an order for costs against a person, the Tribunal must give that person an opportunity to make representations and (where the person is an individual) consider their personal financial means. Legal aid is not available for First-tier Tribunal cases.

10.12.10 Decisions (rule 38) and review of decision (rule 43)

The Information Rights Tribunal must issue its decision in writing by way of a Decision Notice but it may give its decision orally at a hearing with the written decision to follow. The Decision Notice must be provided to each party as soon as reasonably practicable after it has been made and it must include the reasons for the decision and notify the parties of their right of appeal. This is subject to the provisions preventing disclosure of certain information (see **10.12.5**).

If an applicant seeks leave to appeal the Tribunal's decision, the Tribunal can, having regard to its overriding objectives (which are detailed in rule 2), decide to review its decision. It is only permitted to review its 'original' decision if it is satisfied that there was an error of law in the decision. Following a review the Tribunal has the power to amend or correct its decision (see *Nottinghamshire County Council* v. *Information Commissioner* (EA/2010/0142)).

All decision notices are published on the Tribunal's website.

10.13 APPEALS TO THE UPPER TRIBUNAL

Prior to TCEA 2007, appeals from the Information Tribunal were to the High Court but this is no longer the case. Now, appeals are heard by the Administrative Appeals Chamber (AAC) of the Upper Tribunal (hereafter 'the Upper Tribunal') which is a Superior Court of Record with UK-wide jurisdiction. The right of appeal is granted to any of the parties to the Information Rights Tribunal decision, but only on a point of law and subject to permission to appeal.

The Upper Tribunal has four offices in London, Cardiff, Edinburgh and Belfast and an appeal would normally be heard at the office closest to the parties. The AAC panel of the Upper Tribunal can be comprised with different formulations of membership: one judge and two lay members; two judges and one lay member; three judges; or one judge and one lay member.

The Upper Tribunal can give authoritative decisions on the interpretation of EIR 2004.

The following points should be noted:

1. The right to appeal is restricted to those cases which raise a point of law.
2. The Information Rights Tribunal is required to transfer appeals in relation to national security certificates direct to the Upper Tribunal (see **8.3.4**).
3. The Information Rights Tribunal may refer a case or a preliminary issue to the President of the General Regulatory Chamber (GRC) with a request that the case/preliminary issue be considered for transfer to the Upper Tribunal. He will consult with the Chamber President of the AAC as to whether it would be appropriate to transfer the case to be heard in the first instance before the AAC. Cases or issues will only be suitable for transfer where some special feature merits this, for example, where a case raises issues of significant public importance or involves particularly complex issues. The Chambers have produced a joint office note which explains the process.
4. The Upper Tribunal also has jurisdiction to hear certain types of judicial review cases. These are where there is a procedural decision of a First-tier Tribunal which has no right of appeal and in cases which may be transferred to the Upper Tribunal from the High Court.

10.13.1 Permission to appeal

If either party wishes to appeal, they must seek leave to appeal from the Information Rights Tribunal and this must be done no later than 28 days of the applicant receiving the Tribunal's decision notice (or modified/amended notice) (rule 42). On receiving the application to appeal, the Tribunal must first consider whether it needs to review its decision (see **10.12.10**). If the Tribunal decides that it is not going to review its decision or takes no action then it must consider whether to give permission to appeal and must notify the parties of its decision as soon as practicable. The Tribunal can refuse to grant permission to appeal and if it does this it must provide a statement of its reasons and tell the applicant that he or she may make an application direct to the Upper Tribunal.

10.13.2 Grounds for appeal to the Upper Tribunal

It is only possible to appeal against the Information Rights Tribunal's decision on a point of law; this means the appellant must demonstrate that the Information Rights Tribunal made a mistake of law in reaching its decision. This includes appeals on the basis that the Information Rights Tribunal:

- misinterpreted EIR 2004;
- made an order which it is not entitled to make;
- reached a decision which is irrational;
- made a finding of fact without evidence;

- failed to provide adequate reasons for its decision;
- failed to take into account a material consideration or considered an irrelevant one;
- made a procedural error;
- acted in a way that is not compatible with the Human Rights Act 1998.

10.13.3   Further rights of appeal

Beyond the Upper Tribunal an appellate may seek leave to appeal to the Court of Appeal. It is unlikely that leave will be granted unless the case raises important issues of principle or raises questions about the interpretation of European law. The matter can be further appealed to the Supreme Court but only with leave from the Court of Appeal.

At the time of writing, only one EIR case had reached the Court of Appeal and beyond. In 2010 the Supreme Court considered an appeal in *Office of Communications (Ofcom)* v. *Information Commissioner* [2010] UKSC 3; [2010] All ER (D) 167 (Jan).

10.14   COMPLIANCE WITH THE DIRECTIVE AND CONVENTION

As a final note it should be recalled that EIR 2004 gives effect to the United Kingdom's obligations under Directive 2003/4/EC and the Aarhus Convention. A failure to comply with EIR 2004 may, in certain circumstances, constitute a breach of EU law and, as such, an aggrieved the person may lodge a complaint with the European Commission. The European Commission, as 'Guardian of the Treaties' has the power to investigate alleged breaches of EU law and to commence infraction proceedings against the defaulting Member State. Such proceedings may end with the case before the ECJ. The ECJ has the power to issue a judgment against the Member State and to require rectification of the breach. The ECJ also has the power to give authoritative preliminary rulings on the interpretation of the Directive and these rulings are binding on the national court and tribunals. The ECJ is (at the time of writing) considering a request for a ruling from the UK Supreme Court in the *Ofcom* case in relation to the public interest test (see **7.4.2**).

An aggrieved person may also complain to the Aarhus Compliance Committee which, if it accepts the complaint, will investigate the complaint and may direct the government to address any breaches of the Convention. The Convention Compliance Committee has already ruled against the UK in relation to other breaches of the Convention (in relation to costs incurred in judicial review proceedings). It is proving therefore to be a useful further mechanism for the public to challenge breaches of their 'rights' to access environmental information.

CHAPTER 11

Other statutory rights of access to information and public registers

11.1 INTRODUCTION

The reasons why a person or group may want to access environmental information are many and varied, as will be the subject matter of requests. What all applicants are likely to have in common though is a desire to be able to obtain information with relative ease, in the form they requested and at little or no expense. EIR 2004 go a long way to meeting this need. However, there are other 'access' regimes, including the public registers, that provide the public with access to a wide array of information, some of which is obviously environmental. Other regimes provide access to information of such a general or broad nature so as to encompass environmental information.

The aim of this chapter is to provide an overview of some of the other statutory regimes which may be used to access environmental information. The chapter does not endeavour to be exhaustive; the focus is on the principal regimes that provide access to information of an environmental nature. The chapter also briefly examines the extent to which the European Convention on Human Rights (ECHR) provides a right of access to environmental information. In addition, the chapter examines the Re-use of Public Sector Information Regulations 2005, SI 2005/1515.

11.2 PUBLIC REGISTERS

The most important other source of environmental information is that contained within public registers established by environmental and planning legislation. The public registers generally aim to provide the public with information about the way in which the regulatory bodies/planning authorities exercise their pollution control/ planning functions. They are intended to promote transparency and accountability. The extent to which the public registers achieve this aim is a matter of academic opinion and not within the scope of this book.

In broad terms, the public registers are created by either a statute or statutory instrument which requires a public authority to 'maintain' a register of information that is accessible to the public at reasonable times. A public register is essentially an official compilation of information held by a public authority. However, some private sector companies, notably in this context the privatised water and sewage undertakers (the water companies), are also subject to the duty to maintain a public register in relation to the way they exercise certain statutory functions. The requirement to maintain a public register should not be particularly onerous given that in reality most organisations will organise their filing systems in a structured manner which allows them to access documents and information on a specific subject in a single file or archive.

11.2.1 Features of public registers

The statutory provision establishing the public register will usually specify:

- What form the public register may take.
- How and when the information may be accessed.
- Whether the information is available freely. In most instances, inspection is free of charge, but sometimes the statute allows the public authority to levy a reasonable fee for copying entries.
- The information that must be included on the register.
- What information must be withheld, usually on the grounds of national security and at the direction of a Secretary of State or on the grounds of commercial confidentiality. However, see below at **11.2.6**.
- Whether the register will alert the user to the fact that information has been withheld. Typically, the user will not be made aware that information has been withheld on the grounds of national security but will be told that information is withheld for commercial confidentiality reasons.

11.2.2 Form of the public register

The use of the word 'register' can be a little misleading. The information may in fact be maintained in a traditional hard-copy file, in a filing cabinet or in a computer file. Early legislation which pre-dates the advent of the Internet is usually silent on the form of the register whereas more recent legislation will often allow the public authority to decide what form it takes. Rarely is the legislation prescriptive as to form. Hard-copy registers are usually sets of traditional files held within the offices of the authority concerned and may only be inspected by visiting the public authority's offices at reasonable times. Increasingly, however, authorities are making use of scanning and copying techniques to make much of the information available online. For example, the Environment Agency offers online registers which provide summary data backed up by the facility to request further details and copy documents, as well as other registers which are only available for inspection at the Agency's offices.

11.2.3 How and when information can be accessed

This depends on the form of the register. The various statutory provisions establishing the public registers (hereafter referred to generically as 'the public register legislation') generally tend to require that the register be 'open for inspection'. This may mean that a member of the public has to go to the offices of the public authority to examine the information in situ. Sometimes the legislation provides that the public register is held in two places, for example, by the Environment Agency which regulates the activity and the relevant local authority where the regulated activity is located. It would be extremely unusual for the legislation to prescribe when the information can be inspected; in the main, it will require that the information be available for inspection at reasonable times. This will usually be normal office hours but applicants would be well advised to check online or with the regulatory body before embarking on a wasted journey. The Environment Agency's public registers are open for inspection (at least according to the Agency's website) between 9.30 am and 4.30 pm, Monday to Friday (except bank holidays). There is no suggestion in any of the legislation that authorities should make the information available outside normal office hours (although the information may be available online – see below).

11.2.4 Can charges be imposed for inspecting information held on a public register?

Providing the information contained within the public register is environmental information within the meaning of EIR 2004, it can be inspected in situ without any charge to the person wishing to view the information. This is the case even if the statutory provision which established the register provides that charges may be levied for inspection.

   If the information is not environmental information then the question of whether charges may be levied is determined by the legislation establishing the register; however, most statutory provisions require that members of the public may inspect the register for free. It is usual for the relevant statutory provisions to permit the public authority to levy a 'reasonable' charge to cover any photocopying costs. This is often a matter of discretion for the authority concerned, but if the information falls within the broad definition of 'environmental information' under EIR 2004 then the charge must comply with the EIR 2004 requirement of reasonableness (see **6.5** on charges).

11.2.5 What information must be included?

This will be specified by the respective legislation. The public register legislation typically applies to regulatory bodies that have the power to grant permission for some form of conduct and/or have a statutory duty to monitor and enforce such permissions. For example, planning permissions for the development of land;

environmental permits for regulated activities; and trade effluent consents for discharges into sewers. At the risk of generalising, most of the public registers that relate to the exercise of regulatory functions relating to the environment/planning permission contain all or most of the information listed below:

- The application made by the operator for the grant of a license or permit or the developer for planning permission. This will include any supporting documentation including, where applicable, an environmental statement prepared by, or on behalf of, the operator or developer and any environmental investigation reports which were required as part of the application.
- The authorisation/licence/permit/planning permission that was granted in response to the application, including any conditions attached to it. For pollution control permits this will specify in some considerable technical detail what pollutants are permitted to be discharged into given receiving environments.
- Any data supplied by the operator of the regulated activity or developer in compliance with the conditions of the authorisation. For environmental permits, for example, this includes information supplied by operators on emissions into the environment.
- Any information collected by the regulatory body as a result of exercising its inspection powers.
- Any enforcement action taken against the operator of the regulated activity or the developer. This includes formal warnings, cautions, legal notices and prosecutions.
- Details of any offences committed by the operator or developer where the offences relate to a breach of the authorisation or permission.
- Any appeals against the permit/licence and any variations made to the permit/licence after the initial grant.

The precise detail about content will be found in the relevant statute or statutory instrument.

11.2.6 Information excluded from public registers and effect of EIR 2004, reg.5(6)

Many of the statutory provisions which established the public registers were enacted before EIR 2004 came into force in 2005 and enable information to be excluded from the register in a manner that is not wholly consistent with EIR 2004. Typically, the public register legislation permits or requires information to be excluded from the register on the grounds of national security or to protect the commercial confidentiality of the person providing the information. It is usual for the public register legislation to confer on the Secretary of State the power to say what information must be withheld from the public register on the grounds of national security and often there is no duty on the authority maintaining the register to even disclose that information has been withheld on this basis. The second and more frequently used ground for withholding information from the public registers relates to the commercial confidentiality of the person or organisation providing the information; often the public register legislation allows regulatory bodies and the Secretary of State to decide when information should be withheld on this basis.

This raises something of a problem. 'Environmental' information may lawfully be excluded from a public register by virtue of the statutory provision creating the register, but if it were requested under EIR 2004 it may not be exempt from disclosure since EIR 2004 exceptions are more stringent and require the application of the public interest test. The main problem with the discrepancy between the two sources of legislation is that a person may not know to make an information request under EIR 2004 where the register has originally been compiled under the public register legislation, as there may not be a duty on the authority to disclose that information has been withheld. This could mean that some information is potentially 'lost'. The precise relationship between the grounds for exclusion in the public register legislation and the exceptions under EIR 2004 is not clear but the following observations may be made:

1. EIR 2004 do not expressly or impliedly repeal any legislation which excludes information from the public registers.
2. However, if a person makes a request for information under EIR 2004 in relation to information withheld from a public register then the public authority must comply with EIR 2004, reg.5(6), which states that any enactment or rule of law that would prevent the disclosure of information in accordance with EIR 2004 shall not apply. This means the public authority maintaining the register would need to 'dissapply' the statutory provision excluding the information from the register and re-examine whether the information should be disclosed under EIR 2004.
3. In any event, when a court or tribunal is required to interpret national law (and this includes the statutory provisions excluding information from the public registers) then they must do so as to give effect, as far as possible, to the wording and purpose of Directive 2003/4/EC. This applies even if the statutory provision excluding information from the register predates Directive 2003/4/EC (*Marleasing SA* v. *La Commercial International de Alimentacion SA* (Case C-106/89) [1990] ECR I-4135).
4. When taking decisions whether to exclude information from the public registers, public authorities (including the Secretary of State) should have regard to all of the above and take into account the presumption in favour of disclosure required by EIR 2004, reg.12(2).

Information that is not environmental will be subject to the exceptions to disclosure contained within the public register legislation.

11.2.7 Categories of public registers

Public registers can be categorised in different ways, for example, by the type of public authority that maintains them or by the subject matter of the information that is held. Understanding the different categories can help an applicant in deciding which register to search to best provide the information they are after. For example, if a person wants to find out about land use in a particular locality, a good starting point is going to be the local authority in whose area the land is situated. Local authorities are under a duty to maintain various registers, some of which are discussed below, such as the planning register and the contaminated land register. If, on the other hand, a person wants to find out about a particular company and what pollutants it is discharging into the air or a river then the best starting point is likely to be a register held by the Environment Agency. However, local authorities also exercise considerable pollution control functions, and maintain a number of registers about pollution. A belt-and-braces approach may be needed by searching both the Agency's register and the relevant local authority's registers.

11.2.8   Usefulness of the registers

Although there has been considerable academic debate about the value of the public registers in terms of promoting accountability, they do appear to offer a particular benefit to the public; they are relatively simple to use, particularly those registers that are online and easy to navigate. The registers are also very useful where an applicant wants to know about the polluting activities of a particular company which is regulated by a public body, as the relevant public register affords a simple point of access to information about this company (less any information that may have been withheld because an exception to disclosure applies). The information about this company should be located in a single file or archive and therefore be easily accessible to an applicant wishing to see it.

11.3   ENVIRONMENTAL PERMITTING REGISTERS

The public registers of activities regulated by environmental permitting provide a wealth of information about the most polluting activities in England and Wales. Environmental permitting is now the principal mechanism for regulating polluting activities; the environmental permitting regime is provided for by the Environmental Permitting (England and Wales) Regulations 2010, SI 2010/675 (EPR 2010). EPR 2010 consolidate a range of environmental controls into a single system of permitting. Under EPR 2010 various polluting activities (referred to as regulated facilities) are prohibited from operating unless the operation is in accordance with the requirements of an environmental permit. The environmental permitting regime provides for a dual system of regulation; depending on the nature of the activity the regulatory body will either be the Environment Agency or the local authority in whose area the regulated activity takes place. EPR 2010 prescribe the regulatory body for each type of regulated activity. The range of activities that are regulated under the environmental permitting regime is wide and includes:

- waste management (landfill, incineration, recycling);
- seriously polluting activities subject to the system of integrated pollution prevention control (IPPC);
- discharges into water including groundwater;
- radioactive substances;
- closed mining operations.

The regime is to be extended in the future to include water abstraction. Several thousand activities have an environmental permit and details about all of these permits (subject to the application of any exceptions to disclosure) are available for inspection on the environmental permitting public registers. This represents a vast amount of information about private companies and their environmental performance.

The detailed provisions governing the duty to maintain the environmental permitting public registers are contained in EPR 2010, Part 5, regs.45–56 and Sched.24. It is notable that these provisions postdate EIR 2004 and therefore align themselves with EIR 2004, at least in terms of the commercial confidentiality exception to disclosure (see **11.3.3** below).

Both the Environment Agency and the local authorities are obliged to maintain public registers of information about the activities that they regulate. In addition, each local authority is required to include on its register any information which is included on the Agency's public register for which the Agency is the regulator and which is in the authority's area. Therefore, it may make good sense for someone to search the local authority public register in the first instance if he or she is trying to find out about a regulated activity within his or her local area.

One of the criticisms of previous registers was that the legislation did not always specify how frequently information on the public register should be updated. However, EPR 2010, reg.46(7) requires that the Agency/local authority must enter information on its public register as soon as reasonably practicable after it comes within the regulator's possession.

11.3.1 Access to the registers and the form of the registers

A register may be kept in any form but must be freely accessible to the public at all reasonable times and the Agency/local authority must enable members of the public to obtain copies of information on payment of a reasonable charge. Most of the Agency's registers are online but they are also open for inspection Monday to Friday, 9.30 am to 4.30 pm (except bank holidays). Local authorities may have different opening times so members of the public should ring and check with the authority or check for information on the local authority's website.

11.3.2 What information must be included on an environmental permitting public register?

Schedule 24 to the EPR 2010 contains a very long list of what information must be included on a public register. The list is far too long to repeat here; what follows is a summary of the main content:

- Every application made for the grant of an environmental permit or the variation, transfer or surrender of an environmental permit and all supporting documentation including environmental investigation reports.
- All representations made in respect of an application to grant or vary an environmental permit (unless the person making the representation requests that this be withheld; in which case the register will include a statement that a representation was made without detailing it).
- Details of every environmental permit granted by the regulator. Details of any appeals lodged and the outcomes (including any representations made).
- Monitoring data, including data from any inspections by the regulatory body and information supplied by the operator of the regulated activity as required by the environmental permit.
- Details of any convictions or formal cautions for offences under EPR 2010.
- An inventory of certain closed mining waste facilities.
- Details of fees and charges paid to a regulator under EPR 2010.
- The total expenditure of the regulator in exercising its functions under EPR 2010.

The regulator is not required to include any information relating to criminal proceedings, or anything which is the subject matter of criminal proceedings, before those proceedings are finally disposed of. This includes information about prospective criminal proceedings.

11.3.3 Information excluded from a public register

EPR 2010 allow for information to be excluded on two grounds; national security and commercial confidentiality. EPR 2010, reg.46 provides that where information of any description is excluded from any public register, a statement must be entered on the register indicating the existence of information of that description. This is important because it enables members of the public to see that information has been withheld from the public domain.

National security

The issue of whether information should be excluded from an environmental permitting register is always to be determined by the Secretary of State (or the Welsh Minister in Wales) (EPR 2010, reg.47). The Secretary of State can issue two different types of directions to the regulatory bodies.

- First, under EPR 2010, reg.47(1) the Secretary of State may direct that certain specified information or information of a specified description must be excluded from a public register on the grounds of national security. Where the Agency or local authority decides that it is going to withhold information (other than information about radioactive substances) subject to this direction then it must notify the respective Secretary of State/Minister.
- Second, the Secretary of State may issue directions under EPR 2010, reg.47(3) that, in the interests of national security, the regulator must not include certain information on a public register without first referring the matter to the Secretary of State for his determination.

There is also provision for a person to notify the Secretary of State (and also simultaneously the relevant regulator) that in his opinion certain information should be excluded on the grounds that its inclusion would be contrary to the interests of national security. The Secretary of State must be informed what this information is and be given an indication of its apparent nature. The regulatory body cannot include this information on a public register until such time as the Secretary of State decides that it can be included. However, there is nothing in EPR 2010, reg.47 to suggest that information may only be excluded if disclosure would adversely affect national security or indeed that disclosure would not be in the public interest. On this basis, therefore, it is arguable that the prohibition on disclosure is not entirely compatible with EIR 2004. However, given that a Minister of the Crown may issue a Ministerial Certificate preventing disclosure on the grounds of national security, this may, in practice, be a moot point.

Commercially confidential information

It goes without saying that many companies subject to EPR 2010 will want to avoid the disclosure of commercially confidential information. However, EPR 2010 are quite strict in dealing with this and mirror the corresponding provisions of EIR 2004 in that the exception only applies to certain information. Under EPR 2010, s.51(2)(c), for information to be classed as commercially confidential:

(a) the information must be commercial or industrial information;
(b) its confidentiality must be provided by law to protect a legitimate economic interest; and
(c) in all the circumstances, the public interest in maintaining the confidentiality of the information must outweigh the public interest in disclosure.

Ultimately it is up to the regulator to decide whether information should be excluded on the grounds of commercial confidentiality, but when making this decision the regulator must apply a presumption in favour of disclosure (EPR 2010, reg.50(2)(b)). The Secretary of State has the power to 'direct' that certain specified confidential information, or confidential information of a specified description, must be included on the register notwithstanding the confidential nature of the information. However, before he does this he must first consider that the public interest in including such information on the register outweighs the public interest in maintaining its confidentiality (EPR 2010, reg.56). EPR 2010, reg.56 sets out the procedure to be followed:

1. If the regulatory body considers the information is confidential:

    -   when this happens the regulatory body must notify the information subject, who may either consent or object to disclosure within 15 working days after the date of notification;
    -   if the information subject consents to disclosure then the information should be put on the public register;
    -   if the information subject objects then the regulatory body can still override this and make a 'final confidentiality decision' that the information should be included on the register notwithstanding the objection. In addition, the Secretary of State may direct that the information must be included on the register.

2. The person about whom the information relates has notified the regulatory body that it considers the information is confidential and has explained why it/he/she thinks this is the case.

In these circumstances the regulatory body can still decide that the information must be included on the register (by way of a final confidentiality decision) or the Secretary of State may direct that the information must be included.

When the regulatory body is taking a final confidentiality decision in either of the two cases mentioned above, it must take into account the information subject's objections but must also apply a presumption in favour of disclosing confidential information and consider the weight of the competing public interests (maintaining confidentiality against disclosure to the public). When excluding information the regulator needs to take care not to exclude any other information which is not commercially confidential unless the information is not reasonably capable of being separated for the purposes of inclusion on the register. In other words, the regulator should take care when redacting commercially confidential information that it does not exclude other information which should be publicly available.

As a general rule, information which has been withheld on the grounds of commercial confidentiality must be included on the register for four years after the confidentiality decision (or any shorter period specified in that decision) unless the information subject objects. In which case the procedures listed above should be followed again.

Information on emissions cannot be excluded

All of the above is subject to an extremely important caveat; if the information is information on emissions it cannot be excluded from the register. This is entirely consistent with EIR 2004, reg.12(9). For further discussion, see **8.6**.

11.4 PLANNING REGISTERS

The Town and Country Planning Act 1947 established the first public register with information about planning applications; in this respect the planning registers are arguably the first public registers of information about the environment. Under the Town and Country Planning Act (TCPA) 1990, s.69 every local planning authority is under a duty to maintain a public register of the information, currently prescribed under Part 7 (art.36) of the Town and Country Planning (Development Management Procedure) (England) Order 2010, SI 2010/2184 (DMPO 2010). This requires that the planning registers be maintained in two parts.

Part 1 must contain information about planning applications and applications for approval of reserved matters (where outline planning permission has been granted) which have been made or sent to the local planning authority but are not finally disposed of. Part 1 must contain, *inter alia*:

- a copy of the application and any accompanying plans and drawings;
- a copy of any planning obligation or agreement under the Highways Act 1980, s.278 (agreement for the execution of works) in connection with the application;
- particulars of any modification to any planning obligation or s.278 agreement.

Part 2 of the register must contain, *inter alia*, the following in respect of every application for planning permission:

- a copy of the application and the plans and drawings submitted in relation to the application and any accompanying design and access statements;
- particulars of any directions given under TCPA 1990 or DMPO 2010 in respect of the application;
- the decision including details of any conditions attached to the planning permission;
- where the Secretary of State has taken a decision (whether on appeal, where the matter has been referred to him or in respect of urgent Crown development), the Secretary of State's decision, reference number, date and effect of decision;
- the date of any subsequent approval;
- a copy of any planning obligation or s.278 agreement entered into in connection with the decision or taken into account when making the decision;
- particulars of any modifications to, or discharge of, any planning obligation or s.278 agreement;
- particulars of any appeals to the Secretary of State and the date and effect of the Secretary of State's decision;
- details in respect of certificates of lawfulness granted under TCPA 1990, ss.191 or 192;
- information about simplified planning zone schemes in the area.

The registers must be open for inspection at all reasonable times. They must be indexed and there must also be a separate index for applications for developments involving mining operations or the creation of mineral working deposits. The register has to be kept at the principal office of the local planning authority or parts of the register that relate to an area within the authority must be kept at a place within that area or convenient to it. For example, in Northumberland County Council, which is a unitary authority, the register is maintained in the 'old' district area offices. DMPO 2010 allows local planning authorities to make the register open for inspection via the authority's website.

In addition to the above, DMPO 2010, art.37 also provides for a Part 3 to the register, which must contain details of draft and adopted local development orders. DMPO 2010, art.38 makes further provision for a register of stop notices and enforcement notices. This is a useful source of information because it enables members of the public to find out whether the local planning authority has taken any enforcement action in respect of a breach of planning permission. The register must be indexed in such a way as to enable searches by reference to the address of the land.

11.5 CONTAMINATED LAND REGISTERS

Part IIA of the Environmental Protection Act 1990 (EPA 1990) requires local authorities to identify any land within the local authority area that is contaminated and to secure the remediation (clean up) of the land either on a voluntary basis or via the service of a remediation notice. Some sites will be designated as 'special sites' and thereafter responsibility for securing the remediation rests with the Environment Agency.

EPA 1990, s.78R places a duty on the enforcing authority (which is either the local authority in whose area the land is situated or the Environment Agency if the site has been designated as a special site) to maintain a public register of contaminated land. The public register is intended to act as a full and permanent record of all regulatory action taken by the respective enforcing authority in respect of the remediation of the contaminated land and will include information about the condition of the land.

The Environment Agency must send a copy of the details of any special site to the local authority in whose area the special site is situated, which means the information for special sites is available on two registers.

11.5.1 Content of the registers

The registers may be kept in any form but must contain the following information:

(a) remediation notices served by that authority (a remediation notice is a legally enforceable notice which requires the recipient to remediate the land to a standard specified in the notice);

(b) appeals against such remediation notices or charging notices;

(c)   remediation statements or remediation declarations prepared and published under EPA 1990;

(d)   any notice relating to the designation of the land as a special site, including any referrals to the Secretary of State in relation to that decision and any notices terminating that designation;

(e)   any notifications given to the public authority by the person responsible for the remediation of what they claim to have done by way of remediation. This does not constitute any representation on the part of the authority that the thing that has been claimed to have been done has in fact been done;

(f)   details of any convictions for offences under EPA 1990, Part IIA;

(g)   notice that information has been excluded from the register on the grounds of EPA 1990, s.78T;

(h)   any other matters prescribed by the Secretary of State.

(See the Contaminated Land (England) Regulations 2006, SI 2006/1380, reg.13 and Sched.3.) All of this information falls easily within the definition of 'environmental information' under EIR 2004 since it is information about the state of land and measures affecting or likely to affect the state of land. However, the value of the information being available in a specific public register is that it enables an applicant to search for information about a specific area of land/site in order to find out about the state of the land and measures taken to remediate it. The contaminated land registers must be available at reasonable times and free of charge. The local authorities/Environment Agency must give members of the public facilities for obtaining copies of entries, on payment of reasonable charges.

11.5.2 Exclusion from the registers

National security

According to EPA 1990, s.78S, information must be excluded from the register if the Secretary of State considers that its inclusion would be contrary to the interests of national security. The Secretary of State may issue directions specifying information, or descriptions of information, which must be excluded or which must be referred to him for his determination. The register will not show where this has happened. However, see **11.2.6** above.

Commercial confidentiality

Under EPA 1990, s.78T information must be withheld from the register if it relates to the affairs of an individual or business and the information is commercially confidential, unless the person has consented to the information being disclosed. Information is considered to be commercially confidential, in relation to any individual or person, if its inclusion in the register would prejudice to an unreasonable degree the commercial interests of that individual or person. However, any prejudice relating to the value of contaminated land or otherwise to ownership or occupation of the land is to be disregarded for these purposes. If the commercially confidential information is 'environmental' then the only grounds for excluding the information will be those under EIR 2004, but if the information is not environmental then decisions regarding disclosure must be taken by reference to EPA 1990, s.78T.

The Secretary of State can issue directions requiring certain types of information to be included on the register notwithstanding that the information may be commercially confidential. The assumption is that after four years the information is no longer commercially confidential, but the person who provided the information can apply to the authority to maintain the exception after four years have elapsed. The register will explain that information has been withheld on this basis.

11.6 REGISTERS UNDER THE ENVIRONMENT AND SAFETY INFORMATION ACT 1988

The Environment and Safety Information Act 1988, s.1 requires certain public authorities with responsibilities under various legislative provisions to maintain a register of the notices they serve under the different pieces of legislation. These are:

- the Health and Safety Executive (HSE) under the Health and Safety at Work etc. Act 1974;
- local authorities acting as building authorities under the Safety of Sports Grounds Act 1975;
- the Food Standards Agency under the Food and Environment Protection Act 1985;
- the HSE, the Fire and Rescue Authority, the relevant local authority and the fire inspector under the Regulatory Reform (Fire Safety) Order 2005, SI 2005/1541.

The registers contain details of notices served by those authorities under those Acts. The public registers have to be adequately indexed in order that they can be searched by reference to particular premises or persons. The registers and index must be open to inspection by the public, free of charge, at all reasonable hours. The public authority may charge a reasonable fee for providing copies of entries on the register.

Information may be excluded from the register on the grounds that inclusion of an entry on the register would disclose information about a trade secret or secret manufacturing process. Section 4 of the Act details the procedures that are to be followed when a person in receipt of a notice issued by one of the above authorities (the person affected) applies to have information withheld from the register. The person affected must apply in writing within 14 days of the service of the notice for the information to be withheld on this basis.

11.7 LOCAL LAND CHARGES REGISTERS AND PROPERTY SEARCHES

11.7.1 Local land charges register

Under the Local Land Charges Act 1975, s.3 local authorities are under a duty to maintain a local land charges register (LLCR) and an index which enables all entries on the register to be readily traced. The register is not required to be kept in a documentary form. It must be maintained by the 'registering authority' in whose area the land or the land affected by the charge is situated. The register contains details of local land charges which have been acquired by a local authority or National Park authority or a sewerage undertaker that are binding on successive owners of the land affected by the charge. A charge may relate to a prohibition or restriction on the use of land or a positive obligation affecting land. The LLCR includes land charges that are embodied in any condition attached to a consent or licence granted by a local authority (such as a planning permission) or enforceable under a covenant or agreement or imposed by a Minister of the Crown or government department (see LLCA 1975, s.4). A search of the land charges register will reveal the impact of building regulations and traffic/highways control on a particular property or whether the property is listed or subject to a tree preservation order.

11.7.2 Local searches and Form CON29R

The LLCR provides important information to anyone wishing to purchase residential or commercial property land and as such a 'local search' forms a vital part of the conveyancing process. Before EIR 2004 came into force, the local authority would be requested to search the LLCR and also answer certain questions designed to establish whether the property in question was, or might become, affected by certain activities, such as a new road scheme or a compulsory purchase order. To facilitate searches of the LLCR and other public registers held by local authorities, the Law Society devised a standard set of required and optional questions which are contained in Forms CON29R and CON29O. These would be sent to the relevant local authority, who would supply the answers for a fee. It is possible to answer most, but not all, of the questions set out in Form CON29R by inspecting various public registers held by the local authority. The majority of solicitors subcontracted property searches to commercial property search agencies and local authorities have charged for providing this information; the charges represented a significant income stream for local authorities.

11.7.3 Impact of EIR 2004 on charges for property search information

As far as property search questions are concerned, local authorities were able to charge for providing answers to property search questions on a cost recovery basis (the Local Authorities (England) (Charges for Property Searches) Regulations 2008, SI 2008/3248 (CPSR 2008)) and for permitting personal searches of the

LLCR (Local Land Charges Rules 1977, Sched.3, item 5 (now revoked)). However, the advent of EIR 2004 has had a major impact on the capacity of local authorities to charge for the information on the LLCR or indeed for any property information that falls within the broad definition of 'environmental information'. The majority of information required to answer the CON29R questions is environmental information and therefore requests for information using CON29R must be regarded as requests for environmental information under EIR 2004 and subject to EIR 2004 charging provisions. As noted in **6.5** a public authority is not permitted to charge for any in situ inspection of the public registers and is only permitted to levy reasonable charges for providing copies of information. Consequently, EIR 2004 are preventing local authorities from levying charges that they had previously relied upon to generate income. This is proving to be somewhat controversial as manifested by the 16 ICO decisions and two Tribunal decisions to date. (The High Court recently considered whether the Local Government Act 1972 and the CPSR 2008 compel local authorities to allow searches of property search records and concluded that they did not. Unfortunately, the case made no reference to EIR 2004 and therefore added little to the issue – see *One Search Direct Holdings Ltd (formerly SPH Holdings Ltd) (trading as OneSearch Direct)* v. *York City Council* [2010] EWHC 590 (Admin); [2010] All ER (D) 198.)

In the light of these decisions and changes to legislation, the following points need to be considered in relation to the LLCR and property searches:

1. The majority of information provided by local authorities in response to property search enquiries is likely to be environmental, for example, relating to planning permissions, road developments, tree preservation orders, contaminated land, conservation area status, etc. Even though each of the answers on Form CON29R may be a simple yes or no it is necessary to search information which in most cases is environmental.

2. Local Land Charges Rules 1977, Sched.3, item 5 which permitted local authorities to charge for personal searches of the LLCR has been revoked by the Local Land Charges (Amendment) Rules 2010, SI 2010/1812. The explanatory memorandum to the 2010 rules explains that the 1977 rules were amended to remove fees for personal searches because the fees are incompatible with EIR 2004.

3. Under CPSR 2008 the charging provisions do not apply where the local authority is required to provide access free of charge under the provisions of another enactment. This clearly includes EIR 2004.

4. Some local authorities have sought to 'avoid' EIR 2004 by arguing, *inter alia*: the information is not environmental; and unless the applicant makes it clear the request is under EIR 2004 it should not be dealt with as an EIR request (see *North East Lincolnshire Council* FER0326629). Both arguments have been rejected.

5. Under EIR 2004, reg.8(2) a public authority cannot impose any charges on any person who inspects information held on a public register (including the LLCR) or inspects other information in situ at the public authority's offices.

6. A request to inspect information in situ triggers EIR 2004, reg.6(1) (form and format) (*Denbighshire County Council* FER0277170). EIR 2004 does not confer an absolute right to in situ inspection but it may only be refused if it is reasonable to make the information available in a different form or format or the information is already publicly available and easily accessible in another form or format. The fact that the information may be made available via the Form CON29R for a charge does not make it publicly available and easily accessible in another format.

7. Some local authorities have argued that it is not reasonable to allow in situ inspection and have sought instead to provide the information in a collated form, subject to a charge (see *East Riding of Yorkshire Council* v. *Information Commissioner (and Stanley Davies Group Ltd t/a York Place)* (EA/2009/0069). The onus is firmly on the local authority to establish that it is reasonable to provide the information in some other form or format. The Commissioner and Tribunal will examine the arguments very closely and will need clear evidence as to why it is unreasonable to allow in situ inspection.

8. It is not reasonable to refuse inspection merely to justify imposing a charge for making the information available in another format (*Conwy County Borough Council* FER0277395).

9. Other local authorities have permitted in situ inspection but have tried to impose charges. The Tribunal is clear that this constitutes a breach of EIR 2004. (For example, *Wrexham County Borough Council* FER0276442 and *Cheshire West and Chester Council* FER0276228.)

Practical example

East Riding of Yorkshire Council v. *Information Commissioner (and Stanley Davies Group Ltd t/a York Place)* (EA/2009/0069)

York Place is a personal search company providing search services for solicitors. It asked whether it could make arrangements to inspect building control/traffic schemes affecting a certain property. None of the information was subject to an exception to disclosure. The council said the information could not be inspected without further collation and that it would only provide the information in a collated form subject to a reasonable charge for providing it. The council argued that permitting inspection would pose the risk of the applicant accessing personal data and corrupting data that was not locked down; that access to raw data would be unintelligible to the applicant; the council's software licenses did not permit further access to the data; and the records were located in several different locations. The Tribunal considered that the council had not produced sufficient evidence of these claims; for example, it had not acted reasonably in rejecting other means of maintaining security during an inspection. See also *New Forest District Council* FER0308439.

11.8 THE POLLUTANT RELEASE AND TRANSFER REGISTERS: E-PRTR AND UK PRTR

Regulation (EC) 166/2006 established the European Pollutant Release and Transfer Register (E-PRTR) in order to fulfil the requirements of art.5(9) of the Aarhus Convention. The EC Regulation came into force on 24 February 2006. It requires operators of various facilities (listed in the regulation) to report information about the release to air, water and land of specified pollutants; off-site transfers of waste (over certain prescribed limits); and off-site transfers of other prescribed pollutants. Operators have to report the information to the European Commission. The EC Regulation lists 91 key pollutants. The facilities subject to these reporting require-ments are those facilities which are subject to the requirements of Directive 2008/1/EC on integrated pollution prevention and control; they are regulated by the Environment Agency and local authorities under EPR 2010.

The E-PRTR provides (at EU level) a searchable database of data reported annually by 24,000 industrial facilities covering 65 economic activities across Europe. The public can access this register free of charge on the Internet and are able to find information using various search criteria (type of pollutant, geographical location, affected environment, source facility, etc.).

The UK PRTR is also available online. This enables the user to search infor-mation on pollutant release and off-site waste transfer from a variety of industrial sources across the UK where the relevant threshold has been met or exceeded. The dataset is compiled by the Environment Agency, the Scottish Environment Protec-tion Agency, the Northern Ireland Environment Agency and the Department for Energy and Climate Change. Defra is responsible for collating data from local authority sites in England and Wales. It is possible to search the UK PRTR by using the 'What's in your backyard' facility on the Environment Agency's website.

11.9 INFORMATION ASSET REGISTERS

An Information Asset Register (IAR) is an online register/catalogue of unpublished information held by a public authority. The information may be in any form but is commonly a collection of datasets or other raw unpublished information. Each government department or Crown body is responsible for compiling its own register of the information assets it holds. The Office of Public Sector Information (OPSI) is responsible for coordinating the compilation of a government-wide IAR. The IAR does not provide direct access to the information holdings but it does enable the public to search for unpublished information held by government departments which then may be accessible via FOIA 2000 or EIR 2004. Requests for the information from the IAR are dealt with in accordance with FOIA 2000 or EIR 2004 but the scheme is largely intended to facilitate the commercial re-use of public sector information.

11.10   RE-USE OF PUBLIC SECTOR INFORMATION (PSIR 2005)

The fact that information may be in the public domain, either because it is available on a publication scheme or in response to a request, does not necessarily mean it can be used freely by the recipient. Neither FOIA 2000 or EIR 2004 confer any automatic right to re-use the information. It is self-evident that a great deal of the information held by public authorities can be used for significant commercial gain, hence the introduction of the Re-use of Public Sector Information Regulations 2005, SI 2005/1515 (PSIR 2005), which give effect to Directive 2003/98/EC on the re-use of public sector information. PSIR 2005 came into force on 1 July 2005.

PSIR 2005 impose a statutory duty on public sector bodies (defined in PSIR 2005, reg.3 – essentially all government departments (including government trading funds) most National Health Service bodies, local authorities and various non-departmental bodies, such as the Environment Agency). Public sector bodies must provide access to details about re-usable information held by them, preferably by electronic means with an electronic search capacity. This information may be made available via the authority's publication scheme or, as appropriate, the IAR, depending on the nature of the information, but must allow for ready identification of those public sector documents that are available for re-use. PSIR 2005 do not alter the access provisions under FOIA 2000 or EIR 2004; they apply to information once it has been obtained by an applicant or is otherwise accessible by means other than making an information request under FOIA 2000/EIR 2004.

PSIR 2005 only apply to copyright and related rights such as database rights. In the United Kingdom most information produced by the public sector is subject to copyright protection. (Central government documents are covered by the Crown.) This means that the public sector bodies have the legal right to authorise the re-use of the information they produce and they may do this via a permit to re-use under PSIR 2005, reg.7. Applicants may make a request for re-use under PSIR 2005, reg.6 which may be granted subject to conditions or rejected since the public sector body is not under an obligation to permit re-use. Any application to re-use Crown copyright must be sent to HMSO.

PSIR 2005, reg.15 allows a public sector body to charge for re-use but where charges are made then the total income should not exceed the cost of collection, production, reproduction and dissemination of the documents and a reasonable rate of investment.

11.11   SUMMARY OF PRINCIPAL PUBLIC REGISTERS AND SOURCES OF INFORMATION

The following list is not comprehensive. Defra previously produced a list of registers up to February 2008 but has not continued the exercise on the basis that each public authority is required to list their own registers. This is a pity because it means there is no central sources of registers. The Defra register is available at **http://archive.defra.gov.uk/corporate/policy/opengov/eir/pdf/register.pdf**.

Subject matter/where public register is held	Statutory provision where relevant/ comments
Air National Atmospheric Emissions Inventory (NAEI) **http://naei.defra.gov.uk/**	Not specifically a public register. The NAEI compiles estimates of emissions to the atmosphere from UK sources such as cars, trucks, power stations and industrial plant. The website provides a wealth of information about atmospheric pollution.
Coal mining operations Coal Authority	Coal Industry Act 1994, ss.35 and 56.
Coal mining Local authorities	Coal Mining Subsidence Act 1991, s.47. Underground coal mining operations which may result in subsidence in the area.
Contaminated land Local authorities/Environment Agency	EPA 1990, ss.78R–78T and the Contaminated Land (England) Regulations 2006, SI 2006/1380, reg.13 and Sched.3). Land determined to be contaminated and details of remedial actions required or undertaken. See **11.5**.
Control of Major Accidents and Hazards (COMAH) The Health and Safety Executive and Environment Agency acting jointly.	Control of Major Accident Hazards Regulations 1999, SI 1999/743, Sched.8. Not available electronically.
Eco Management and Audit Scheme (EMAS) **www.iema/net/ems/ukregister**	Article 6 of Regulation (EC) 761/2001 of the European Parliament and of the Council of 19 March 2001 allowing voluntary participation by organisations in a community eco-management and audit scheme. Information about UK organisations registered for the EMAS scheme.
Environmental permitting Local authorities/Environment Agency **www2.environment-agency.gov.uk/epr**	Part 5 of the Environmental Permitting (England and Wales) Regulations 2010, SI 2010/675. See **11.3**.
Food safety Local authorities	Article 6(2) of Regulation (EC) No 852/ 2004 of the European Parliament and of the Council of 29 April 2004 on the hygiene of foodstuffs.

Forestry Register of grant scheme and felling applications Register of environmental impact assessments **www.forestry.gov.uk/forestry**	Environmental Impact Assessment (Forestry) (England and Wales) Regulations, SI 1999/2228, reg.24.
Genetically Modified Organisms (GMOs) Register of consents for release of GMOs Defra	EPA 1990, ss.111 and 112 and Genetically Modified Organisms (Deliberate Release) Regulations 2002, SI 2002 /3188.
Land County Councils, Metropolitan Councils, District Councils and the Council of any London Borough	Commons Registration Act 1965 Commons Act 2006 require registers of common land and town and village greens to be maintained.
Local Land Charges District councils, county borough councils, council of any London borough and the Common Council of the City of London	LLCA 1975 (see **11.7**)
Litter control areas Lists all street litter control notices County councils, county borough councils, district councils, London borough councils, the Common Council of the City of London and the Council of the Isles of Scilly	EPA 1990, s.95. Need not be kept in documentary form. Available for inspection at reasonable time for free. Copies available on payment of reasonable charge.
Marine licensing Marine Management Organisation Licenses issued in respect of deposits at sea for both construction related activities and disposal of dredged or other materials	Marine and Coastal Access Act 2009, s.101 and Marine Licensing (Register of Licensing Information) Regulations 2011, SI 2011/424.
Pesticides Defra, Health and Safety Executive, Fire Authority, Secretary of State, the council of any London borough, the Common Council of the City of London, district councils, county councils, county borough councils	Environment and Safety Information Act 1988. Notices issued under Food and Environment Protection Act 1958, s.19 relating to the unlawful use, sale, supply, advertisement or importation of pesticides.
Planning District planning authorities, council of every metropolitan district or London Borough	TCPA 1990, ss.69 and 188. Every application for planning permission, decisions taken, any environmental impact assessment documentation, enforcement actions. See **11.4**.

Planning (hazardous substances) The Hazardous Substances Authority	Planning (Hazardous Substances) Act 1990, s.28. Consents to allow hazardous substances on or in land.
Pollutant Release and Transfer Register Environment Agency European Environment Agency	Regulation (EC) No 166/2006 of the European Parliament and of the Council of 18 January 2006 concerning the establishment of a European Pollutant Release and Transfer Register and amending Council Directives 91/689/EEC and 96/61/EC. See **11.8**.
Radioactive substances Environment Agency	Was the Radioactive Substances Act 1993, s.39, now repealed and replaced by EPR 2010.
Sewer maps Private sewerage undertakers	WIA 1991, s.199.
Trade effluent consents Private sewerage undertakers	WIA 1991, s.196.
Tree preservation orders Local planning authority	Regulations 3(3) and 6(c) of the Town and Country Planning (Trees) Regulations, SI 1999/1892, regs.3(3) and 6(c).
Water quality Environment Agency Identifies water quality objectives and water quality sampling and remedial works	WRA 1991, s.190.
Water supply maps Private water companies	WIA 1991, s.198.
Waste carriers and waste brokers Environment Agency	Control of Pollution (Amendment) Act 1989, s.2 and the Controlled Waste (Registration of Carriers and Seizure of Vehicles) Regulations 1991, SI 1991/1624, reg.3. Register must be indexed and arranged so that members of the public can readily trace information contained in it. Free of charge.
Waste electrical and electronic equipment (WEEE) public registers Environment Agency	Waste Electrical and Electronic Equipment Regulations 2006, SI 2006/3289, as amended. Lists of registered WEEE producers, WEEE compliance schemes, approved authorised treatment facilities and approved exporters. Online, complied annually.

Water abstraction	WRA 1991, s.189, as amended. Details of water abstraction and impounding licenses granted under WRA 1991, Part II.

11.12   OTHER STATUTORY SOURCES

11.12.1   The Public Records Act 1958

The Public Records Act 1958 requires public bodies, including central government departments, to consider whether their administrative and departmental records need to be permanently preserved. Most documents to be preserved must be transferred to the National Archives for safekeeping and to afford the public access under FOIA 2000 or EIR 2004, unless, for example, they need to be retained for administrative or other purposes.

11.12.2   Local government information

There are a number of statutes which provide access to certain information held by local authorities. These have developed over time since the Public Bodies (Admissions to Meetings) Act 1960, which gave the press the right to be supplied with a copy of the agenda for certain local government meetings. The principal provision is now the Local Government Act (LGA) 1972 which was amended by Local Government (Access to Information) Act 1985. Part VA of LGA 1972 provides for public and press access to certain local authority council meetings subject to certain limits when the public may be excluded. The public may be excluded from a council meeting at a particular point if it is likely, in view of the matter that is being discussed, that if the public were present, confidential information would be disclosed to them in breach of the obligation of confidence (LGA 1972, s.100A). Additionally, the council can vote to exclude the public from parts of a meeting where certain 'exempt' information is being discussed. Exempt information is described in LGA 1972, Sched.12A. This includes information:

- about an individual;
- which is likely to reveal the identity of an individual;
- relating to the financial or business affairs of any particular person (including the authority holding that information);
- relating to any actual or contemplated consultations or negotiations, in connection with any labour relations matter arising between the authority or a Minister of the Crown and employees/office holders;
- in respect of which a claim to legal professional privilege could be maintained in legal proceedings;

219

- which reveals that the authority proposes to serve a notice on a person (under any enactment) where the notice requires the person to do something or to make an order or direction under any enactment;
- relating to any action taken or to be taken in connection with the prevention, investigation or prosecution of crime.

Part VA of LGA 1972 also provides that certain documents must be made available for the public to inspect. These relate to meetings of the council, including committee and sub-committee meetings, and include:

- Copies of agendas for council meetings and any reports submitted for consideration at such meetings. However, where the report or parts of a report relate to matters which will be discussed at part of the meeting where the public may be excluded, then this information should not be available for inspection either. Copies of the documents that can be disclosed must be made available for inspection at least five clear days before the meeting except where the meeting is convened at shorter notice or a later agenda item is added; in which case the information must be made available from the time the meeting is convened or the item added. One further qualification is that the information cannot be made available to the public until copies have been made available to council members. Agenda items and reports should be left open for inspection for six years.
- Copies of the minutes of council meetings (excluding minutes relating to those parts of the meeting from which the public was excluded). These must be made available for a period of six years following the meeting.
- A list and a copy of the background papers used by an officer of the council when compiling any report which can be disclosed to the public. These papers do not actually have to be left open for inspection provided that they are supplied as soon as reasonably practicable if someone makes a request to see them. Background reports must be kept for four years.

The Local Government Act 2000 gives local authority executives some discretion as to whether it holds its executive or executive committee meetings in public or private. It also permits local authorities to provide public access to minutes of local authority executive committee meetings held in private (s.22) and also through a public register of members' interests (s.81).

11.13 ACCESS TO EUROPEAN UNION INFORMATION

The Aarhus Convention extends to bodies established by the EU Treaties and as a signatory to the Convention it was necessary for the EU to adopt legislation to ensure it complied with the access to information provisions of the Convention. Accordingly, Regulation (EC) 1049/2001 of the European Parliament and Council (OJ L 145/43, 31.5.2011) provide for access to environmental information held by the European Parliament, Council and Commission. Any citizen of the EU and any natural or legal person residing or having a registered office in an EU member state has a right of access to documents of institutions, subject to the principles and conditions defined in the Regulation. It is not within the scope of this book to explore the substantive content of Regulation 1049/2001. However, it should be noted that where a public authority of a member state receives a request for a document in its possession, originating from an EU institution, the member state is required to consult with the EU institution concerned unless it is clear that the document must or must not be disclosed. For further information on access and transparency relating to European Union information see the Europa website (**www.ec.europa.eu/transparency/access_documents/index_en.htm**).

APPENDIX

The Environmental Information Regulations 2004

Made 21st December 2004

Coming into force 1st January 2005

Whereas a draft of these Regulations has been approved by resolution of each House of Parliament in pursuance of paragraph 2(2) of Schedule 2 to the European Communities Act 1972;

Now, therefore, the Secretary of State, being a Minister designated for the purposes of section 2(2) of the European Communities Act 1972 in relation to freedom of access to, and dissemination of, information on the environment held by or for public authorities or other bodies, in exercise of the powers conferred on her by that section, makes the following Regulations:

PART 1   INTRODUCTORY

1.   Citation and commencement

These Regulations may be cited as the Environmental Information Regulations 2004 and shall come into force on 1st January 2005.

2.   Interpretation

(1)   In these Regulations–

'the Act' means the Freedom of Information Act 2000;
'applicant', in relation to a request for environmental information, means the person who made the request;
'appropriate records authority', in relation to a transferred public record, has the same meaning as in section 15(5) of the Act;
'the Commissioner' means the Information Commissioner;
'the Directive' means Council Directive 2003/4/EC on public access to environmental information and repealing Council Directive 90/313/EEC;
'environmental information' has the same meaning as in Article 2(1) of the Directive, namely any information in written, visual, aural, electronic or any other material form on–
    (a)   the state of the elements of the environment, such as air and atmosphere, water, soil, land, landscape and natural sites including wetlands, coastal

and marine areas, biological diversity and its components, including genetically modified organisms, and the interaction among these elements;

(b) factors, such as substances, energy, noise, radiation or waste, including radioactive waste, emissions, discharges and other releases into the environment, affecting or likely to affect the elements of the environment referred to in (a);

(c) measures (including administrative measures), such as policies, legislation, plans, programmes, environmental agreements, and activities affecting or likely to affect the elements and factors referred to in (a) and (b) as well as measures or activities designed to protect those elements;

(d) reports on the implementation of environmental legislation;

(e) cost-benefit and other economic analyses and assumptions used within the framework of the measures and activities referred to in (c); and

(f) the state of human health and safety, including the contamination of the food chain, where relevant, conditions of human life, cultural sites and built structures inasmuch as they are or may be affected by the state of the elements of the environment referred to in (a) or, through those elements, by any of the matters referred to in (b) and (c);

'historical record' has the same meaning as in section 62(1) of the Act;

'public authority' has the meaning given by paragraph (2);

'public record' has the same meaning as in section 84 of the Act;

'responsible authority', in relation to a transferred public record, has the same meaning as in section 15(5) of the Act;

'Scottish public authority' means–

(a) a body referred to in section 80(2) of the Act; and

(b) insofar as not such a body, a Scottish public authority as defined in section 3 of the Freedom of Information (Scotland) Act 2002;

'transferred public record' has the same meaning as in section 15(4) of the Act; and

'working day' has the same meaning as in section 10(6) of the Act.

(2) Subject to paragraph (3), 'public authority' means–

(a) government departments;

(b) any other public authority as defined in section 3(1) of the Act, disregarding for this purpose the exceptions in paragraph 6 of Schedule 1 to the Act, but excluding–

(i) any body or office-holder listed in Schedule 1 to the Act only in relation to information of a specified description; or

(ii) any person designated by Order under section 5 of the Act;

(c) any other body or other person, that carries out functions of public administration; or

(d) any other body or other person, that is under the control of a person falling within sub-paragraphs (a), (b) or (c) and–

(i) has public responsibilities relating to the environment

(ii) exercises functions of a public nature relating to the environment; or

(iii) provides public services relating to the environment.

(3) Except as provided by regulation 12(10) a Scottish public authority is not a 'public authority' for the purpose of these Regulations.

(4) The following expressions have the same meaning in these Regulations as they have in the Data Protection Act 1998, namely–

    (a)   'data' except that for the purposes of regulation 12(3) and regulation 13 a public authority referred to in the definition of data in paragraph (e) of section 1(1) of that Act means a public authority within the meaning of these Regulations;

    (b)   'the data protection principles';

    (c)   'data subject'; and

    (d)   'personal data'.

(5)   Except as provided by this regulation, expressions in these Regulations which appear in the Directive have the same meaning in these Regulations as they have in the Directive.

3. Application

(1)   Subject to paragraphs (3) and (4), these Regulations apply to public authorities.

(2)   For the purposes of these Regulations, environmental information is held by a public authority if the information–

    (a)   is in the authority's possession and has been produced or received by the authority; or

    (b)   is held by another person on behalf of the authority.

(3)   These Regulations shall not apply to any public authority to the extent that it is acting in a judicial or legislative capacity.

(4)   These Regulations shall not apply to either House of Parliament to the extent required for the purpose of avoiding an infringement of the privileges of either House.

(5)   Each government department is to be treated as a person separate from any other government department for the purposes of Parts 2, 4 and 5 of these Regulations.

PART 2   ACCESS TO ENVIRONMENTAL INFORMATION HELD BY PUBLIC AUTHORITIES

4. Dissemination of environmental information

(1)   Subject to paragraph (3), a public authority shall in respect of environmental information that it holds–

    (a)   progressively make the information available to the public by electronic means which are easily accessible; and

    (b)   take reasonable steps to organize the information relevant to its functions with a view to the active and systematic dissemination to the public of the information.

(2)   For the purposes of paragraph (1) the use of electronic means to make information available or to organize information shall not be required in relation to information collected before 1st January 2005 in non-electronic form.

(3)   Paragraph (1) shall not extend to making available or disseminating information which a public authority would be entitled to refuse to disclose under regulation 12.

(4)   The information under paragraph (1) shall include at least–

    (a)   the information referred to in Article 7(2) of the Directive; and

    (b)   facts and analyses of facts which the public authority considers relevant and important in framing major environmental policy proposals.

5. Duty to make available environmental information on request

(1) Subject to paragraph (3) and in accordance with paragraphs (2), (4), (5) and (6) and the remaining provisions of this Part and Part 3 of these Regulations, a public authority that holds environmental information shall make it available on request.

(2) Information shall be made available under paragraph (1) as soon as possible and no later than 20 working days after the date of receipt of the request.

(3) To the extent that the information requested includes personal data of which the applicant is the data subject, paragraph (1) shall not apply to those personal data.

(4) For the purposes of paragraph (1), where the information made available is compiled by or on behalf of the public authority it shall be up to date, accurate and comparable, so far as the public authority reasonably believes.

(5) Where a public authority makes available information in paragraph (b) of the definition of environmental information, and the applicant so requests, the public authority shall, insofar as it is able to do so, either inform the applicant of the place where information, if available, can be found on the measurement procedures, including methods of analysis, sampling and pre-treatment of samples, used in compiling the information, or refer the applicant to a standardised procedure used.

(6) Any enactment or rule of law that would prevent the disclosure of information in accordance with these Regulations shall not apply.

6. Form and format of information

(1) Where an applicant requests that the information be made available in a particular form or format, a public authority shall make it so available, unless–

    (a) it is reasonable for it to make the information available in another form or format; or

    (b) the information is already publicly available and easily accessible to the applicant in another form or format.

(2) If the information is not made available in the form or format requested, the public authority shall–

    (a) explain the reason for its decision as soon as possible and no later than 20 working days after the date of receipt of the request for the information;

    (b) provide the explanation in writing if the applicant so requests; and

    (c) inform the applicant of the provisions of regulation 11 and of the enforcement and appeal provisions of the Act applied by regulation 18.

7. Extension of time

(1) Where a request is made under regulation 5, the public authority may extend the period of 20 working days referred to in the provisions in paragraph (2) to 40 working days if it reasonably believes that the complexity and volume of the information requested means that it is impracticable either to comply with the request within the earlier period or to make a decision to refuse to do so.

(2) The provisions referred to in paragraph (1) are–

    (a) regulation 5(2);

    (b) regulation 6(2)(a); and

    (c) regulation 14(2).

(3) Where paragraph (1) applies the public authority shall notify the applicant accordingly as soon as possible and no later than 20 working days after the date of receipt of the request.

8. Charging

(1) Subject to paragraphs (2) to (8), where a public authority makes environmental information available in accordance with regulation 5(1) the authority may charge the applicant for making the information available.

(2) A public authority shall not make any charge for allowing an applicant–

    (a) to access any public registers or lists of environmental information held by the public authority; or

    (b) to examine the information requested at the place which the public authority makes available for that examination.

(3) A charge under paragraph (1) shall not exceed an amount which the public authority is satisfied is a reasonable amount.

(4) A public authority may require advance payment of a charge for making environmental information available and if it does it shall, no later than 20 working days after the date of receipt of the request for the information, notify the applicant of this requirement and of the amount of the advance payment.

(5) Where a public authority has notified an applicant under paragraph (4) that advance payment is required, the public authority is not required–

    (a) to make available the information requested; or

    (b) to comply with regulations 6 or 14,

unless the charge is paid no later than 60 working days after the date on which it gave the notification.

(6) The period beginning with the day on which the notification of a requirement for an advance payment is made and ending on the day on which that payment is received by the public authority is to be disregarded for the purposes of determining the period of 20 working days referred to in the provisions in paragraph (7), including any extension to those periods under regulation 7(1).

(7) The provisions referred to in paragraph (6) are–

    (a) regulation 5(2);

    (b) regulation 6(2)(a); and

    (c) regulation 14(2).

(8) A public authority shall publish and make available to applicants–

    (a) a schedule of its charges; and

    (b) information on the circumstances in which a charge may be made or waived.

9. Advice and assistance

(1) A public authority shall provide advice and assistance, so far as it would be reasonable to expect the authority to do so, to applicants and prospective applicants.

(2) Where a public authority decides that an applicant has formulated a request in too general a manner, it shall–

    (a) ask the applicant as soon as possible and in any event no later than 20 working days after the date of receipt of the request, to provide more particulars in relation to the request; and

    (b) assist the applicant in providing those particulars.

(3) Where a code of practice has been made under regulation 16, and to the extent that a public authority conforms to that code in relation to the provision of advice and assistance in a particular case, it shall be taken to have complied with paragraph (1) in relation to that case.

(4) Where paragraph (2) applies, in respect of the provisions in paragraph (5), the date on which the further particulars are received by the public authority shall be treated as the date after which the period of 20 working days referred to in those provisions shall be calculated.

(5) The provisions referred to in paragraph (4) are–

    (a) regulation 5(2);

    (b) regulation 6(2)(a); and

    (c) regulation 14(2).

10. Transfer of a request

(1) Where a public authority that receives a request for environmental information does not hold the information requested but believes that another public authority or a Scottish public authority holds the information, the public authority shall either–

    (a) transfer the request to the other public authority or Scottish public authority; or

    (b) supply the applicant with the name and address of that authority,

and inform the applicant accordingly with the refusal sent under regulation 14(1).

(2) Where a request is transferred to a public authority, for the purposes of the provisions referred to in paragraph (3) the request is received by that public authority on the date on which it receives the transferred request.

(3) The provisions referred to in paragraph (2) are–

    (a) regulation 5(2);

    (b) regulation 6(2)(a); and

    (c) regulation 14(2).

11. Representations and reconsideration

(1) Subject to paragraph (2), an applicant may make representations to a public authority in relation to the applicant's request for environmental information if it appears to the applicant that the authority has failed to comply with a requirement of these Regulations in relation to the request.

(2) Representations under paragraph (1) shall be made in writing to the public authority no later than 40 working days after the date on which the applicant believes that the public authority has failed to comply with the requirement.

(3) The public authority shall on receipt of the representations and free of charge–

    (a) consider them and any supporting evidence produced by the applicant; and

    (b) decide if it has complied with the requirement.

(4) A public authority shall notify the applicant of its decision under paragraph (3) as soon as possible and no later than 40 working days after the date of receipt of the representations.

(5) Where the public authority decides that it has failed to comply with these Regulations in relation to the request, the notification under paragraph (4) shall include a statement of–

    (a) the failure to comply;

    (b) the action the authority has decided to take to comply with the requirement; and

    (c) the period within which that action is to be taken.

PART 3   EXCEPTIONS TO THE DUTY TO DISCLOSE ENVIRONMENTAL INFORMATION

12.   Exceptions to the duty to disclose environmental information

(1)   Subject to paragraphs (2), (3) and (9), a public authority may refuse to disclose environmental information requested if–

    (a)   an exception to disclosure applies under paragraphs (4) or (5); and

    (b)   in all the circumstances of the case, the public interest in maintaining the exception outweighs the public interest in disclosing the information.

(2)   A public authority shall apply a presumption in favour of disclosure.

(3)   To the extent that the information requested includes personal data of which the applicant is not the data subject, the personal data shall not be disclosed otherwise than in accordance with regulation 13.

(4)   For the purposes of paragraph (1)(a), a public authority may refuse to disclose information to the extent that–

    (a)   it does not hold that information when an applicant's request is received;

    (b)   the request for information is manifestly unreasonable;

    (c)   the request for information is formulated in too general a manner and the public authority has complied with regulation 9;

    (d)   the request relates to material which is still in the course of completion, to unfinished documents or to incomplete data; or

    (e)   the request involves the disclosure of internal communications.

(5)   For the purposes of paragraph (1)(a), a public authority may refuse to disclose information to the extent that its disclosure would adversely affect–

    (a)   international relations, defence, national security or public safety;

    (b)   the course of justice, the ability of a person to receive a fair trial or the ability of a public authority to conduct an inquiry of a criminal or disciplinary nature;

    (c)   intellectual property rights;

    (d)   the confidentiality of the proceedings of that or any other public authority where such confidentiality is provided by law;

    (e)   the confidentiality of commercial or industrial information where such confidentiality is provided by law to protect a legitimate economic interest;

    (f)   the interests of the person who provided the information where that person–

        (i)   was not under, and could not have been put under, any legal obligation to supply it to that or any other public authority;

        (ii)   did not supply it in circumstances such that that or any other public authority is entitled apart from these Regulations to disclose it; and

        (iii)   has not consented to its disclosure; or

    (g)   the protection of the environment to which the information relates.

(6)   For the purposes of paragraph (1), a public authority may respond to a request by neither confirming nor denying whether such information exists and is held by the public authority, whether or not it holds such information, if that confirmation or denial would involve the disclosure of information which would adversely affect any of the interests referred to in paragraph (5)(a) and would not be in the public interest under paragraph (1)(b).

(7)   For the purposes of a response under paragraph (6), whether information exists and is held by the public authority is itself the disclosure of information.

(8) For the purposes of paragraph (4)(e), internal communications includes communications between government departments.

(9) To the extent that the environmental information to be disclosed relates to information on emissions, a public authority shall not be entitled to refuse to disclose that information under an exception referred to in paragraphs (5)(d) to (g).

(10) For the purposes of paragraphs (5)(b), (d) and (f), references to a public authority shall include references to a Scottish public authority.

(11) Nothing in these Regulations shall authorise a refusal to make available any environmental information contained in or otherwise held with other information which is withheld by virtue of these Regulations unless it is not reasonably capable of being separated from the other information for the purpose of making available that information.

13. Personal data

(1) To the extent that the information requested includes personal data of which the applicant is not the data subject and as respects which either the first or second condition below is satisfied, a public authority shall not disclose the personal data.

(2) The first condition is–

    (a) in a case where the information falls within any of paragraphs (a) to (d) of the definition of 'data' in section 1(1) of the Data Protection Act 1998, that the disclosure of the information to a member of the public otherwise than under these Regulations would contravene.

        (i) any of the data protection principles; or

        (ii) section 10 of that Act (right to prevent processing likely to cause damage or distress) and in all the circumstances of the case, the public interest in not disclosing the information outweighs the public interest in disclosing it; and

    (b) in any other case, that the disclosure of the information to a member of the public otherwise than under these Regulations would contravene any of the data protection principles if the exemptions in section 33A(1) of the Data Protection Act 1998 (which relate to manual data held by public authorities) were disregarded.

(3) The second condition is that by virtue of any provision of Part IV of the Data Protection Act 1998 the information is exempt from section 7(1) of that Act and, in all the circumstances of the case, the public interest in not disclosing the information outweighs the public interest in disclosing it.

(4) In determining whether anything done before 24th October 2007 would contravene any of the data protection principles, the exemptions in Part III of Schedule 8 to the Data Protection Act 1998 shall be disregarded.

(5) For the purposes of this regulation a public authority may respond to a request by neither confirming nor denying whether such information exists and is held by the public authority, whether or not it holds such information, to the extent that–

    (a) the giving to a member of the public of the confirmation or denial would contravene any of the data protection principles or section 10 of the Data Protection Act 1998 or would do so if the exemptions in section 33A(1) of that Act were disregarded; or

    (b) by virtue of any provision of Part IV of the Data Protection Act 1998, the information is exempt from section 7(1)(a) of that Act.

14. Refusal to disclose information

(1) If a request for environmental information is refused by a public authority under regulations 12(1) or 13(1), the refusal shall be made in writing and comply with the following provisions of this regulation.

(2) The refusal shall be made as soon as possible and no later than 20 working days after the date of receipt of the request.

(3) The refusal shall specify the reasons not to disclose the information requested, including–

    (a) any exception relied on under regulations 12(4), 12(5) or 13; and

    (b) the matters the public authority considered in reaching its decision with respect to the public interest under regulation 12(1)(b) or, where these apply, regulations 13(2)(a)(ii) or 13(3).

(4) If the exception in regulation 12(4)(d) is specified in the refusal, the authority shall also specify, if known to the public authority, the name of any other public authority preparing the information and the estimated time in which the information will be finished or completed.

(5) The refusal shall inform the applicant–

    (a) that he may make representations to the public authority under regulation 11; and

    (b) of the enforcement and appeal provisions of the Act applied by regulation 18.

15. Ministerial certificates

(1) A Minister of the Crown may certify that a refusal to disclose information under regulation 12(1) is because the disclosure–

    (a) would adversely affect national security; and

    (b) would not be in the public interest under regulation 12(1)(b).

(2) For the purposes of paragraph (1)–

    (a) a Minister of the Crown may designate a person to certify the matters in that paragraph on his behalf; and

    (b) a refusal to disclose information under regulation 12(1) includes a response under regulation 12(6).

(3) A certificate issued in accordance with paragraph (1)–

    (a) shall be conclusive evidence of the matters in that paragraph; and

    (b) may identify the information to which it relates in general terms.

(4) A document purporting to be a certificate under paragraph (1) shall be received in evidence and deemed to be such a certificate unless the contrary is proved.

(5) A document which purports to be certified by or on behalf of a Minister of the Crown as a true copy of a certificate issued by that Minister under paragraph (1) shall in any legal proceedings be evidence (or, in Scotland, sufficient evidence) of that certificate.

(6) In paragraphs (1), (2) and (5), a 'Minister of the Crown' has the same meaning as in section 25(3) of the Act.

PART 4   CODE OF PRACTICE AND HISTORICAL RECORDS

16.   Issue of a code of practice and functions of the Commissioner

(1)   The Secretary of State may issue, and may from time to time revise, a code of practice providing guidance to public authorities as to the practice which it would, in the Secretary of State's opinion, be desirable for them to follow in connection with the discharge of their functions under these Regulations.

(2)   The code may make different provision for different public authorities.

(3)   Before issuing or revising any code under this regulation, the Secretary of State shall consult the Commissioner.

(4)   The Secretary of State shall lay before each House of Parliament any code issued or revised under this regulation.

(5)   The general functions of the Commissioner under section 47 of the Act and the power of the Commissioner to give a practice recommendation under section 48 of the Act shall apply for the purposes of these Regulations as they apply for the purposes of the Act but with the modifications specified in paragraph (6).

(6)   For the purposes of the application of sections 47 and 48 of the Act to these Regulations, any reference to–

    (a)   a public authority is a reference to a public authority within the meaning of these Regulations;

    (b)   the requirements or operation of the Act, or functions under the Act, includes a reference to the requirements or operation of these Regulations, or functions under these Regulations; and

    (c)   a code of practice made under section 45 of the Act includes a reference to a code of practice made under this regulation.

17.   Historical and transferred public records

(1)   Where a request relates to information contained in a historical record other than one to which paragraph (2) applies and the public authority considers that it may be in the public interest to refuse to disclose that information under regulation 12(1)(b), the public authority shall consult–

    (a)   the Lord Chancellor, if it is a public record within the meaning of the Public Records Act 1958; or

    (b)   the appropriate Northern Ireland Minister, if it is a public record to which the Public Records Act (Northern Ireland) 1923 applies,

before it decides whether the information may or may not be disclosed.

(2)   Where a request relates to information contained in a transferred public record, other than information which the responsible authority has designated as open information for the purposes of this regulation, the appropriate records authority shall consult the responsible authority on whether there may be an exception to disclosure of that information under regulation 12(5).

(3)   If the appropriate records authority decides that such an exception applies–

    (a)   subject to paragraph (4), a determination on whether it may be in the public interest to refuse to disclose that information under regulation 12(1)(b) shall be made by the responsible authority;

    (b)   the responsible authority shall communicate its determination to the appropriate records authority within such time as is reasonable in all the circumstances; and

     (c)   the appropriate records authority shall comply with regulation 5 in accordance with that determination.

(4)   Where a responsible authority is required to make a determination under paragraph (3), it shall consult–

     (a)   the Lord Chancellor, if the transferred public record is a public record within the meaning of the Public Records Act 1958; or

     (b)   the appropriate Northern Ireland Minister, if the transferred public record is a public record to which the Public Records Act (Northern Ireland) 1923 applies,

before it determines whether the information may or may not be disclosed.

(5)   A responsible authority which is not a public authority under these Regulations shall be treated as a public authority for the purposes of–

     (a)   the obligations of a responsible authority under paragraphs (3)(a) and (b) and (4); and

     (b)   the imposition of any requirement to furnish information relating to compliance with regulation 5.

PART 5   ENFORCEMENT AND APPEALS, OFFENCES, AMENDMENT AND REVOCATION

18.   Enforcement and appeal provisions

(1)   The enforcement and appeals provisions of the Act shall apply for the purposes of these Regulations as they apply for the purposes of the Act but with the modifications specified in this regulation.

(2)   In this regulation, 'the enforcement and appeals provisions of the Act' means–

     (a)   Part IV of the Act (enforcement), including Schedule 3 (powers of entry and inspection) which has effect by virtue of section 55 of the Act; and

     (b)   Part V of the Act (appeals).

(3)   Part IV of the Act shall not apply in any case where a certificate has been issued in accordance with regulation 15(1).

(4)   For the purposes of the application of the enforcement and appeals provisions of the Act–

     (a)   for any reference to–

        (i)   'this Act' there shall be substituted a reference to 'these Regulations'; and

        (ii)   'Part I' there shall be substituted a reference to 'Parts 2 and 3 of these Regulations';

     (b)   any reference to a public authority is a reference to a public authority within the meaning of these Regulations.

     (c)   for any reference to the code of practice under section 45 of the Act (issue of a code of practice by the Secretary of State) there shall be substituted a reference to any code of practice issued under regulation 16(1);

     (d)   in section 50(4) of the Act (contents of decision notice)–

        (i)   in paragraph (a) for the reference to 'section 1(1)' there shall be substituted a reference to 'regulation 5(1)'; and

        (ii)   in paragraph (b) for the references to 'sections 11 and 17' there shall be substituted references to 'regulations 6, 11 or 14';

   (e)   in section 56(1) of the Act (no action against public authority) for the words 'This Act does not confer' there shall be substituted the words 'These Regulations do not confer';

   (f)   in section 57(3)(a) of the Act (appeal against notices served under Part IV) for the reference to 'section 66' of the Act (decisions relating to certain transferred public records) there shall be substituted a reference to 'regulations 17(2) to (5)';

   (g)   in paragraph 1 of Schedule 3 to the Act (issue of warrants) for the reference to 'section 77' (offence of altering etc. records with intent to prevent disclosure) there shall be substituted a reference to 'regulation 19'; and

   (h)   in paragraph 8 of Schedule 3 to the Act (matters exempt from inspection and seizure) for the reference to 'information which is exempt information by virtue of section 23(1) or 24(1)' (bodies and information relating to national security) there shall be substituted a reference to 'information whose disclosure would adversely affect national security'.

(5)   In section 50(4)(a) of the Act (contents of decision notice) the reference to confirmation or denial applies to a response given by a public authority under regulation 12(6) or regulation 13(5).

(6)   Section 53 of the Act (exception from duty to comply with decision notice or enforcement notice) applies to a decision notice or enforcement notice served under Part IV of the Act as applied to these Regulations on any of the public authorities referred to in section 53(1)(a); and in section 53(7) for the reference to 'exempt information' there shall be substituted a reference to 'information which may be refused under these Regulations'.

(7)   Section 60 of the Act (appeals against national security certificate) shall apply with the following modifications–

   (a)   for the reference to a certificate under section 24(3) of the Act (national security) there shall be substituted a reference to a certificate issued in accordance with regulation 15(1);

   (b)   subsection (2) shall be omitted; and

   (c)   in subsection (3), for the words, 'the Minister did not have reasonable grounds for issuing the certificate' there shall be substituted the words 'the Minister or person designated by him did not have reasonable grounds for issuing the certificate under regulation 15(1)'.

(8)   A person found guilty of an offence under paragraph 12 of Schedule 3 to the Act (offences relating to obstruction of the execution of a warrant) is liable on summary conviction to a fine not exceeding level 5 on the standard scale.

(9)   A government department is not liable to prosecution in relation to an offence under paragraph 12 of Schedule 3 to the Act but that offence shall apply to a person in the public service of the Crown and to a person acting on behalf of either House of Parliament or on behalf of the Northern Ireland Assembly as it applies to any other person.

(10) Section 76(1) of the Act (disclosure of information between Commissioner and ombudsmen) shall apply to any information obtained by, or furnished to, the Commissioner under or for the purposes of these Regulations.

19.   Offence of altering records with intent to prevent disclosure

(1)   Where–

(a) a request for environmental information has been made to a public authority under regulation 5; and

(b) the applicant would have been entitled (subject to payment of any charge) to that information in accordance with that regulation,

any person to whom this paragraph applies is guilty of an offence if he alters, defaces, blocks, erases, destroys or conceals any record held by the public authority, with the intention of preventing the disclosure by that authority of all, or any part, of the information to which the applicant would have been entitled.

(2) Subject to paragraph (5), paragraph (1) applies to the public authority and to any person who is employed by, is an officer of, or is subject to the direction of, the public authority.

(3) A person guilty of an offence under this regulation is liable on summary conviction to a fine not exceeding level 5 on the standard scale.

(4) No proceedings for an offence under this regulation shall be instituted–

(a) in England and Wales, except by the Commissioner or by or with the consent of the Director of Public Prosecutions; or

(b) in Northern Ireland, except by the Commissioner or by or with the consent of the Director of Public Prosecutions for Northern Ireland.

(5) A government department is not liable to prosecution in relation to an offence under paragraph (1) but that offence shall apply to a person in the public service of the Crown and to a person acting on behalf of either House of Parliament or on behalf of the Northern Ireland Assembly as it applies to any other person.

20. Amendment

(1) Section 39 of the Act is amended as follows.

(2) In subsection (1)(a), for 'regulations under section 74' there is substituted 'environmental information regulations'.

(3) After subsection (1) there is inserted–

'(1A) In subsection (1) 'environmental information regulations' means–

(a) regulations made under section 74, or

(b) regulations made under section 2(2) of the European Communities Act 1972 for the purpose of implementing any Community obligation relating to public access to, and the dissemination of, information on the environment.'.

21. Revocation

The following are revoked–

(a) The Environmental Information Regulations 1992 and the Environmental Information (Amendment) Regulations 1998 except insofar as these apply to Scottish public authorities; and

(b) The Environmental Information Regulations (Northern Ireland) 1993 and the Environmental Information (Amendment) Regulations (Northern Ireland) 1998.

Index